Place and Space in Modern Fiction

UNIVERSITY PRESS OF FLORIDA / STATE UNIVERSITY SYSTEM

Florida A&M University, Tallahassee
Florida Atlantic University, Boca Raton
Florida Gulf Coast University, Ft. Myers
Florida International University, Miami
Florida State University, Tallahassee
University of Central Florida, Orlando
University of Florida, Gainesville
University of North Florida, Jacksonville
University of South Florida, Tampa
University of West Florida, Pensacola

Wesley A. Kort

University Press of Florida
Gainesville · Tallahassee · Tampa · Boca Raton
Pensacola · Orlando · Miami · Jacksonville · Ft. Myers

Place and Space

in Modern Fiction

PR
888
.P525
K67
2004

Copyright 2004 by Wesley A. Kort
Printed in the United States of America on recycled, acid-free paper
All rights reserved

09 08 07 06 05 04   6 5 4 3 2 1

ISBN 0-8130-2731-4
A record of cataloging-in-publication information is available
from the Library of Congress.

The University Press of Florida is the scholarly publishing
agency for the State University System of Florida, comprising
Florida A&M University, Florida Atlantic University, Florida
Gulf Coast University, Florida International University, Florida
State University, University of Central Florida, University of
Florida, University of North Florida, University of South
Florida, and University of West Florida.

University Press of Florida
15 Northwest 15th Street
Gainesville, FL 32611-2079
http://www.upf.com

Also by Wesley A. Kort

Shriven Selves: Religious Problems in Recent American Fiction (1972)
Narrative Elements and Religious Meaning (1975)
Moral Fiber: Character and Belief in Recent American Fiction (1982)
Modern Fiction and Human Time: A Study in Narrative and Belief (1985)
Story, Text, and Scripture: Literary Interests in Biblical Narrative (1988)
Bound to Differ: The Dynamics of Theological Discourses (1992)
"Take, Read": Scripture, Textuality, and Cultural Practice (1996)
C. S. Lewis Then and Now (2001)

Contents

Preface

This book began when I developed a course to serve as part of a program that I taught in England beginning in the summer of 1987 and in several subsequent summers. I developed this course because the narrative language of place and space was next on my agenda, but I also thought that the course would allow me to talk about modern fiction in relation to particular places in England, some of which we could visit. The pedagogical benefits of joining encounters with places like Salisbury, London, and Dorchester to encounters with significant sites in fictional narratives were powerful. This fortified my sense of the complex interactive relations that occur between our experiences of places and the role of places in narratives. As the students' own narratives of their time in England were dominated by the places where they stayed and visited, so the narratives we studied were shaped by the force and significance of place. It was not difficult to bring home to students the need to be more attentive than they otherwise would be to the roles of place and place-relations in fictional narratives and the importance of narratives for our relations to places.

As I mentioned, I developed the course also because narrative place and space were next on my scholarly agenda. This book, then, completes a set of four studies on the languages of narrative and stands alongside studies of the narrative languages of teller (1972), of character (1982), and of action and event (1985). The theory of narrative that underlies this project will, however briefly, be taken up in the introduction. Let me say here that it supports two principal points: First, narratives are constituted by four languages, any one of which can be a dominant, and, second, narrative discourse is potentially adequate to articulate a person's or people's world because a world is constituted by responses to four sets of uncertainties that the languages of narrative address or keep at bay.

Although a study of one of the languages of narrative runs the risk of separating it from the whole, the advantages of such a study outweigh the disadvantages. All the languages of narrative and the uncertainties to which they draw attention and to which they respond are sufficiently important to warrant the risks of treating each in relative isolation. However, it should be said that, while primary attention to place at the expense of the other languages of narrative is a distortion, I have tried to limit distortion by choosing narratives in which the language of place and space is prominent, if not dominant.

It would not have occurred to me to develop the course in which this book finds its origins, or at least to develop it in the way that I did, if it had not been for David Jasper, who invited me, while I was on sabbatical leave in Germany in 1986, to lecture at the University of Durham. We taught the program together in Durham during several summers. I also taught the program there with Terry Wright, from the English department at the University of Newcastle. These people, along with several others who participated in the program both in Durham and, later, in Cambridge, became valuable resources, and I am grateful to them. I especially want to mention J. R. Watson, who also read an earlier version of the book manuscript.

I completed a rough draft of the book while I worked, during the 1999–2000 academic year, as a senior fellow in the Erasmus Institute at the University of Notre Dame. I am grateful to the institute; its director, James Turner; and my own university for the time I was given for this project. My year at the institute was a rewarding period in my career, and it was an unaccustomed pleasure to work with people genuinely interested in the work of their colleagues and willing to take the time to understand and respond helpfully to it. I also gave the gist of this study as a paper for a seminar at the American Academy of Religion on Constructions of Space. I want to thank Jim Flanagan, the chair, and all the participants in the seminar for their interest in my paper and their encouragement. Finally, I gave a similar paper for a faculty colloquium in my own department, and several of my colleagues, especially Kalman Bland, offered helpful commentary and challenges.

Indeed, one of the benefits of the rather long period of time separating the beginnings of this project in Durham, England, and its completion now in Durham, North Carolina, is that I have had the benefit of talking with many students and scholars about it. It has been an undertone in my work for fifteen years, even though I completed and published four other books in the meantime. In addition, the fact that I have lived with this project for so long means that I have seen the questions of spatiality and human place-relations come increasingly to the fore in literary, cultural, religious, and theoretical work of various kinds. I am grateful, then, for all to which this study exposed me. It is my hope that my contribution to what has become a very big and timely topic of study and conversation will provoke responses that will open up potentials and problems in the understanding of human spatiality that I still insufficiently understand or may have overlooked completely.

Introduction

Narrating Place-Relations

There is no obvious way to begin a discussion of human place-relations and spatiality in modern culture. There are few if any conventions that shape spatial analyses and theories. Discussions of human spatiality are shaped more by the diverse interests of those who engage in them—architectural, geographical, social scientific, literary, cultural critical, philosophical, religious, and so on—than by agreement. One consequence of this scattering is that the categories that control discussions of human spatiality are not fixed. As the editors of a recent volume on space point out, the term "space" is used "with such abandon that its meanings run into each other before they have been properly interrogated."[1] A second consequence is that questions of places and of our relations to them appear more elusive and complex than, perhaps, they need to. A third is that in this area there are many competent and interesting contributors but no dominant or authoritative voice, school, or method.

Another way to make this point is to say that place and space have not had the kind of systematic and widespread attention in modernity that has been given to time and temporality. Perhaps this is because time, by its vulnerability to abstraction and measurement, is more philosophically engaging than space. Kant, in his early discussions of space, subordinates spatiality to temporality precisely because spatial relations are more physical. Time, thereby, is judged as more universal, and time, he contends, includes, with everything else, space.[2] Michel Foucault gives a different answer. He believes that questions of place and space have been the province of military and political interests, largely leaving to philosophy the more abstract problem of time.[3] A third answer lies in an argument I recently made that a major shift in early modern culture occurred with Vico's application of Bacon's method of reading nature to reading history. Bacon read nature as a second scripture that was not optional but necessary if one is to know God, and Vico applied that practice to reading the history of nonbiblical peoples as scripture. Hegel added a crucial ingredient to Vico's shift when he dissolved the distinction between the histories of biblical and nonbiblical peoples and posited reading history as a way by which the effects of Providence are actualized. In the eighteenth and nineteenth centuries, reading history as scripture, while at first it complemented reading the Bible, eventually displaced it.[4]

Without attempting to be exhaustive, I want to suggest another answer to the question of why in modern culture theories of time and history upstage theories of space and place. Modern culture was able to adjust to the loss of shared religious beliefs as they apply to temporality as it was not able to adjust to that loss in regard to spatiality. The loss of a shared ultimate beginning and ending, of Creation and Apocalypse, was redressed by the elevation of moments within history as decisive. Christianity already had done this by affirming the birth of Jesus as a beginning point that rivaled, if it did not overshadow, the beginning marked by Creation. Marking historical watersheds and distinguishing periods in history became part of Christian culture, and in the modern period identifying epochs and contrasting eras became characteristic acts, if not self-defining obsessions. Monarchies, political revolutions, radical cultural shifts: these all serve to mark decisive beginnings and endings, and modern culture can, perhaps, be no more accurately characterized than by the assumption it carries about itself as a period sharply distinguished in nature and value from what preceded it.

The erosion of the dominant religious view regarding ultimate places and their stabilizing and normative status could not so readily be redressed. The growth of cities in the nineteenth century did not add to but diluted the authority and prestige of their resident churches. The distinction between sacred and profane, while in some respects it may have become clearer, also became less important. Indeed, authority and prestige shift to the nonecclesiastical monuments of urban space. The relation of human orientations and interests to good and evil places, ultimately to heaven or to hell, along with the authority those locations traditionally carried, dwindled in their public currency. No culturally shared or conventionally stable alternatives were found by which the relation of particular places to the contrary poles of ultimate good and evil could be judged.

Time and history have largely defined modern culture, consequently, more than have space, place, and understandings of them. But in recent decades this situation has been altered. Fredric Jameson writes, "I think it is at least empirically arguable that our daily life, our psychic experience, our cultural languages, are today dominated by categories of space rather than by categories of time, as in the preceding period of high modernism proper."[5] Michel Foucault also notes the recent cultural turn from the dominance of time to a dominance of place and space: "the present epoch will perhaps be above all the epoch of space. We are in the epoch of simultaneity: we are in the epoch of juxtaposition, the epoch of the near and the far, of the side-by-side, of the dispersed. We are at a moment, I believe, when our experience of the world is less that of a long life developing through time than that of a network that connects points and intersects with its own skein."[6] The influential geographer Edward Soja argues that one of the most important intellectual and political developments of the latter half of the twentieth century is that "a growing community of scholars and citizens has, for perhaps the first time, begun to think about the spatiality of human life in much the same way that we have persistently approached life's intrinsic and richly revealing historical and social qualities."[7] If such a shift has occurred, and I think that it has, it could be taken as one of the signs that distinguish modernity from the rise of a postmodern culture.

However, I think it is mistaken to distinguish a postmodern from a modern culture sharply. Nineteenth- and twentieth-century cultural history, while it gave a temporal orientation to modernity, was also a history of changing places, relations to place, and spatial understandings. That history came to be read as an increasingly costly one. Places and relations to them formed a subtext to the progressive "scriptural" text of modern history. This subtext gradually, although at times also abruptly, emerged as dominant. Perhaps it would be helpful to rehearse some moments in this subtext and to suggest how and why its dominance occurred.

One often noted change in England in the early part of the nineteenth century was its shift from an agricultural to an industrial society. Agricultural products, both for consumption and manufacture, were increasingly imported, especially from the Americas and Australia. This change in large part accounts for an accompanying move from a rural and small town to an urban population. By the mid-nineteenth century, the balance tipped demographically in placing a majority of the population in cities. During the same time, imperialism and colonialism changed England from a small island nation to the center of a world empire. This expansion brought with it its own questions and problems so that by the end of the nineteenth century the relation of England to people in faraway places and other cultures began to be seen as complicated and often problematic. All of these changes affected London in particular, since it underwent rapid growth and emerged not only as a huge city relative to the rest of England but also as a great commercial center. Its identity was as much determined by the empire and its relations to other great cities as to the rest of England. Since London needed to be connected and in constant reliable contact with other cities, efficient means of transportation and communication developed, and they altered spatial orientations. In all these respects, London was not an exception or aberration but an epitome and norm. As Malcolm Bradbury puts it, "London increasingly comes to typify the great city of modernity.[8] These many changes—industrialization, urbanization, empire, and transportation/communication—while concentrated in London, were widely felt, and they combined to create enormous shifts in place-relations and orientations to and understandings of human space. While nineteenth-century culture must be understood in terms of its preoccupation with history, that history must also be understood as marked by place changes, spatial dislocations, and reorientations.

From the Romantics down to the close of the nineteenth and opening years of twentieth century, this history of change began to be read as taking a toll on the well-being of English life, including its moral and spiritual well-being. While there was much on the surface that spoke of confidence and optimism, there was also a growing sense of foreboding. It became difficult for some to read this history as a story of progress, particularly as a story of the coincidence of English history and divine Providence. As the society was becoming complex, destabilized, and dislocated, its religious identity became, especially after 1859, less assured. Evolutionary theories and German biblical scholarship had their impact on English culture at just the time when it was becoming, for these other reasons, less unified and secure. And London, the principal product of this history of change, came increasingly to be viewed as a "modern Babylon," a place offering "manifold opportunities for Sin."[9]

The minority voices of concern and warning turned into a widespread sense of loss during and after the First World War. All of the misgivings about changes wrought by events in the nineteenth and early twentieth centuries found their justification and intensification in a war that was, among other things, dislocating and disorienting. History could now be read far more clearly as a story not of advancement but of loss, even of violence and of a human evil heretofore concealed by the deceptions and illusions of culture. This reading of history continued in the twentieth century and found support in economic depression and, even more, in the Second World War. What emerged to displace a confidence in and identification with history was a sense of having been betrayed by it, "conned," as William Golding put it, into a great "mincing machine."[10]

Along with an altered sense of history's meaning, of history not as support but as betrayal, late modern culture, increasingly in the second half of the twentieth century, could no longer look to history as a source of cultural identity and unity. Rather than thinking of history as culturally inclusive, the particularity of peoples, their separate histories and social locations, came increasingly to the fore. As Gianni Vattimo puts it: "There is no single history, only images of the past projected from different points of view. It is illusory to think that there exists a supreme or comprehensive viewpoint capable of unifying all others."[11] This relativizing of history deprived it of its capacity to unify diverse peoples, and places more and more performed that function, especially urban locations and markets. Advanced capitalism and economic relations increasingly served to unify peoples spatially, howbeit commercially, with the effect of what we now refer to as globalization.

This brief and selective history supports the claim that attempts clearly to date the ending of modernism slight the continuities that tie the present with the early decades of the nineteenth century. Along the way, important shifts were noticed, whether Henry Adams's 1900, Virginia Woolf's 1910, or D. H. Lawrence's 1915, but these mark changes in awareness, signals that what had been going on for some time should be taken starkly into account.[12] The subtext of rapidly changing places began to challenge the "scriptural" status of history. A shift becomes noticeable in the last quarter of the nineteenth century—I mark it with Hardy—and it continues to the present day. We are beginning now to read places as our cultural "scriptures" and to identify and evaluate ourselves and other people spatially. This is why spatial orientation and place-relations are basic to what is often referred to as a postmodern culture. The primary texts of postmodern discourses are spatial, and their principal interpreters are cultural critics, theorists, and human or cultural geographers. The problem is that, as I said at the outset, their language lacks conventions. Modern hermeneutics, whether biblical or secular, is still dominated by temporal categories, and reading and interpreting the text of human spatiality needs a more usable theory. We should see that need before turning our attention toward meeting it.

Cultural Studies and the Language of Place

Taking our starting point from what Jameson calls "today," we can recognize the language of space as dominant for the discourses of late modernism. As Mike Crang and Nigel Thrift put it, "Space is the everywhere of modern thought."[13] We should look at some evidences of this present dominance of spatial language before turning to the problem that, I hope, begins now to emerge, namely that, as mentioned at the outset, we lack a stable way of talking about place and space at just the time when spatial texts have become scriptural.

One reason why the language of space dominates Jameson's "today" is that the so-called postmodernist reaction to modernism was focused by architectural theory and design. The distinctions and contrasts available in the shift from styles characteristic of modernism to those in reaction to them are easily recognizable. Photographs of the architecture of Las Vegas in the conversion narrative of architectural theorist Robert Venturi, for example, add visual clarity to written distinctions between modern and postmodern like those attempted by David Harvey and Jean-François Lyotard.[14]

The prominence of spatial language for Jameson's "today" is also due to the debt that cultural studies owe to critical sociologies. These analyses designate social placements and offer topologies of social distinctions. While countered by such sociologists as Anthony Giddens with his category of "structuration" and by all historical sociologists, sociology has a decidedly synchronic thrust that carries over into cultural studies. For example, Pierre Bourdieu in *Distinction* analyzes taste not by means of a hermeneutics of history and tradition, as does Hans-Georg Gadamer, but in terms of class-specific social location.[15]

In addition, cultural studies that are oriented by discourse analysis, often under the influence of Michel Foucault, chart or measure the locations granted discourses by institutions. Such acts of locating tend to de-temporalize and to spatialize the analysis of discourses.[16] Rather than charted by intellectual history, knowledge is located spatially in terms of structures and resources, political and economic, that establish and sustain them.

Also, the coherence and uniformity that marked Marxist theories of history are generally eschewed in a postmodernist ethos, and such post-Marxist social theorists and critics as Ernesto Laclau and Chantal Mouffe use spatial metaphors to play down social history and the teleologies it implies.[17] What Lyotard calls metanarratives, defined as temporal orderings, tended to govern Marxist analyzes, and, since in a postmodern ethos they become suspect, more spatial and synchronic descriptions of political and economic conditions emerge.

Finally, a commonly employed form of argumentation in cultural studies "today" tends toward spatial language. It could be called an argument from synecdoche. Because cultural analyses such as those offered by Fredric Jameson, Jean Baudrillard, or Marshall Berman cannot treat contemporary culture in its entirety, they regularly use one aspect or detail of the culture in order to characterize the whole. Highways, film, cell phones, and other forms of technology, communication, and transportation are offered as particular points where or from which the total culture can be viewed.[18] Such juxtapositions of particular and general, of detail and the whole, are spatial in conception and effect.

The spatial language and orientations of such postmodern discourses, although dominant, tend to be free-floating and abstract. This has been noted by theorists and critics who, like Edward Said, have concerns for or attachments to particular places. Said sees the widespread interest of literary and cultural theory in "writing" and intertextuality, for example, as spatial but, at the same time, as separating texts from their relations to specific locations by relating them instead to one another. The spatial qualities of textuality should not, he argues, abstract texts from particular, material spatial factors. His point represents a relevant intervention into the general direction toward the *atopic* condition of postmodernist spatial discourses.[19]

Indeed, current cultural studies, by virtue of a somewhat phobic attitude toward "reality," seem condemned to occluding the particularity of sites and the dynamics of specific place-relations. In this respect, they continue rather than counter the dominant attitude of the modern period toward places and space. The shift from temporal to spatial language indicates less a change in relations to actual places or locations than a change in the way cultural theorists establish and interpret the primary texts of the present cultural situation.

Jacques Derrida, in fact, attributes the current dominance of spatial language not to actual places or attitudes toward them but to the need for warranting voice. Geological, architectural, and urban metaphors are indispensable for granting modern discourses the weight of placement in a culture in which speakers are often abstracted from actual locations or decline to declare their particularity.[20] He invokes the biblical narrative of the city and tower of Babel as a metaphor descriptive of spatial language use. As the diversification of languages gave rise to a cacophony of particular and partial discourses in the Babel story, so the language of space in contemporary discourses should call attention to specificity and partiality. Postmodern discourses should spell an "end to the plan of domination" by combining the language of position with that of dislocation.[21] It is questionable that this call has been heeded.

As though picking up Michel Foucault's challenge that space often appears as a philosophical exile and as needing a home that geography should grant it, Edward W. Soja asks cultural theorists to recognize that human interests are "space-forming and space-contingent," products as well as producers of spatiality. In order for this to be recognized, cultural studies should not be carried on in a language that "submerges and peripheralizes the spatial imagination."[22] Soja, drawing heavily on the work of Henri Lefebvre, has been among American theorists most highly effective in addressing the neglect of spatial issues in the human sciences and the inadequacy of current spatial theories. His challenge is well worth heeding: "Whenever you read a sentence that empowers history, historicality, or the historical narrative, substitute space, spatiality, or geography and think about the consequences."[23]

Despite efforts of many voices to resist it, however, the tendency of postmodern cultural and literary studies is to allow spatial language to remain abstract and rhetorical. This is said not to blame but to record the hold that displacement has on the language of space and place. The placelessness of the language of place and space in current cultural studies is produced by the abstract way in which space has tended to be treated in much of modern culture. Abstract space, unlike its Newtonian partner absolute time, has not, in the modern period, been adequately relativized. Spatial language may be so difficult to tie down because the primacy of absolute or abstract space seems consistent with common sense. People commonly think that particular places, places with qualities, are housed by an inclusive space that is itself uniform and without qualities. Inclusive abstract space is taken as primary and its particularizations as temporary and derivative. As Edward Casey puts it, "Once it is assumed (after Newton and Kant) that space is absolute and infinite as well as empty and a priori, places become the mere apportionings of space, its compartmentalizations."[24] This notion seems confirmed by models close to home. Our houses provide a general space that is subdivided into rooms with particular qualities and uses. The notion that space is first of all general and without qualities and that particular places with qualities are secondary and temporary has proven to be too firmly a part of Western culture to be dislodged by the move from modernism to whatever one calls the culture that today we are in. It represents the clearest instance in the culture of a lingering idealism, and it continues to determine how we think about and relate to space and place.

Space divorced from qualities and specific human interests also assumes authority because it is amenable to rational and mathematical languages and is therefore basic to planning, designing, and mapping. Such acts are crucial particularly to constructing, maintaining, and visualizing the massive social spaces that largely define modern culture. As Lefebvre puts it: "The thesis of an inert spatial medium where people or things, actions and situations, merely take up their abode, as it were, corresponds to the Cartesian model (conceiving of things in their extension as the 'object' of thought) which over time becomes the stuff of 'common sense' and 'culture.' A picture of mental space developed by the philosophers and epistemologists thus becomes a transparent zone, a logical medium."[25] Thus arise the pervasive assumptions about space both in modern and postmodern culture: that abstract space is primary and antecedent to particular places and that space is inherently free from qualities.

Finally, abstract space has such authority in our spatial language because it is so often and so easily related to social space, and social space dominates our spatial awareness. The language of social space tends toward abstraction because we think of the social whole as antecedent to its parts. We tend to posit society as a general container unifying the differing and at times contending segments or locations of the society. The scientific interests of sociology privilege quantification, and abstract social space gives itself to geometric and other mathematical mappings. Our interests in social space, then, resist specificity, and they tend to subordinate particular human places.[26]

When we think of space, especially social space, in an abstract way, great harm can be done. The imperialist colonial enterprise is inconceivable apart from such ingrained habits of mind. Newly occupied lands became vulnerable to planning imposed on them by minds conditioned by abstract ways of viewing places. Particular places and the relations of their inhabitants to them could simply be subsumed by rational categories that could legitimize economic and political agendas. Mary Louise Pratt, working with travel books about Africa written by visiting Europeans in the nineteenth century, for example, details how little interest was taken by the colonists in the relation of the indigenous people to their locations and in the particular qualities of those places. The general landscape was emphasized.[27] Operating with similar critical tools, Timothy Mitchell shows how French and British colonists imposed an order on Egyptian societies that was assumed to be not order of a particular kind but order itself. This order, which identified certain arrangements in social space as consistent with rationality, could be imposed as unproblematic and requiring acceptance by Egyptians as their ticket for access to the advances of modern culture. The effect was to control a society under the pretext that abstract arrangements made society more fully human.[28] A third example is offered by William Pietz in his study of the creation of the "fetish" as a Western notion applied to non-Western cultures. This category allowed colonized cultures to be viewed as unpredictable and even irrational. In order to stabilize economic transactions, these societies were required to submit to uniform commercial planning, which entailed suppressing or marginalizing practices determined by specific locations. Again, admission to the fully human (that is, modern) world was thought of as synonymous with attitudes toward space that favored abstraction, quantification, and rational, economic transactions.[29]

Abstract space is particularly consistent with a social space determined by economic interests. Such a space gathers into itself, so to speak, all particular places, defines them, and assigns them their value. The primacy of economic interests in the construction of social space allows other forms of place-relations to be devalued. An inclusive economic system discounts not only particular values but also the value of particularity, including relations with particular places. As Lefebvre points out, spaces, when absorbed by such abstract notions, conceal both the historical conditions that gave rise to them and the actual differences between them in order to conform them to an imposed rational homogeneity.[30]

However, while cultural theory and criticism, especially postcolonial theory and criticism, are sensitive to the havoc wrought by imposing abstract notions of space on particular locations, cultural studies do not counter the real or potential damage such language warrants by challenging it with a more adequate theory of human place-relations. Current theory and criticism have not thrown cultural studies back on their resources to forge a hermeneutics of spatial texts that will enhance the particularity of places and of the relations of humans to them. This may be due to the close ties between postmodernist and economic interests. Architecture, for example, which so influences the styles and attitudes of postmodernism, is heavily dependent upon economic conditions even while it is irreverent toward them.[31] Robert Venturi, for example, can celebrate the architecture of Las Vegas without adequately noting the commercialization of human interests and the commodification of pleasure that are so much a part of that setting. When cultural studies employ an abstract spatial language they betray their lingering attachments to—even, perhaps, their dependence on—the economic system that so fully forms modern and postmodern attitudes.

It is my opinion that the language of place and space in current cultural studies maintains its currency not because of its inherent stability and significance but negatively, by virtue of its contrary relation to modernity, particularly modernity defined by history. In other words, the language of place and space, to the degree that it is stable and has meaning and force, holds a derived, oppositional position. What is needed, then, is to identify a cultural location where the language of place and space has a rightful role, generates positive content, emphasizes the particularity of places and of people's relations to them, and stands not in opposition but in relation to the language of actions and events, of time and history. We find this, I believe, in modern narrative discourses.

Spatial Language and Narrative Discourse

Narrative theory, however, is unprepared to respond to this challenge or invitation. This is because narrative theory, rather than doing justice to the full potential of spatial language in narrative discourse, subordinates it. It does this primarily by making temporal language, that is, the language of actions and events, central to narrative discourse, thereby subjecting narrative to the dominant discourses of modernity.

In my view, narrative discourses potentially challenge modernity or surface its subtext by giving prominence to the language of place and space. In narrative discourse, spatial language can generate a significance of its own without being separated from the other languages of narrative, including the language of action and event. The necessary and potentially prominent role of place and space in narrative discourse and its embeddedness among the other languages of narrative provide at least a partial remedy to the current pervasive deficiencies of spatial understandings, such as abstraction, fragmentation, and opposition to temporality. The language of place and space is always a part of narrative discourse and can be a principal locus of a narrative's power and significance. Places in narrative have force and meaning; they are related to human values and beliefs; and they are part of a larger human world, including actions and events.

To establish the importance of narrative place, we must first challenge the disparagement of narrative discourse in postmodernist cultural and literary studies, a disparagement epitomized by Lyotard. This disparagement is due to the habit of defining narrative primarily in terms of time and temporality. As we have seen, postmodernism marks the emergence of spatial language as a dominant over temporality. Narrative, therefore, has been a victim of the general turn of the culture away from the language of time and history. We are not accustomed to thinking of narrative when we think about place and space. Recognizing the role of spatial language in narrative discourse and rehabilitating narrative in current cultural theory are, therefore, mutually reinforcing projects.

The rehabilitation of narrative depends upon resisting the widespread assumption that the dominant language of narrative must be the language of temporality. We need not look far to find examples of recent theorists who define narrative temporally and by doing so contribute to its disfavor in present cultural studies. Frank Kermode, for example, defines human time as basically an undifferentiated succession of "now" points, and he treats narratives as responses to that situation. Narratives grant order to time by giving to mere sequence a beginning and, more important, an ending. Kermode's theory of narrative as a concord-producing response to the actual nonconnectedness of events appears to grant cultural significance to narrative by giving it soteriological functions; narratives and the practices of reading and interpreting them heal the split that people otherwise suffer between the reality of events in their noncoherence and the need of people to understand events as related to one another and to a significant beginning and end.[32] However, by defining narrative in primarily temporal terms, Kermode restricts the relevance of narrative and narrative theory to current cultural studies.

Gérard Genette goes further and is more deliberate than Kermode in dismissing the language of space from an account of what narratives are or do. Genette defines narrative as "the representation of an event or sequence of events, real or fictitious, by means of language and, more particularly, by means of written language."[33] Narratives contain both "actions and events, which constitute the narration in the strict sense and, on the other hand, those objects and characters that are the result of what we now call *descrip-*

tion."[34] Genette does not take these two kinds of language as actual or potential equals. Lest we misunderstand him, he sharpens his point: "narration is concerned with actions or events considered as pure processes, and by that very fact it stresses the temporal, dramatic aspect of the narrative; description, on the other hand, because it lingers on objects and beings considered in their simultaneity, and because it considers the processes themselves as spectacles, seems to suspend the course of time and to contribute to spreading the narrative in space."[35] For Genette, description impedes and even halts the main business of narrative, which is to represent actions and events. Consequently, he not only relegates "description" to a secondary role in narrative but even considers "description" and its spatial effects not to be constitutive parts of narrative. A description does not become part of the narrative but "forms a sort of cyst that is very easy to recognize and to locate."[36] He concludes that narrative, because it cannot exist without descriptions, never appears in pure form; "narrative exists nowhere, so to speak, in its strict form. The slightest general observation, the slightest adjective that is little more than descriptive, the most discreet comparison, the most modest 'perhaps,' the most inoffensive of lyrical articulations introduces into its web a type of speech that is alien to it, refractory as it were."[37] Rather than include the language of space in his account of narrative discourse, Genette defines narrative as a pure form that always, due to contamination by spatial language, appears in compromised and attenuated ways. Knowing that narratives inevitably contain spatial language, he brackets out such language in order to produce a definition of narrative as unlike any narrative that actually exists.

Paul Ricoeur commits himself as well to the primacy of the language of action and event in narrative discourse. This commitment arises from the constant interest in human temporality that controls his work. Ricoeur is not first of all interested in narrative, as he is also not first of all interested in the many other topics he has taken up in his work—metaphor, symbol, interpretation theory, or the dialectics of ideology and utopia, for example. In all these topics, he is interested first of all in human temporality, and these topics grant ways to explore the mysteries and problems of that philosophical and even theological topic. Consequently, he gives his attention primarily to plot in narrative and to the relation of events to patterns of coherence or "followability."[38]

Seymour Chatman favors time in narrative for a somewhat different reason. Influenced by Russian formalism, he distinguishes the *fabula* of a narrative from its *sujet,* and this ends, as for most who follow this path, in a separation of events in their putative sequence from events as they are presented in the narrative. Narrative, then, is a combination of temporal material and a certain treatment of it.[39] Though coming at the matter from a very different starting point, Chatman's theory ends up looking much like Kermode's.

If in narrative theory space is taken into account at all, it will, as J. J. van Baak says, be "viewed in its subordinate and subservient role in relation to the other thematic blocks: space providing formally indispensable locations for occurrences, characters, their actions and experiences."[40] While most often subordinated to the language of action and event, critics and theorists also subordinate spatial language to the other languages of narrative. Leonard Lutwack, for example, subordinates place and space to character, and Carl Darryl Malmgren subjects place and space to a dominant interest in narrative point of view.[41] Critics and theorists who elevate character or point of view to perpetual prominence are similar to Kermode, Genette, Ricoeur, and Chatman in taking one of the languages of narrative discourse and lifting it to a permanently dominant and defining position. Rarely is such elevation given to the language of place and space, however. Narrative theorists, then, regularly manifest two errors. First, they allow their theoretical interests to confine them to, or to privilege, one of the languages of narrative. Second, while differing as to which of the languages they choose for privileged and even exclusive attention, they agree that, if the language of space has a role at all in narratives, it will likely not be a prominent or, even less, a dominant one.

Despite a widespread disregard for the language of place and space in narrative by modern theoretical and critical discourses, there are exceptions, and I should note some of them. Edward Said, to whom I already have referred, provides one. He points out that we read particular novels with such attention to temporality that we overlook the function in them of space, geography, and location. More important, we place novels, in our general account of their cultural role, in a historical context, that is, as providing one of the ways by which English society appropriated its past, adjusted to its present, and anticipated its future. However important that role may be in accounting for the novel in the formation of English consciousness, it is also the case that the English novel granted its readers a spatial sense of England not only as centrally located relative to outlying areas but also as relating those areas to England in imperial terms. From Defoe through Austen, during the whole of the nineteenth century and well into the twentieth century, distant lands not only are out there but they also, by being under English control, can, without serious question, be visited and referred to, thereby being incorporated into a continuous spatial compass.[42]

Jeffrey R. Smitten stresses spatiality in his study of Hawthorne's *The House of the Seven Gables*. The house not only contains but even sponsors events and actions.[43] He suggests that narratives can be called spatial whenever attention is given to environments that become distinguishable from human control, that is, whenever places take on a power or significance of their own.

Joseph A. Kestner also respects the language of space in narrative, and he supplies some helpful terminological distinctions. He defines *place* in contrast to *space* as particular in contrast to general, and he arranges narrative places into scene, setting, space, environment, and atmosphere, moving, in that order, from the most particular to the most general. He also suggests a grammar of locations that can be drawn from narrative conventions, locations that recur and have significance because certain kinds of people predictably inhabit them or because certain actions are likely to occur there.[44] Kestner is less successful, in my opinion, when he attempts to tie kinds of spatial language in narrative to kinds of visual art—narrative scenes to painting, descriptions of character to sculpture, and the total arrangement of a narrative's parts to architecture.[45]

Finally, Sharon Spencer traces an increasing occurrence of the language of place in twentieth-century narrative. She sees literary modernism as a watershed in narrative form, by which an emphasis on temporality is replaced by an emphasis on space.[46] While I agree with Spencer that the language of space is prominent and at times even dominant in the narrative discourses of literary modernism, I do not think that a gap between modernist and earlier narrative discourses is opened by a shift to spatial language. I think the more reliable move is to normalize the language of space as a constitutive part of narrative discourse rather than to make its increasing role definitive of a new narrative mode.

If we recognize the constitutive role of spatial language in narrative discourse and do that without denigrating the other languages of narrative, we end with a more complex and variable understanding of narrative discourse than is otherwise available. Such a theory of narrative recognizes the variety of languages in narrative discourse and the ability of any one of them to be prominent or even to dominate the others. The languages that constitute narrative discourse can be designated as the languages of character, of actions and events, of the teller's interests or attitudes, and of place or environment. This does not mean that these four languages are parts of narrative the way, as one theorist put it, "engine, chassis, and wheels are parts of a car."[47] Narrative discourse is not a process by which preexisting discourses are brought into relation to one another. Narrative discourses are not secondary and derivative but primary and generative. And one of the evidences of narrative's status is that the four languages that constitute narrative discourses are always already not only present but related to and interactive with one another. However, the fact that in particular narratives these four languages are always already present, related, and interactive does not mean that all four must be of equal importance. The point is that the language of place and space is always operative in narrative, always related to narrative's other languages, and potentially as able as the others to be prominent and even dominant in a particular narrative discourse.

When readers take note of the language of space in a narrative, they usually do so by referring to "setting." But "setting" condemns the language of place to inherently passive and secondary roles. "Setting" suggests background, necessary, perhaps, but never, like the other languages of narrative, foregrounded. Also, the other terms imply content, while "setting" seems to lack it; the term sounds empty as well as passive. We say of someone that "he is a character" or that "she has character." "Plot" also gets infusions of significance because we use the term as a synonym for scheme and design. And tone—the language of material choice, of attitude toward the material, and of style—has connotations of color, evaluation, and relationships. "Setting" is an inadequate term for covering the possibilities of the language of space in narrative discourse because place and space need not stand only as background and need not lack force and significance.

Indeed, spatial language in a narrative can be active, meaningful, and primary. The various locations of a narrative can be read as constituting a kind of "geographical synthesis" in the narrative analogous to the kind of synthesis of actions and events we refer to as the narrative's plot.[48] A narrative's "geography" can set limits and boundaries to the narrative world, determining, for example, what occurs, what is possible, and what can and cannot be expected. In addition, the language of space can set conditions, either negatively or positively arrayed, that resist or enhance the interests or attitudes of characters or narrators. As J. E. Malpas says, "we understand a place and a landscape through the historical and personal narratives that are marked out within it and that give that place a particular unity and establish a particular set of possibilities within it."[49] Because the language of place plays such roles it may be better to refer to a narrative's "atmosphere," "environment," or "geography" instead of "setting." "Atmosphere" allows for a range of density and pressure, and an "environment" can be hostile, suggesting force and significance. We think of geography as granting circumscription, designating places, and clarifying relations between them.

While places in narratives can have force and significance, their value is not constant and predictable. Differing places can evince a range of positive and negative qualities. While conventions help readers to interpret the language of space in a narrative, there is lack of stability in the conventional meaning of locations. This is due not only, as Edward Soja points out, to the fact that in our culture a split has occurred between spaces and their meanings but also to the fact that the meanings of spaces are complex and ambiguous.[50] The result of this lack of agreement in the evaluation of places is that spatial values, ranging from strongly negative and feared to strongly positive and desired, are as primary as the locations to which they variously are related.

The language of place becomes prominent in a narrative not only when it is strongly evaluated but also when the reader is transported to an unaccustomed place or when a familiar place is radically altered. Such impertinence generally occurs by encounters with places that have a negative relation to the well-being of the characters or narrator. Characters and narrators raise questions about their locations more readily when they are radically altered or have become unpleasant than when locations are customary and support their interests. Some of the most striking instances of space-dominated narratives in this century—*The Plague* of Albert Camus, for example, or Franz Kafka's *The Trial*—draw the attention of characters and narrators to their environments because conditions arise that make a familiar place strange and a supportive place antagonistic.

When the language of place, environment, or atmosphere is prominent or dominant in a narrative, the other languages of the narrative tend to be deformed toward it. This dynamic among the languages of narrative discourse deserves comment.

The language of place in a narrative is often subordinate to the language of character, as when descriptions of a room or house serve to indicate a character's personality, tastes, or social standing. The language of space can be subordinate to plot, as when it provides places where events can occur. However, the language of space begins to dominate character and plot when it determines the characters that are likely to appear in certain locations or the kinds of events that occur. So, institutions—hospitals, prisons, the military—are arenas that determine who will appear and what kinds of things will go on. Kinds of buildings, differing rooms of a house, open fields, and other locations can affect character and plot. The language of place becomes even more determining when, as in several narratives to be studied later, action or characters are restricted to a particular place. Characters are thrown or held together by the confines of the space, and they are forced by place to deal not only with one another but also with the spatial conditions that they share.

When the language of space becomes dominant in a narrative, especially by bearing negative or threatening potential, characters are more determined by their situations than they otherwise would be and are put into more reactive than initiative roles. In an environment of a heavily negative kind, survival rather than development and enrichment becomes the major concern. Characters are flatter and have fewer options. Such conditions give rise to what has been variously referred to as the vanishing hero, the pariah, the exile, and the stranger in modernist narratives. When place takes on characteristics of an antagonist, characters find themselves attacked not by other human beings but by pervasive, indefinable, and malignant spatial conditions, and they are not likely to know how to contend with them. Rather than a human antagonist against whom, even in defeat, a character can achieve some stature by virtue of resistance, an indefinite set of negative conditions can reduce characters to bewildered helplessness and their responses to impulsive or desperate reactions that may worsen their situations. Characters also tend to become, when determined by the language of antagonistic space, little more than types of responses to the conditions. So, in *The Plague* we have characters that are embodied examples of a range of human reactions to a terribly negative situation. An allegorical meaning-effect begins to emerge in such a narrative whereby characters represent human types—in this case, the person of reason, the person of faith, the person of courage, and the coward, for example.

When the language of space dominates a narrative, its plot is also flattened. Not as much can happen. A heavy atmosphere can even break the continuity of time, and plot becomes more episodic. Actions and events are more causally related to the conditions than to one another. Rather than having a significance of its own, the time of the narrative can easily become the time it takes for the conditions to expose themselves and to exert their effects or the time it takes for the characters and narrator to explore the environment.

Domination by the language of space will also alter the role of the teller in a narrative. When the language of space dominates, the material of the narrative is not so much chosen by as forced on the teller. The attitude of the teller also becomes not one of moral evaluation, which would give tone the authority of judgment as well as selection, but one of uncertainty and obsession. And word choice will be determined by the urgency of the situation rather than by the richness of the teller's vocabulary or the skills and resources of the teller that would require more relaxed conditions. The language will tend to be spare and unadorned, a language that reports conditions and their details objectively and dispassionately. One finds, for example, a cool, even eerie detachment of tone in Elie Wiesel's *Night,* by which a horrible place is described in a quite matter-of-fact way.

Important as these consequences of a dominant and negative language of space are for the language of tone, even more significant consequences arise from the rhetorical effects of a dominant language of negative space. The language of negative place in a narrative helps to create a relationship between the narrator and narratee. A common threat or situation of stress can be posited under which both narrator and narratee stand, and between them a communal identity of the distressed, of victims, or of survivors can develop. This consequence of negative space becomes important for modernist narratives because they are written in increasingly complex social and cultural situations. In these situations, authors and readers cannot be counted on to have much in common. The loss of a shared world, of encompassing values and interests, between narrator and narratee, requires techniques for establishing relations between them. The language of negative place is a very effective way of producing that result. In fact, it could be argued, in reply to Sharon Spencer, that one of the reasons for the rise in prominence of the language of space, especially negative space, in fictions of the modernist period is the need to create shared situations when they are no longer readily provided culturally. The modernist description of "the human condition" as problematic and threatening is inseparable from this rhetorical need and potential.

A sharp rise in prominence of the language of space over the other languages of narrative occurs in modernist writing, although that rise is not as sudden or unprecedented as Spencer suggests. Lee T. Lemon, in an essay on the language of environment in nineteenth-century English fiction, charts a developing interest during that period in what he calls a "hostile universe."[51] While places in Jane Austen's novels are shaped to support the needs and interests of characters, in the fiction of Thackeray, the Brontë sisters, and Dickens environment becomes increasingly prominent, complicated, and even threatening. In *Wuthering Heights* (1847), for example, the environment exerts force on the characters and complicates their relationships. Characters are affected by aspects of their locations that they neither control nor understand.

Indeed, one could go back further to point out that Defoe placed characters in strong relation to places. Social and natural contexts are recognized as forces, and environment has consequences for human needs and potential. And one could refer to the epic tradition and to biblical narrative as demonstrating how places are not only prominent but exert influence on characters and action. In other words, the potential prominence of the language of place in narrative discourse is not uniquely actualized by literary modernism.

Finally, we should note that the language of place and space, which is always present in narrative, is given prominence in modern fiction not only for reasons internal to the narratives but also because of the larger cultural context. The narratives I shall examine give prominence to the language of place because they contend with their environments. They serve to make the language of place specific and related to human interests and contend with cultural attitudes and practices that undervalue or distort places and human relations to them. This means that these texts need not be validated by or subjected to some kind of spatial theory in order to be significant players in spatial discourse but, rather, that the spatial theory implicit in them needs to be released, organized, and placed in a complementary and correcting relation to other theories. These narratives do not simply depend upon theories or cultural assumptions about places and the relations they have to human needs and values. They generate and contend for certain understandings of human spatiality. The main purpose of this study is to release their potential contribution to current understandings of human place-relations.

Toward a Narrative-Based Theory of Place-Relations

My aim is to derive from texts of six modern writers the outlines of a theory of human place-relations that is incipient in their narrative discourses. In the narratives I have chosen the language of place and space is prominent, if not dominant. The incipient theory drawn from them has been turned back onto the texts as principles of organization. I shall describe the organization and thereby outline the theory. This anticipates the third part of the study, in which the incipient theory is elaborated by bringing it into conversation with other, diverse theories of human spatiality.

There are three components of the theory of human place-relations derived from the narratives and turned back onto them as a structure for this study. The first distinguishes between kinds of human place-relations. The three kinds of human place-relations clarify one another by contrast, although each also has its own distinguishing characteristics. This means that there are differential relations between the three kinds. Having a relation to one kind of place is to a large degree defined as not having a relation to one of the other two kinds.

The narrative discourses that I shall examine differ from one another, then, in the prominence given to one rather than to either of the other kinds of place-relations. While all of the discourses agree that the present state of places and of the relations of people to them in the culture are faulty and that these faults have consequences for human moral and spiritual well-being, they disagree about which kind of place-relation needs most to be corrected. They differ by giving prominence to one of the three kinds of place-relations.

One kind of place-relation can be housed under the category of "cosmic or comprehensive space." This is a sense of placement within a space that precedes, outstrips, and includes humans and their constructions. Often this kind of place-relation is associated with nature, but nature, by the close of the nineteenth century, has become sufficiently problematized to prohibit its simple identification with comprehensive space. Nature is not clearly and finally distinguishable from culture, although some locations and phenomena, like wilderness and storms, are more natural than cities and other human constructions. Natural locations or situations often are used to suggest or represent cosmic or comprehensive space, but such space is not, without qualification, identifiable as natural space.

The second kind of place-relation is social or political. Such space is created by the relations of people to one another, the structure of those relations, and the laws and mores that regulate them. The narratives I shall examine identify modernity with the rise to dominance of social, particularly urban, space. Indeed, one of the problems they seem in consort to expose is that human place-relations are swamped by the power and pervasiveness of social, political space. For all of them, modern social space is problematic not only because it dominates other kinds of places but also because modern social spaces are constituted in ways that resist positive relations with them. Texts that emphasize social space as primary have the job of clarifying what a more viable or humanly enhancing kind of social, political space would be.

The third kind of place-relation I designate as "personal or intimate." I avoid using the term "private" because it suggests ownership, and ownership is not necessary to relations with personal or intimate places. Ownership as definitive of personal space reveals its domination by social space. One of the difficulties with personal, intimate space, as with comprehensive space, is to free it from social space, especially social space as structured by economic determinations.

These three kinds of space or place-relations structure the study because the writers are arranged according to them. In each of the first two parts of the study, I shall move from cosmic, comprehensive (Hardy and Greene) to social, political (Conrad and Golding), and to personal, intimate (Forster and Spark) space.

The incipient theory in these narratives not only posits human spatiality as complex by being constituted of three kinds of place-relations but also reveals that human place-relations are two-sided. On one side, they are physical. Without physicality there can be no place-relations, only substitutes for or images of them. However, place-relations also have a spiritual side. They have a significance or attraction that cannot wholly be accounted for. Having said this, however, it also appears that while place-relations include both sides, one side will be perceived or presented as more needed and valued than the other.

The two-sided character of human place-relations, which is the second aspect of the theory of human spatiality drawn from the narratives, is also turned back on them as an organizing principle. The first part of the study deals with three early modernists—Hardy, Conrad, and Forster—who have two things in common. First, they respond to the deficiencies and potentials of human place-relations by attempting to invoke values and orientations located in the past. Second, all three of them present narratives that imply a diagnosis of contemporary place-relations that targets a lack of physicality. The narratives of all three direct attention to the primacy of the physical in place-relations. We shall have to see what this means, then, for comprehensive, social, and intimate place-relations. Meanwhile, the second part of the study deals with three later modernists—Greene, Golding, and Spark —whose fiction depicts the spiritual more than the physical side of place-relations. In addition, as much as the fiction of the early modernists directs attention to the past, the fictions of the later modernists direct attention to the future. Instead of retrieval, we find search and projection. Using Paul Ricoeur's categories, I have called these two sides or directions in the language of place-relations "archaeological" and "teleological."[52]

The third aspect of the theory is more implicit to the whole of the study. This pertains to the depiction or adumbration by the fiction of positive place-relations. All six writers agree that modern spaces and place-orientations are harmful, especially to moral and spiritual well-being; that human beings have a great need and potential for positive relations to places; and that positive place-relations can be both imagined and experienced. It is not, therefore, the negative in modern place-relations that these narratives emphasize. Negative places and placelessness are preliminary in their work to the more important task of retrieving or adumbrating positive place-relations. The principal value of these texts, it seems to me, is that they counter either implicitly or explicitly the problem that places and place-relations have become with positive alternatives.

Commonly, positive place-relations are characterized by the feeling of being "at home." But "at home" tends to favor intimate space, although one can be, as William James put it, at home in the universe, and one can feel at home in a social setting. I find "at home" an inadequate designation for positive place-relations not only because it favors intimate space but also because it smacks too much of arrival and permanence. Indeed, this reservation should be underscored, because it would be best, with all the attention I shall give to place-relations, not to begin talking about place-relations as though they are fixed and represent "rootedness." People move between places as well as dwell in them. Indeed, one feature of a more fully human sense of place-relations—a feature that narrative secures—is the important relation of placement to human mobility and temporality. Placement and movement imply, clarify, and stimulate one another. I have tried to incorporate some of these complexities by characterizing positive human place-relations as "accommodating." I end each discussion of the six narratives I have chosen for more detailed study by rehearsing the characteristics of positive place-relations implied or advocated by each, characteristics that allow the six otherwise diverse narratives to support a single norm.

These three components of the incipient theory of place-relations derived from the fictions—that human spatiality is constituted of three kinds of place-relations, that these relations are two-sided or two-directional, and that all place-relations can be evaluated by the use of the single norm of "accommodating"—are individually dealt with in the third part of the study and placed in conversation with other prominent and diverse theories of human spatiality. These conversations allow the incipient theory not only to draw from others but also to amend and correct them.

In the conclusion, I shall return to the question of sharp dichotomies in the language of place. Returning to some of the points made in this introduction, I shall look at the sharp distinctions drawn by modern theorists between secular or profane and sacred spaces. I shall argue that a negative assessment of social places and place-relations, particularly regarding urban space, has become a fact in cultural studies. This factual profane is then used to steady and grant significance to individually sponsored theories or constructions of "sacred" place. Whether these constructions and theories are sponsored by secular or religious interests, by political or aesthetic dispositions, they all depend on agreement concerning the factual profane. I shall argue that the factual profane is a rhetorical construction and that various forms of sacred space should be theorized not on such a narrow and vulnerable basis but on a more adequate theory of positive place-relations, a theory that this study is designed to advance.

Part One

Early Modernists and the
Archaeology of Place-Relations

1

Thomas Hardy

Facing the Physicality of Comprehensive Space

By treating Thomas Hardy as an early modernist I do not posit a sharp discontinuity between his fiction and the Victorian novel. Indeed, as Lee Lemon points out, during the nineteenth century, hostile environments became increasingly forceful in English fiction, and Lemon places Hardy at the end of this development.[1] However, one can also say that places and place-relations take on new dimensions and force in Hardy's fiction.[2] His architectural training, his sojourn in London, his attachments to the open spaces of southwestern England, and his sense of England as a bellwether of modern Western adjustments to a changing sense of cosmic and cultural location seem to have made Hardy unusually sensitive to human placement and place-relations. Hardy was aware of and affected by what I called earlier a history of changing places and spatial orientation, and his fiction is in great measure a response, even a counterthrust, to that history.

Hardy was aware of the traumatic consequences for spatial orientation that arose in English culture from the impact of Darwin and the work of other natural and social theorists. The principal consequence was to subvert an anthropocentric cosmos. There are probably few if any more important yields to Hardy's work than this: people can no longer think of the world anthropocentrically, that is, as established with them and their well-being in mind. His awareness of cultural change and the spatial qualities of his fiction have much to do with one another. And this relation locates him not only at the end of the development that Lemon charts but also as an early contributor to what follows.

Some implications of Hardy's cultural awareness need to be emphasized.

He believed, first of all, that recent changes force people to recognize the truth about the world in which they live and about themselves. These recognitions about cosmic placement expose cultural confinement and illusion. Second, the uncertain, unsettling qualities of the world in which humans now find themselves need not create pessimism or defiance toward the conditions of life, although they require attention and radical adjustment. Third, this attention and adjustment, while disconcerting, have positive moral and spiritual consequences. They create integrity and, more important, a charitable attitude not only toward other people but also toward all living creatures. The force of his fiction, then, is to subvert the sense of privilege, security, and centrality that had come to be basic to cultural self-understanding and to keep this disorientation from undermining human values. Relation to the comprehensive reality of life calls for, if it does not produce, a capacity for truth and kinder, more compassionate attitudes toward fellow creatures.

Relation to the force of comprehensive space, then, opens Hardy's work to religious attitudes, but these attitudes are not primarily Christian. Hardy's work more frequently calls attention to pre-Christian attitudes, both local and distant, that, we are asked to believe, reveal more awareness of the actual conditions of life than does contemporary English culture, especially in its Christian form. As Raymond Williams put it, for Hardy "traditional religion had taught the essential mystery of human existence but had simultaneously offered ways through and beyond it, in worship and charity."[3] The new cosmic awareness made ancient forms of religious belief and practice more relevant to the present situation than were the cultural and religious institutions of England. His response to the trauma of spatial disorientation and of the ambiguous relation of human well-being to cosmic conditions took the form, then, of retrieval. Pre-Christian cultures indigenous to the countryside, classical culture, and Old Testament texts, especially the Wisdom books, provide moral and spiritual resources for relating to the conditions that comprehend human life as they have recently been exposed.

Another way of saying this is that evolutionary theories and *Essays and Reviews* pried Hardy, along with many of his contemporaries, from orientations that had given Christian support to anthropocentrism. However, unlike many of his contemporaries, Hardy did not shift to antireligious ideologies.[4] He did not move from the comforts of one kind of certainty to those of another kind.[5] Rather, his fiction places human life in the midst of uncertainty. We are led by his fiction to conclude that only people unprotected by the certainties of Christian and secular doctrines are able to appreciate the actual placement of human life and the truthfulness and charity that this placement can create. True, Hardy, as one commentator puts it, "whole-heartedly rejects the conventional Christian myth of a benevolent universe,"[6] but, rather than exchange Christian for secular certainty or certainty of a benevolent for certainty of a malignant universe, he located himself not in dogma but before what he took to be reality. His fictions primarily make available the force of that comprehensive, cosmic reality and the significant moral and spiritual benefits that are created by awareness of and relation to it.

Cultural dislocation, therefore, plays a role in Hardy's fiction that is penultimate to relocation. And the new location is defined primarily by what for Hardy was physical reality. He does not draw attention to the physicality of space primarily by means of human labor, although labor, kinds of work, and idleness are major matters in his fiction.[7] Nor does he secure the physicality of place by means of the human body, particularly the sexed body, although sexuality in his fiction is a recurring and at times a defining dimension of particular human locations.[8] While human labor and human sexuality are crucial to securing the physicality of place for Hardy's fiction, the principal locus of physical space is reality itself as a forceful, comprehensive physical environment. Recognition of and alignment with that reality offer a greater degree of truthfulness and charity than do the dogmas and institutions of both Christian and secular culture.

The reader of Hardy is led to conclude, then, that the present traumatic dislocations offer an opportunity as well as a loss, an opportunity for a more accurate and moral understanding of human beings, their relation to the world, and their obligations toward one another. He valued Darwin because of the uncertainties created by his theories rather than because of the scientific certainties his views might sponsor.[9] Indeed, "Hardy, though he is aware of the known, emphasizes the unknown far more than the scientist does."[10] The force and significance of the unknown in the comprehensive physical environment of life can impart integrity and, even more, wisdom to human beings.

However, embodiments of an integrity and wisdom drawn from relations to the physical reality that comprehends human life are not frequently found among Hardy's characters. This would have required making the language of character dominant in his fiction rather than the language of place. His characters present types of responses or relations to the circumstances and forces that affect their lives, and some are judged to be more adequate than others. Few, however, reach normative status. Indeed, the attitudes of most characters are inadequate, mistaken, or destructive for self and others. It is this, as much as the conditions of life, that casts over his fiction bleak shadows. His plots, while they reveal the impact on characters of the harsh conditions under which they live, also reveal the consequences of their failure to take those conditions fully enough into account.

Rather than to his characters, therefore, it is to the narrators of his fictions that we should look for examples of Hardy's most fully advocated attitude toward the newly recognizable location of human life. His narrators model the kind of relation to comprehensive reality that his work promotes. They have this authority not by drawing attention to themselves but rather by bringing into focus the comprehensive physical environment of human life.

The narrative that gives us fullest access to the kind of place-relations advocated by Hardy's fiction is *The Return of the Native*. I shall look first at how space and place-relations are narrated in this text. Then I shall turn to some of his other work in order to expand and complicate the sense of place it provides.

I

The narrator of *The Return of the Native* does not locate himself within the story's temporal setting but within present time, which has become uncertain. It is for the sake of present time that he narrates. He shares this temporal position with his reader and draws continuities or analogies between it and both the earlier time of his narrative's setting and the cultures of pre-Christian peoples. He contends, for example, that he and his readers resemble the contemporaries of Aeschylus in that now even children recognize what only a few ancients did, namely, "the defects of natural laws" and the "quandary" humanity is in because of them (*RN*, 1:206).[11] He turns the attention of his readers to the heath and its inhabitants of the previous generation as though to something useful for the present that can be retrieved from that location and culture. Those people, like pre-Christians, lived in situations more exposed to the actual physical conditions of human life than do modern Englishmen. Appreciation for them and their situation will be helpful to readers now.

The true, actual context of human life is recognizable on the heath, for one thing, because of its northern location. Southern regions lull people into inattention or keep them in innocence regarding the conditions that affect human well-being. Warm and gentle climates offer illusions of harmony between human needs and the conditions of life, but the North divests people of such comforts. It forces them to recognize that the realities affecting human life are not predictable and are often hostile.[12] This potential for revealing the truth about human life will increasingly attract people to northern exposures where a second renaissance will occur—or already is beginning: "The time seems near, if it has not actually arrived, when the chastened sublimity of a moor, a sea, or a mountain will be all of nature that is absolutely in keeping with the moods of the more thinking among mankind. And ultimately, to the commonest tourist, spots like Iceland may become what the vineyards and myrtle-gardens of South Europe are to him now; and Heidelberg and Baden be passed unheeded as he hastens from the Alps to the sand-dunes of Scheveningen" (RN, 1:5). To some degree, the problems that Eustacia Vye has with the heath arise from her ties with southern Europe. She is unable to accept the truthfulness of reality as exposed by the heath and is drawn to the illusion of more comforting and flattering locations. In contrast, Clym Yeobright, who feels drawn to the heath, is related by the narrator to northern cultures, to the world of Rembrandt and Dürer.

Another reason why the narrator turns to the heath and its inhabitants is that they have not been fully colonized by English political and ecclesiastical institutions. On the heath, people live unprotected by the institutions and doctrines that reach out from the religious and political centers of society, and they consequently are not protected or abstracted from the harsh conditions of their physical surroundings. This means that the heath's culture, the language and rituals of its people, bears the marks of its comprehensive location, a location that is actual and specific.

Christianity's ecclesiastical structure has little more than a token presence on the heath; it is as though Christianity never really took hold. Christian holidays, such as Christmas, are marked more by the St. George play with its ties to ancient rituals of natural renewal than by rehearsals of the Gospels. Pagan rituals and pre-Christian beliefs have more force than their Christian replacements. The people's rites acknowledge the enduring tenure of ancient divinities. As the narrator says, "fragments of Teutonic rites to divinities whose names are forgotten, seem in some way or other to have survived mediaeval doctrine" (RN, 2:479). It is not as though awareness of the actual physical conditions of life cancels religious beliefs and practices. Rather, religions of the past, by being formed in exposure to those conditions, are more relevant to the specific realities of the people's location. The Celts, Saxons, and Romans who lived in the region were more aware of their actual circumstances than people in Christian cultures are likely to be, and traces of those cultures remain because Christianity, very likely due to its lack of relevance to the particularities of the place, failed to take hold on the heath or to suppress former shrines, practices, and beliefs.

Nor have English political and social structures and practices been able to impose themselves between the people and their environment. Guy Fawkes Day is celebrated on the heath not as a political festival but as a ritual that defies the oncoming darkness of winter. The narrator wants the reader not to miss this point: "Indeed, it is pretty well known that such blazes as this the heathmen were now enjoying are rather the lineal descendants from jumbled Druidical rites and Saxon ceremonies than the invention of popular feeling and Gunpowder Plot" (*RN*, 1:18–19). The fall rituals and the May Day celebration on the heath mark a society more related to ancient than to modern culture.

Ancient cultural inscriptions make the heath a significant resource for the narrator's audience, which he implicitly constructs as people having found current ecclesiastical and political structures inadequate to the conditions of life recently exposed. The narrator directs readers to a location where they can find an example of culture geographically and temporally close by that takes into account rather than conceals the comprehensive physical reality in relation to which life must be lived.

The heath and the physical reality it exposes are placed in sharp contrast to social, especially urban spaces. While it may be too much to say that the novel evokes a "spirit of place in terms of two locations, representing two states of mind or ways of life,"[13] it is true that life on the heath is advocated in contrast to living in cities. Budmouth, London, and especially Paris are attractive alternatives for some of the characters because cities appeal to desire and divert attention from the comprehensive realities under which people must live. Clym's assessment of Paris as a place of pretension, deception, and greed was made possible because he had grown up on the heath. His early conditioning by the heath allowed him to see it as the standard of reality by which Paris in contrast could be judged as artificial and frivolous. The heath puts in sharp contrast urban environments that entice people toward vanity and self-deception.

With these general characteristics of the heath in mind—that its northern location exposes people to the harsh but true conditions of human life, that pre-Christian cultures still active there are more suited to and responsive to those conditions than are English ecclesiastical and political institutions, and that the heath stands in contrast to modern cities as actual and true to artificial and vain—we can describe more specific characteristics of the heath. We should notice that they are both negative and positive.

The negative conditions of the heath are registered by the inability of people to be fully prepared for its harsh realities. Conditions associated with the heath, rather than receding to a background position, constantly impose themselves, and people must contend with them. Storm is the heath's love, wind its friend, and civilization its enemy (*RN*, 1:6–7). The heath is more likely to separate and isolate people than to enfold and join them. And its force and breadth throw into contrast the temporary and fragile standing of human lives and cultures. Its principal human monuments are ancient burial sites.

However, the heath also has positive qualities.[14] For example, it can, by its expanse, enlarge human awareness, and the narrator both advocates human expansiveness and defers to the heath as producing it. In addition, by always being noticeable and never out of sight, the heath exerts a steadying influence or counterweight for the "mind adrift on change, and harassed by the irrepressible New" (RN, 1:7). Finally, its particularity grants the heath a kind of significance that, because it cannot be captured by language, provides a resonant counterpart to human words and actions.[15] The heath, therefore, is only partially recorded in the narrative and in the language and behavior of the culture produced on it. This combination of negative and positive effects makes the heath a deeply ambiguous place: "The heath is to be hated as much as worshipped, feared as much as admired, respected as much as challenged."[16]

All of this is preparatory for the narrator's principal point, namely, that transitions and the uncertainty that they cause are basic to life and come to awareness by the physical conditions of living on the heath. The power and significance of the heath are particularly recognizable in moments of transition. The narrator stresses transitions and the places between alternatives that transitions expose. Indeed, the major point of difference between life lived on the heath and life contained by political, religious, and social structures can be located precisely here: on the heath the full grandeur and uncertainty of transitions can be felt, while the constancy of institutions shelters people from the uncertainty created by change. We find this emphasis already on the opening page: in the "transitional point of its nightly roll into darkness the great and particular glory of the Egdon waste began, and nobody could be said to understand the heath who had not been there at such a time" (RN, 1:4). The force and significance of transition can in part be measured by the uncertainty it creates in and for human attitudes and behavior: "To do things musingly, and by small degrees, seemed, indeed, to be a duty in the Egdon valleys at this transitional hour, for there was that in the condition of the heath itself which resembled protracted and halting dubiousness" (RN, 1:12). Transition in natural conditions—diurnal, lunar, seasonal, annual—create points between states, interstices and thresholds, to which the narrative is particularly oriented. It is particularly uncertainty, "dubiousness," that fascinates the narrator and holds special meaning for him. Transitions create uncertainty and are marked; the winter solstice is the time of Clym's arrival; the wedding of Thomasin and Wildeve occurs on December 24; in the month of March, the heath awakens "from winter trance" (RN, 1:234); the maypole marks the advent of spring.

The dubiousness created by such transitions is echoed in or reinforced by the locations of several characters. The reddleman, for example, holds a transitional position as one of a class becoming extinct in Wessex, something like the dodo bird of the previous century (RN, 1:10). Thomasin and

Eustacia, whose fathers were musicians and died young, were exposed to transitions in their lives. Wildeve, trained as an engineer, now operates an inn and is uncertain in social location.[17] Clym was dislodged from his place in Paris when he reached a transitional point in his life, "the stage in a young man's life when the grimness of the general human situation first becomes clear and the realization of this causes ambition to halt awhile. In France it is not uncustomary to commit suicide at this stage; in England we do much better, or much worse, as the case may be" (*RN*, 1:232). Indeed, the entire culture of the heath is in a state of transition. Its pastoral isolation is beginning to be disrupted by the introduction of the railway. The rustics of the former generation were not literate, while those of the present are. And the major characters appear to represent influences that may threaten, distract, or alter the rustics, as with Susan Nunsuch and Charley. Since the narrator tells us that the qualities of the heath are revealed in moments of transition, of protracted "dubiousness," we can infer that characters and cultures are most fully revealed in transitional states as well.

Moments of transition and the crossing of thresholds revealed in and by the heath are so important to the narrator because they resemble the situation in which he finds himself and locates his audience, that is, betwixt and between the ending of an inadequate culture and the advent of its more adequate replacement. As the heath is most fully revealed in times of transition, human realities are most fully revealed in times of cultural transition or change. As Raymond Williams puts it, thereby making Hardy's point characteristic of literary modernism: "[T]he real Hardy country, I feel more and more, is that border country so many of us have been living in: between custom and education, between work and ideas, between love of place and experience of change . . . for in Britain generally this is what has been happening: a moving out from old ways and places and ideas and feelings; a discovery in the new of certain unlooked-for problems, unexpected and very sharp crises, conflicts and desire and possibility."[18] Hardy reads the consequences of transition in English culture not as superficial or temporary but as exposing realities that should not again be covered up. Experiences of the reality betwixt and between human constructions are authoritative because they expose people to what comprehends and locates human life. By attention to transitions readers can exchange their primary attachment to the partial and temporary structures of rationally, politically, religiously, or scientifically defined locations for the dubious actuality of physical, comprehensive space.

While the transitional place between structures commends itself by its physical reality, it is a dangerous place for people unaware of its hazards. The benefits of living betwixt and between, of living with uncertainty and "dubiousness," come only to those trained by exposure to avoid rashness, illusion, and excess. As we shall see, it is not surprising that Wildeve and Eustacia meet their ends violently, as it is not surprising that they do so in the weir located on the boundary between the heath and the meadow.

The narrator's ability to face uncertain reality and not to flee it to the security of some protective certainty or to deny it in favor of some comforting illusion is the narrative's implied norm. One attribute or consequence of this normative stance is the comprehensive perspective that it grants. A person so positioned is not surprised or taken off guard by change, as would be one with narrower views and more limited interests. Breadth and poise are closely tied. In addition, a wide perspective is able to encompass compassionately all creatures of the earth, including animals. This range of the narrator's attention should not be confused with abstraction or with the disinterested detachment assumed by intellectuals.[19] The narrator, while standing back and viewing all of life, is marked by sympathy and affirmation rather than by disinterest. Finally, an inclusive perspective embraces the contraries or antinomies of life—gain and loss, chance and necessity, the beautiful and sublime, courage and folly. The narrator's attitude, its stability, range, complexity, and sympathy, are products of his sustained attention to the transitional and unsettling conditions of life's physical environment.

The normative attitude of the narrator is warranted by contrast with the characters who, while variously judged, all fall short of that norm. The principal meaning-effect of the language of character in the narrative is to reveal kinds of responses to the conditions of life exposed on the heath. There are three kinds of characters, three types of responses, in the novel.

The rustics provide the first. They go about their lives, continue their traditions, and know their environment. Since these characters have sometimes been seen as props or as chorus, we should recognize, it seems to me, how they are valued in the economy of the book. They bear some resemblance to more highly favored characters such as Venn, who, like them, knows the heath and moves about on it, and Clym, who is willing to work on the heath and to adjust his life to it. They are naturally integrated with their place, a characteristic conveyed by their dialect, which reveals the close ties of place and language to one another.[20] They are also resourceful and even defiant. While they show a good bit of curiosity in and some strong responses to people more wealthy, sophisticated, and mobile than themselves, they are not dislodged by them from their own culture, one rooted in ancient beliefs and practices and able to sustain them as individuals and as a community in their difficult physical surroundings. Let us call them and the relation to the heath that they represent "innocence."

The second type is formed by characters who are acquainted with and oriented to possibilities outside and in contrast to the heath. The first of these is Mrs. Yeobright. She differs from the "rustics" because of her discontent with her surroundings. She wants something better for her niece Thomasin, if not for herself, and she looks beyond the heath, like Moses from the mountain before he died, to a more desirable place: "At moments she seemed to be regarding issues from a Nebo denied to others around" (*RN*, 1:37). Living vicariously an escape from the heath that she cannot herself effect, she wants a husband better than Venn and Wildeve for Thomasin and a better life for Clym than Eustacia and the heath can provide. She is a disappointed woman, a victim of a conflict between her self-image or aspirations and the actual conditions of her situation.

Wildeve is a more developed example of discontent with the heath. He hates it and longs for other places. He is a man of desire and sentiment. Impulsive and restless, he does not sleep well, and he easily falls under the power of Eustacia. He neither recognizes the conditions of life nor develops appropriate attitudes toward them. He is a man who seems permanently unsettled in regard to his work. His uncertainty and transitional state are feeble or false versions of the narrator's positive evaluation of "dubiousness." Wildeve's vacillations are a sign of his weakness, the power of desire and illusion over him, rather than of a strength earned by facing reality.

Eustacia also resists and resents the heath. She longs to be delivered from it and looks for a great love as her form of rescue. She subjects all of her powers and her relationships to this goal. Since she manipulates other people, we can conclude that she dislikes the heath because she cannot conform it to her desires. It is also clear that her manipulation of people manifests her disdain for them, and she despises her fellow creatures as much as she hates nature (*RN*, 1:229). The object of her resentment gradually enlarges to include the whole world (*RN*, 2:436). She ends thinking of herself as Heaven's victim (*RN*, 2:442).

This second group of characters, with their negative attitudes toward the heath, are sharply distinguished from the rustics because, unlike the rustics, they imagine locations free from the harsh realities exposed by the heath. The most arresting and provocative of them is Eustacia. What they have in common is that all have allowed their desires and expectations to grow in separation from the actual conditions of their environment. Since for the narrator this physical environment has the potential of clarifying the location of all human life, these characters, by turning from it and toward some other place, are attempting to locate themselves not in reality but in fabricated or illusory space, in locations without physicality. Let us call the relation to place exposed by these restless and distracted characters "knowledge."

The third group of characters stands in a more positive relation to the heath. Thomasin is the least developed among them. She is more like the rustics than the others in this group; she is innocent, but she is also self-conscious in her relation to her location. Her sober, measured qualities arise from her basic acceptance of the heath: "Egdon in the mass was no monster whatever, but impersonal open ground. Her fears of the place were rational, her dislikes of its worst moods reasonable" (RN, 2:453). Thomasin reflects on the heath more than do the rustics, but she does not judge it negatively, as do those in the previous group, in terms of some other, more comforting places. She is peaceful and deliberate, a person of integrity and constancy.

Venn shares with others in this third group an affinity with the heath, a knowledge of and appreciation for it. He can maneuver over the terrain even in the dark. And the heath has created in him a patience and self-disinterestedness that grant him moral stature. He is not self-seeking, and this puzzles Eustacia: "The reddleman's disinterestedness was so deserving of respect that it overshot respect by being barely comprehended; and she almost thought it absurd" (RN, 1:185–86). Venn is a wanderer, a kind of gypsy or border figure, and he thereby takes into himself the characteristics of transition of which the heath makes the narrator so aware. In this regard it is helpful to contrast him with Wildeve, who is also in a state of transition. But Wildeve is in transition by indecision and by an inability or refusal to locate himself. Venn is in transition by virtue of his adaptability to change. In addition, Venn is a hurt man who, rather than respond in anger to his hurt and what occasioned it, has grown compassionate and tries to help others. He is a liaison figure and a kind of trickster. He is a charitable man covered by devil-like red.

The third and most favored figure in this group and among all the characters is Clym. His life is closely tied to the heath: "He was permeated with its scenes; with its substance, and with its odors. He might be said to be its product" (RN, 1:213). He affirms the heath as much as Eustacia denies it: "'To my mind it is most exhilarating, and strengthening, and soothing. I would rather live on these hills than anywhere else in the world'" (RN, 1:229). He is aware of the heath's druidical associations. When afflicted he could rebel, we are told, but he does not. Rather than pity himself, he wills the well-being of others.

Those in this third group have "knowledge" of the kind that the second group possess, but they also have a relation to their location that characterizes those in the "innocent" group. Their response should be identified as a combination of knowledge and innocence that the term "wisdom" best conveys. This wisdom takes the most complicated and articulated form in the character of Clym.

The wisdom of Clym is revealed first of all in his judgment that Paris is a place of vanity: "'I get up every morning and see the whole creation groaning and travailing in pain, as St Paul says, and yet there am I trafficking in glittering splendors with wealthy women and titled libertines, and pandering to the meanest vanities'" (*RN*, 1:215). He recognizes the pretensions and illusions of urban society and returns to the heath in order to find a more valid way of life. At first he brings with him new ideas that he wants to promulgate, utopian ideas, but his experiences of the heath's harsh physicality reduce his expectations. He gradually becomes a teacher whose message is "knowledge of a sort which brings wisdom rather than affluence," ennoblement rather than submission (*RN*, 1:211). He learns before he teaches, and he gradually adjusts his goals and expectations to reality. He concludes, "'But the more I see of life the more do I perceive that there is nothing particularly great in its greatest walks, and therefore nothing particularly small in mine of furze-cutting'" (*RN*, 2:315).[21] He compares himself to Job but does not attempt thereby to elevate his own state: "'In the words of Job, "I have made a covenant with mine eyes; why then should I think upon a maid?"'" (*RN*, 2:494). At the very end of the novel, he has chosen for his text a passage from 1 Kings that depicts Solomon, the biblical patron of wisdom, with his mother, Bathsheba. The morality he teaches is not confined to a particular tradition or institution but affirms "the opinions and actions common to all good men" (*RN*, 2:507). And his sense of human life and its value is not to be taught in abstraction from but in the immediate and pressing context of the heath.

What matters most is the positive relation of Clym to the heath. His exposure to the heath's harshness requires accommodations by him, and those changes in expectation are a measure of his increasing wisdom. The heath, in turn, becomes a fitting arena for Clym to carry on his pedagogical program because it is, along with him, a teacher of wisdom. There is mutuality between them. In addition, Clym relates to the heath as to something commodious. It joins the past to the future and the physical to the moral and spiritual. The past is located in the ancient monuments and rituals, and the future is adumbrated in the teaching ministry that is his work. The relation of the physical to the moral and spiritual is secured not only by rituals but also by the moral integrity and charitable qualities of people like Clym and Venn, qualities causally related to the heath. But Clym's relation to the heath is not altogether secure. He is aware of its negative qualities, and his return is not a completion, not a finality. Last, his relation to the heath is a kind of gift, a welcomed alternative to and relief from other sites. It is a relation that he needs and cannot himself provide. His wisdom requires the heath, and the sense of reality that Clym has there is not simply his projection.

While Clym is most highly favored among the characters by the narrator, he is not fully advocated as a paradigm for human response to the conditions of human life revealed by comprehensive space especially in moments of transition. While the narrator judges Thomasin, Venn, and Clym more favorably than others, he does not fully endorse any of them. The position he most fully advocates is his own, his comprehensive range, sympathetic and observant attitude, and sober appreciation for life. He is, in other words, the kind of teacher, the kind of artist and thinker, that Clym is struggling, haphazardly, to become. The characters enable the narrator to clarify the relation to the conditions of life exposed on the heath that he himself models and advocates. This relation is advanced as available and appropriate for the reader in the present time of cultural transition and loss of certainty.

From among the narrator's pre-Christian sources for articulating this position, the biblical wisdom literature, to which Clym in particular is related, seems most useful. Biblical wisdom grants authority to those conditions that comprehend human constructions, and it directs the attention of the reader both to the harshness of those conditions and to their grandeur and beauties. The wisdom literature is didactic, and its reader is directed to the physical context of human life as a source of learning; primarily one learns from it that life is more complex and precarious than one expects or desires it to be. Experience, though harsh, can produce respect for life, a sense of what is and what is not important, and a recognition of the magnitude, complexity, and power of the encompassing environment in which humans find themselves. By means of these general characteristics, biblical wisdom literature helps the narrator of *The Return of the Native* to clarify and affirm the reality and uncertainty in which he and his readers must now locate themselves.

II

The ties between narrative and place are deep and constant in Hardy's fiction. In *Desperate Remedies,* Cytherea Graye, on seeing the old manorhouse for the first time, asks the coachman if horrid stories are told about it. She wonders, that is, if it has been narrativized. The coachman replies that stories are not told of it and that this lack is unfortunate. "'Tis jest the house for a nice ghastly hair-on-end story, that would make the parish religious,'" he says. "'Perhaps it will have one some day to make it complete; but there's not a word of the kind now'" (DR, 69). This dialogue foreshadows what transpires in the narrative, and it clarifies in Hardy both the primacy of places in their specific physicality and the need to articulate the incipient relations of physical places to their spiritual potentials by means of narrative. As Philippa Tristram puts it, Hardy's "houses become something much more than mere settings; they are stories in stone."[22] Places have force and significance, and stories can actualize the force and significance of places and the relations that people have to them. Place-relations serve to make people "religious" more effectively than do Christian institutions and doctrines.

Just as deep in Hardy's work is his belief that place-relations are threatened by an English culture that is disrespectful of the particularity of place. *Under the Greenwood Tree* narrates the cultural conflict created when the vicar intervenes in the traditions of the village by replacing the string players in the church with an organ. The vicar positions himself not in the actual place of the local people but in an abstract social space of urban England and the national church.[23] The vicar's disregard for his specific location and his orientation to an abstract social space causes painful consequences. The novel makes it clear that it is not only urban spaces like London that threaten the integrity of local sites but also the wider environment created by economic, social, and institutional connections. Social space, for all its power and significance, fails, by want of physicality and specificity, to grant a person a relation to reality. The moral and religious force and significance of place-relations do not come from outside but arise from particular physical locations and the ties of people to them.

The physicality of place-relations often is suggested in Hardy's fiction by the land and those who work it. This is clear in *Far from the Madding Crowd*. For one thing, we are given detailed descriptions of physical landscapes. In addition, buildings are described and evaluated in terms of their relation to the land. The barn, for example, is given careful attention: its "lanceolate windows, the time-eaten archstones and chamfers, the orientation of the axis, the misty chestnut work of the rafters, referred," we are told, "to no exploded fortifying art or worn-out religious creed" (*FMC*, 166). The narrator contrasts the barn to the castle and the church, buildings tied to political and religious interests. The barn's relation to the physical land gives it enduring significance; it survives the transition from "medievalism" to "modernism," as it is put, because it defers to the actual physical conditions of life.

The importance of the physical aspects of place-relations for moral integrity is depicted by the novel in the figure of Gabriel Oak, a man who stands tall in Hardy's work. Oak frames the narrative and reveals the fruits of being grounded in a specific physical location. As his name suggests, he is attached to the land and attuned to his physical context. He can tell time by the stars, read the signs of approaching storms, and attend to sick animals. Oak absorbs the terrible loss of his herd, driven to the chalk-pit by his young sheep dog. His moral stature is secured by the courage he reveals in fighting fires and protecting the harvest from impending storm.

When the narrator comments that Oak's "special power, morally, physically, and mentally, was static, owing little or nothing to momentum as a rule" (*FMC*, 11), he does not mean that Oak defies the vicissitudes and uncertainties of life but that, by being located, he bends with them. Oak's steadiness stands in contrast both to the impervious constancy of ecclesiastical and political institutions and to the inconstancy of the crowd. People, especially those in cities, are driven by fashion. Pointless movement and instability also mark the attitudes of several characters: Fanny Robin, Mr. Boldwood, Frank Troy, and, most of all, Bathsheba Everdene. Impulsive, unrealistic, and detached, they are easily tossed about by circumstances, victims of folly, and, as Oak judges Bathsheba at the outset, of vanity. In contrast to them, Oak and the narrator provide examples of flexible stability. This quality is the consequence of being related to a spatial reality that Hardy locates primarily in the land. Oak's primary orientation to the physical conditions of comprehensive space commends his deportment and validates his position as a man of wisdom, after whom, if the reference to the first of the biblical Psalms is implied, he is named.[24]

Hardy also makes clear that social space is secondary to physical, comprehensive space in *The Mayor of Casterbridge*. The relatively favorable depiction of social space in the novel is noteworthy, and the reason for it is that the borders between Casterbridge and the countryside are permeable.[25] Even people relatively distant from the agricultural base of the society maintain a strong interest in it: "And even at the dinner parties of the professional families the subjects of discussion were corn, cattle disease, sowing and reaping, fencing and planting; while politics were viewed by them less from their own standpoint of burgesses with rights and privileges than from the standpoint of their county neighbors" (*MC*, 70). Deference to the wider physical landscape seems positively to affect the boundaries internal to the social space of Casterbridge, such as those between classes. Comprehensive physical space allows all people, despite their social differences, to be related to one another as well as to the land upon which all depend.[26]

The quite favorable depiction of Casterbridge may also be due to the town's relations with its pre-Christian history. We are told that it bears Roman imprints; it "announced old Rome in every street, alley, and precinct. It looked Roman, bespoke the art of Rome, concealed dead men of Rome" (*MC*, 80). The roads in the countryside also follow Roman precedents. Indeed, the town has closer ties to Rome than to the period of "modernism" (*MC*, 30), and Roman imprints are deeper than those of Christian institutions.

We saw that in *The Return of the Native*, Hardy places characters in difficult locations in order to reveal various responses to them, responses that are evaluated by the narrator. We have this, as well, in *Tess of the D'Urbervilles*. Some responses lead people who face the difficulties of their locations to form supportive communities, while other responses lead people to aggravate their circumstances by an orientation to self-gratifying projections. For example, Tess and her younger brother, Abraham, set off in the morning darkness to do their father's work because he, suffering the effects of celebrating his newly discovered lineage, is unable to make the deliveries of honey himself. While traveling, Abraham imagines that the stars he sees are worlds more desirable than his own, and Tess allows the passing trees and hedges to be "attached to fantastic scenes outside reality" (*TD*, 34). The children are lured by their difficult conditions into sleeplike fantasies. As a result, the horse, crucial to their family's well-being, is gored by the morning mail-cart. The conclusion to be drawn is clear: adversity calls attention to reality, but it can also distract attention from reality to unreal alternatives. When that happens, an already difficult situation will become worse. Indeed, poverty and vulnerability to losses mark Tess's life. A positive consequence of these physical conditions is the rapport created between Tess and other people similarly situated. She has a close feeling for her family; the milk-maids who work together form a loyal group; and the days of intimacy Tess shares with Angel toward the close of the novel are made intense by the threats exerted by their social contexts. But adversity, while it can create rapport between people similarly situated, can also produce desires for "fantastic scenes outside reality": the milk-maids long for Angel; the Stokes family desires cultural capital; Angel's father is absorbed by beliefs in supernatural Providence; Angel's brothers fancy themselves as elevated above others because of their associations with the university and the church; Angel hopes to find a better life in Brazil; and Tess's parents take the unexpected news of their descent from a prestigious family as an occasion to project themselves into a fantastic future.

It would be a mistake to think that for this and other Hardy novels the conflict between what people find in life and what they desire, the conflict between their "inherent will to enjoy," and "the circumstantial will against enjoyment," reveals that the conditions of life are evil and human desires are good (*TD*, 365). For one thing, much in the situations of characters that counters their well-being is caused by, rather than imposed on, them. For example, Alec, whether as rich man or Pauline evangelist, is possessive and life-denying. Angel, while more attractive than Alec, acts, as he later realizes, in a cruel and unforgiving way toward Tess. In addition, much suffering is caused by unjust laws and social practices, by the intrusion of machinery into rural life, and by the hard lot imposed by the society on women—"The Woman Pays," as the title of one section puts it. Comprehensive physical space appears less malicious or contrary to human well-being than social space. In fact, the narrator depicts many positive moments in the course of times and seasons, such as the coming of spring and dawn: "the luminary was a golden-haired, beaming, mild-eyed, god-like creature, gazing down in the vigour and intentness of youth upon an earth that was brimming with interests for him" (*TD*, 109). This means that the conclusion Tess draws about the plight of human beings, one in which, we are told, she goes beyond Solomon in judging life not as "vanity" but as "*injustice*, punishment, exaction, death," is extreme and distorted (*TD*, 353). The narrator refers to such a response as "modernism." Preferred is the attitude of the man with a "Cosmopolitan mind" that Angel met in Brazil, an attitude inclusive "as of the whole of the terrestrial curve" (*TD*, 433). His perspective is also contagious; it gives to Angel a more charitable, less short-sighted judgment of Tess, for example. It is a perspective like the narrator's, one that attends primarily to the larger, even cosmic, context of human actions and attitudes. Tess reveals such wisdom when she recognizes in the dead and dying pheasants wantonly killed by hunters that her own suffering, in comparison and in company with theirs, is not so exceptional and perhaps not even so great as she previously had thought.

A final point to make about Hardy's depiction of human place-relations is that he attacks the authority of what Henri Lefebvre calls "monumental" space. "Monumental" space consists of those structures that make visible both the largely invisible distinctions that constitute social space and the often invisible rules and power by which those distinctions are maintained.[27] The fullest example of this is Hardy's subversion of Oxford's authority in and through its role in *Jude the Obscure*.

Jude, the product of a family that was violently dissolved, is looking for stability. His two mistakes are to interpret his own insecure and uncertain position in the world as an anomaly, as a problem that needs to be solved, and, even more, to think that society, especially if he gains access to its cultural capital, will provide him the stability he craves. Jude looks to Christminster (Oxford) as a monumental space that epitomizes cultural authority and social value and that can therefore provide the stabilization and elevation he needs. Christminster is for him a "heavenly Jerusalem" (*JO*, 16). He longs for it as a young lover desires his mistress. It is a city of light, a garden of Eden (*JO*, 22). When oriented toward it, he feels "nursed on the supernatural" and led by Providence (*JO*, 105). The great spirits of Christminster seem yet to walk its streets. However, this social and cultural acme does not carry the saving power that Jude attributes to it. One reason is that Christminster has repressed its indebtedness to pre-Christian cultures, which in the novel are evaluated as more vital and accommodating than the Christian culture that supplants them. Christminster is abstract, pretentious, and impervious to change.

Jude, by combining real dilemmas, adversities, and conflicts in life with those produced by a mistaken evaluation of "monumental" space, becomes ambiguous. Nature's harsh law, as it is put, of "mutual butchery" conspires with social pretension and exclusion to produce and aggravate personal suffering (*JO*, 364). The reader is left with the question of how to sort out what, in the suffering of people, is caused by conditions they cannot control and what is caused by their mistaken and foolish values and decisions. The characters are correspondingly complex. Arabella is a victim, but she is also manipulative, self-interested, and opportunistic. Sue, irresolute, "capricious," and petulant, moves from pagan to Christian convictions as such moves seem appropriate to protect her from the full realities and responsibilities of marriage (*JO*, 186). Richard Philloston, although a model for Jude, also appears, for reasons not wholly developed, in a constant state of decline. Finally, Jude errs by allowing his ambitions to blind him to the values in his actual conditions—access to learning (books and lectures), a trade (stonemason), and people to love.

The uncertainty presented to the reader by many Hardy narratives, then, is that the characters are harshly and unjustly dealt with by circumstances while at the same time they aggravate their situations with unhelpful goals and, under pressure, reveal many faults. Despite Hardy's many references to Job, readers cannot simply place themselves in the familiar situation of sympathetic identification with innocent victims of harsh events and circumstances. While readers are led to sympathize with characters because they are unjustly treated, readers also are led to judge them because they bring at least some misfortune on themselves.[28] Hardy, in other words, places the reader in a position betwixt and between the circumstances of life and the responses to those circumstances expressed by the attitudes and actions of his characters. The reader is able neither wholly to condemn nor to commend. The principal consequence of this positioning is to keep the texts from becoming an alternative to the difficult but necessary task of accommodating oneself to the ambiguities but also the steadying physical realities of comprehensive space.

III

The many references in Hardy to biblical wisdom literature are relevant to the power and significance of comprehensive space in his fiction. To say this is neither to discount the roles of other pre-Christian texts and prototypes, both classical and archaic, nor to confer on Hardy's work a biblically derived legitimacy. I want only to point out that Hardy's cultural location in change or transition is one that the wisdom texts of the Old Testament helped him to affirm and clarify. For the biblical wisdom literature has several emphases directly relevant to Hardy's needs: experience teaches; human societies are complex and human relations uncertain; and, most of all, the primary, defining arena of human life, rather than being provided by religious or social institutions, is to be found in the physical cosmos as principal site of divine manifestation.

True, biblical wisdom texts refer to the cosmic context of human life as to a divine construction. But the sense of that context advocated by biblical wisdom is not, by virtue of belief in a Creator, something benign, constant, and consistent with human interests. That cosmic context is as forbidding and disruptive to human life as it is supportive, and Hardy makes enough references to Job to reveal his interest in that side of human experience. In wisdom texts, as in Hardy, the comprehensive space that precedes and contains human life is both contrary and complementary to human nature. While reality is often antagonistic, it also holds a positive potential for actualizing the human capacity for truth, integrity, and compassion. Hardy's view of the cosmic conditions of human life is as complex as that of biblical wisdom. Both emphasize the predictability and the unpredictability of events, the favorable and unfavorable relation of natural conditions to human well-being, and the importance and unimportance of human beings in the cosmic whole.

Hardy drew on his familiarity with biblical wisdom texts, therefore, to illuminate the comprehensive physical context of human life. He does so to counter the applicability and adequacy of dogmatically defined and institutionally specific forms of biblically sponsored belief to the present cultural situation. In addition, he employs wisdom texts because they were important for people in the situations he narrates, particularly people living by their own wits under the taxing conditions of rural and small-town settings in the decades of his youth. The wisdom literature serves to warrant for his own day the move that Hardy sees as inevitable for the culture, namely, from the certainties and securities of political and religious institutions and dogmas to the dubiousness of life in relation to forces of reality exposed by transition.

Biblical wisdom texts, then, form for Hardy a vestibule on his way not only out of the biblical tradition but also out of textuality and to exposure to the physically forceful qualities of the comprehensive human context. The wisdom literature allows this use to be made of it because it presents neither a theory of the context of human life nor precise rules as to how one should confront its uncertainties. Indeed, what is so fascinating about the cosmos, for wisdom texts, is that both it and how people should respond to it cannot be fit into formulas. The context of human life challenges human expectations by its force and unpredictability, by being worse and better than expected, and by evading human comprehension by its mysteries. For these reasons, the power and presence of deity are related in wisdom literature to the comprehensive physical context of human life.

However, by granting primacy to comprehensive, cosmic place-relations, Hardy does not direct the reader, as the wisdom texts do, from cosmic realities to their Creator. The mysteries of comprehensive space do not defer to what transcends them. If there is anything divine in Hardy's fiction that impinges on human life, it cannot be separated from the events, circumstances, and conditions of physical space as they are made especially clear and forceful in times of transition.[29] The actual conditions of life are narrated as themselves mysterious, as both fascinating and repulsive, supportive and antagonistic, generative and destructive. People related to the physicality of comprehensive space will be deepened and enlarged by the unpredictable and forceful physical environment that precedes and overarches human life.

The narrativization of place-relations in Hardy's novels, then, directs attention to the conditions of human life as themselves worthy of respect, if not of reverence. The ambiguity of human life's conditions always puts human beings betwixt and between, always in a situation of uncertainty, of both support and threat, attachment and distance. The powers resident in that environment require from human beings an elementary caution and humility and can evoke a commonality with and even a sympathy for all forms of life. The primacy of cosmic circumstances means that a life lived in protection from them or in disregard or defiance of them will not only be false but also will be reduced and even destroyed.

While Hardy's fiction recalls English culture to its earlier, pre-urban attention to physical, comprehensive space, his work is not nostalgic. Hardy does not want to reverse the course of events, however much he is critical of the illusory and untenable attitudes toward their places characteristic of modern people. He does not call for a return to simpler or earlier forms of human community. Indeed, people in close proximity to the harsh conditions of life are not always beneficially affected by them and not always rightly related to them. Nor—and this is even more to the point—do those who live in urban settings necessarily give themselves to vanity. This is because the conditions of life, while more readily recognized in the countryside than in the city, are most fully revealed in transitions, in positions betwixt and between, and transitions and dubiousness can be found in human life variously located. While it may be more difficult to encounter the effects of transitions in cities, given the illusion of permanence produced by the institutions and monumental spaces of cities, they can also be encountered there. Indeed, the present transition precipitated by the end of a culture marked by Christian and political certainty is more felt in urban than in rural locations. Hardy makes clear to the readers that this transition is not exceptional or temporary but revelatory of the actual situation in which people live. Rather than resist it, readers should attend to it as granting not only truth but such moral and spiritual values as humility and compassion.

The great transitions palpably felt on the heath and the transitions in English culture of which the narrator of *The Return of the Native* is so aware cast into doubt the permanence and adequacy of the culture's institutions and dogmas. Transitions make clear that human constructions, no matter how extensive or impressive, are, relative to comprehensive space, temporary and partial. True, Hardy may also have more immediate goals in mind; for example, he may have wanted English society to recognize its dependence on agricultural economy, and he may have wanted English culture to protect rather than to absorb local traditions. These more proximate values depend, however, on a shift of focus to the widest angle. People exposed to seasons and storms and people who express their location in their language are more likely than urban people to recognize the vulnerability of human constructions relative to the larger comprehensive context of human life. One need not move from London to Higher Bockhampton to undergo that shift, although such a move could very likely help. Hardy suggests that recognition of cultural transitions in his readers can become the basis upon which the corrective and productive consequences of looking beyond human constructions can arise.

Hardy narrates, then, the most extensive and inclusive kind in the repertoire of human place-relations. He deals with what geographers refer to as "landscape." Implicit in his narratives of "landscape" is a negative response to the gradual substitution of urban space for landscape, but he does this neither by retrieving a Romantic model of nature nor by positing the natural as something apart from culture. Orientation to cosmic or comprehensive space rests on a cultural evaluation of what is real and must first of all be taken into account. This means, to put it differently, that "landscape" for Hardy is read. The reader, especially under the tutelage of narrators such as those created in his fiction, can become aware not only of the power of transitions but also of what they reveal about the context of human life and the uncertainty that comprehensive physical space beneficially imparts to human enterprises. Indeed, English culture from Bacon to Hardy had read landscape like a text. As Brian Stock puts it, "our notion of landscape contains within it an already conceptualized notion of the reading process."[30] Hardy's narratives reinstate and reinforce the textuality of "landscape," of spatial location that is comprehensive or cosmic. He stands, therefore, as an appropriate, even indispensable participant in the modern reconstruction of place and place-relations.

2

Joseph Conrad

Labor and the Physicality of Social Space

A move from Hardy's fiction to Conrad's requires a change of focus. Rather than to cosmic, comprehensive space, attention turns now to social space. True, there are seascapes and other wide-angle descriptions in Conrad's fiction, as in Hardy's fiction we encounter towns and other social spaces, but Conrad sees the principal problems with human place-relations in modern culture as sited in social space. Rectification of those problems must begin with its reconstitution.

In Hardy's narratives of comprehensive space, locations, such as the heath, endure while people come and go. But in Conrad's fiction, places, because they are primarily social, are not easily separable from characters. One could almost remove characters in a Hardy novel and look at the places that they occupy, but in Conrad's fiction there is more continuity between people and place. This leads some readers to take the language of character to be dominant in Conrad's work, but the reason for this close tie between the languages of space and of character in his fiction is that space is primarily social.[1]

In addition, the narrators of Hardy's fiction are conscious of the conditions under which characters live, express attitudes concerning those conditions, judge characters as to how they respond to them, and relate quite directly to the narratee. But Conrad's narrators seem less conscious of the situation in which characters live, and their judgments and beliefs are less accessible or reliable than Hardy's. His narrators seem often as affected by the problematic situations that they present as are the characters. The lack of clarity and integrity in Conrad's narrators and implied authors creates uncertainty about moral judgments being made or implied and the norms that govern them. These unreliable narrators and abstract tellers are so provocative that some readers think that narrative point of view produces the dominant language of Conrad's fiction and the principal locus, however ambiguous, of its meaning and force.[2]

When we consider the language of events and actions in the work of the two writers, more similarities appear. In the narratives of both, unexpected events and impulsive actions, moments that radically affect the development of the plot, occur. Disruptive and accidental events and acts of thoughtlessness and betrayal stand out in the plots of both writers. In Conrad, such events are combined with aspects of the spy novel and the adventure tale. The results tend to draw the attention of some readers away from the language of space and place and lead them to take Conrad's plots as the principal source of his narratives' force and meaning.[3]

Despite the importance of the other narrative languages in Conrad's fiction, however, I believe that it is primarily to places and the actual and potential relations of people to them that attention should be directed. It is possible to say of his fiction—as did his friend Richard Curle—that "atmosphere is not simply a background, it is an essence vitally affecting the spirit of the work."[4] "His atmosphere is indeed at times so strong with the menace of disaster or the promise of delight that it becomes acutely oppressive."[5] I agree.

As already indicated, the spatial language of Conrad's fiction is directed toward social space, to the life of people together, to the basis and structure of that life, and to the authority that legitimizes and maintains order. This does not mean that for Conrad social space is all-inclusive, as is social space for many spatial theorists. Indeed, when social space excludes or discounts the other kinds of human space, it is, for Conrad, diseased. But comprehensive or cosmic space and personal or intimate spaces, while needing to play their roles, are subservient in his fiction to social space.

Like Hardy's, Conrad's fiction emphasizes the physicality of place-relations, and he locates the physicality of social space in human labor. This physical emphasis counters the social spaces typical of modern Western culture in Conrad's fiction because modern social spaces seem increasingly, almost inevitably, to ignore or even to repress their physicality and to become increasingly abstract. When social space becomes abstract, it exchanges the substantial relations that people otherwise would and should have to places and to other people for formal relationships. This is a sign, along with its ability to obscure comprehensive and to swamp personal spaces, that modern social spaces have become diseased.

Conrad's stress on the physicality of social space does not mean that he ignores its actual or potential moral and spiritual aspects. As with Hardy, attention to the physicality of places is morally productive. For both writers, morality is not imposed on human situations from above but arises from the relations of people to their situation and to one another, and in Conrad these relations are marked by the mutuality and loyalty that working together can generate. The physical grounding of social space in human labor carries the moral content of trust between people. Social spaces that become abstract in Conrad's fiction are spaces that, conversely, are marked by a severance from their physical base and by betrayals and conflicts between people and between people and their locations. When diseased, a social space—which should keep order and direct human activities and, at the same time, allow for individual initiatives and contributions to the whole—suffers a falling out between these two sides of its life. The failure of social space to sponsor mutuality between differing people becomes, in its extreme form, a pitting of autocratic and anarchic people against one another.

It will be important, when we look at Conrad's fiction, to distinguish the contraries endemic to social spaces from the many other contraries characteristic of his work. People often comment on Conrad's antinomies: West and East, North and South, Ego and Id, reason and emotion. One reader asserts that "the antinomies between the West and Asia/Africa/Latin America, or between North and South, are ultimately transmitted as the antagonism between Ego and Id, Reason and the Irrational, consciousness and the Unconscious."[6] I think that for understanding Conrad, terms that are less psychological and more social and political serve us better. Viable social spaces in Conrad's fiction hold human contraries together in interdependent relations. A social space is diseased when differences between people become antagonisms, especially when autocracy and anarchy divide social space against itself.

The principal cause of disease in social space for Conrad is its abstraction from its physical base in human labor. When that occurs human relations lose vitality and reality, determined as they become by impersonal and purely formal connections. The fullest example of this is the social space that shapes *The Secret Agent*. I shall comment first on this novel, then on the two political novels that stand, chronologically, on either side of it, and finally on some of Conrad's other fiction.

I

In sharp contrast to *The Return of the Native,* which opens with a description of the heath, *The Secret Agent* opens with a description of an urban street and the shop from which Verloc emerges. The adjectives "small" and "grimy" prepare the reader for a description of London inattentive to its expanses and splendors. The reader will look in vain for evidences in the London setting of what Henri Lefebvre calls monumental space, the visible markers or signs that warrant the order that structures the society. The well-known buildings, squares, and statues that suggest religious and political legitimacy and stability are missing. This absence emphasizes that social space, according to Conrad, is expressed in and maintained by invisible and not visible means. Lines of connection, boundaries, prohibitions, and directives structure and even determine social space. Accuracy of depiction regarding social space, then, especially in an urban setting—in this case a world capital—requires the impertinence of ignoring familiar landmarks. Attention is turned, instead, to the more important but largely hidden lines of connection and separation that structure social space by means of exclusion and inclusion. These lines are drawn by international as well as by local interests and by economic as well as political power.

The reader also finds that London does not constitute a finite social space but is all-inclusive; "for all its miscellaneity and intricacy [it] is perceived as a monad, an organism in itself."[7] The lives of its inhabitants are contained within it and conditioned by it. There are no alternative place-relations, either in the countryside outside the city or in domestic personal places. Social space in the novel invades personal or intimate and occludes cosmic or comprehensive spaces.

Further, the reader finds London to be not diverse and exhilarating but homogeneous and drab. It is described with the language of dissolution—wetness, darkness, and fog. Indeed, rather than support and release human lives, it confines and threatens them. It is labyrinthine. The city suggests evil, even hell. As one reader puts it, "The action of the novel begins, in fact, with a contrast between secular and spiritual cities established by an allusion to the rusted treasures of the earth that moth and rust corrupt."[8]

The reader also notices that, with all the attention given to social space, there is little that is open or public about the lives of people and their relationships. Indeed, people, even people who live together, seem isolated and concealed from one another. There is little common life. The whole middle range of life, what lies between isolation and large, anonymous crowds, the range of urban life generally occupied by other institutions and associations—churches, clubs, schools, concerts, and so on—is missing. Although the anarchists associate, they have nothing substantial in common. People who live close to one another, as does the family of Verloc, are not open and candid with one another. This lack of intermediate social space, of spaces created by mutual interests and effort, this division of social space between the all-inclusive and the isolated, is a consequence of polarization, in diseased social space, between the inclusive and particular.[9]

The reader also finds that connections between individuals are primarily formal, professional, or economic. These relations create lines of connection between people who are, in position and interest, sharply different from one another. The professor and Vladimir, the anarchists and the police, Michaelis and the lady patroness, even Winnie and Verloc: these paired contraries have little in common. This means that their relations, which are important for the sustainability and relative coherence of the whole, are formal rather than substantial. Moreover, people recognize neither mutual dependence nor how their relations are created and controlled by the social whole. The characters become simple integers in a mathematics that no one of them fully appreciates or understands. This has the effect of making them and their work not the creators of the social structure and its relationships but the means by which particular positions within the social structure are maintained. The position or function within the system becomes more important than the person holding or performing it. The structure, it could almost be said, uses people to sustain itself. "Agent," as applied to Verloc, refers to him not as an actor but as a means, as in our use of the word in "cleaning agent."[10] People see other people as means.

Finally, the subordination of people to functions and offices and of functions and offices to one another, a subordination that makes people not innovative and substantial but derivative and instrumental, renders the physicality of people irrelevant to the constitution of social space. We are aware of the bodies of people—the obesity of Michaelis, Verloc, and Vladimir, for example—but this physicality makes no contribution to the construction and maintenance of the social space. Rather than being basic to the structure of social space, physicality is absorbed by it. It is reified, as is Winnie's body, or it is employed as a tool, as Verloc uses Stevie as a carrier and as the professor turns his body into a weapon.

Social space, when defined by offices or political and economic relations rather than by mutual interests and work, becomes abstract, and its power and significance shift from its actual physical source to a derivative mental status. Characters are defined by positions rather than by particular abilities and potentials. They are less connected to one another than to sets of formal arrangements that determine them and their relationships. This abstract quality marks all human relations in the novel. Even sex is narrated not as a form of physical relationship but as a commodity in Verloc's shop or as determined by the economic interests that gave rise to his marriage.

While—or, perhaps, because—the characters are determined in their personal and social relationships by an impersonal, all-inclusive social grid, they are also defined by sharply focused, even obsessive interests. Sir Ethelred, who sits at the very center of the empire, is obsessed with time and fishing industries. Vladimir despises the survival of liberalism in England. The assistant commissioner worries about public opinion. Inspector Heat focuses sharply on his investigation. The professor concentrates on devising a perfect detonator. Michaelis works in his prisonlike room on his autobiography and utopian vision. Ossipon reduces everything he can to scientific terms and to his preoccupation with women and wealth. Obsessions serve to isolate more than particularize people and to abstract them from rather than relate them to one another.

Finally, the characters, while greatly reduced in their potential by the functions and offices they serve, carry swollen evaluations of their own importance. The anarchists, for example, prize their individuality too highly to make common cause or form consensus with others, and they deceive themselves by underestimating how dependent they are on the social, economic, or political conditions that they oppose. Verloc's self-assessment of his professional value is exaggerated and is clearly at odds with the sharply negative evaluation given him by the first secretary of the embassy.

The conditions of the social space invade and shape the personal space of the Verloc household. The question is whether or not the household presents a viable alternative to the social space. Karen Piper, working from the references both by Conrad and the text to the narrative as a "domestic tragedy," thinks that it does. But the structures and forces that shape the larger setting are not discontinuous with those that shape the domestic location. There is no entry to their home other than through the pornographic shop, and the family structure has an economic rather than a physical or emotional base. Piper suggests that while Winnie may have entered the relationship for economic reasons, Verloc seems to have not. But Verloc's position as purveyor of shady wares and his wanton use of Stevie cast doubts on his attitudes toward and constructions of personal relationships.[11] As Aaron Fogel points out, "The family has no comic, lively, or sentimental language of its own . . . to set against state-forced dialogue."[12] The financial support of the family, which is provided by Verloc's questionable business and political activities, is far from steady and dependable. Despite the infirm financial base of the family structure and Verloc's unreliability, Winnie and her mother and brother base their well-being on him. When that reliance is betrayed by Verloc, the resulting exposure of his relation to her and her brother has the marks not of something exceptional but of something consistent with the whole to which Winnie mistakenly had thought her family was an exception. The domestic events are tragic because they are determined by malignant forces that lie outside the relationship and that lead to violence.

As there are no intimate or personal spaces that stand apart from the determining force of social space, so there is no access to comprehensive space, to a larger spatial context in which London could be placed. There is no viable countryside and the sky seems to be incorporated by the urban landscape. The sun, for example, is described in the opening chapter as "punctual," as though it obeys the clock, and in terms of the color that it gives to buildings. And the turn of the season from late winter to early spring has little palpable effect on the lives, activities, or relations of people.

The Secret Agent gives us social space, therefore, in an abstract expressionist style. The geometrical framework of the total composition determines the positions and relationships of the figures in the work. This framework, which organizes and controls London and its life, is invoked from behind or beneath the surface of the largely unnarrated, even absent variety and vitality that one ordinarily ascribes to human activities and relations in urban settings. The structure of this social space is abstract and formal, and those characteristics are reinforced by the language of geometry in the novel. Stevie is obsessed with circles. The sign of agent Verloc's professional identity was a triangle. Most of all, the social space is constituted by lines of connection that relate and differentiate offices and functions within the structure, lines that connect contraries, such as the anarchists and the police. The novel as abstract painting or as x-ray reveals the skeletal structure of the social space. As Aaron Fogel puts it, "The novel is a skeleton covered by a careful literary robe of scorn."[13] What makes for its chilling effect is the realization that the skeleton is all there is, that there is no vitality, no flesh or warmth, no social life. The narrator says of the city, "In its breadth, emptiness, and extent it had the majesty of inorganic nature, of matter that never dies" (*SA*, 30).[14] The reader, accustomed to regard London as vital and attractive, is caught off guard, realizing that this exposure of an abstract social structure is not whimsical but definitive.

It is not surprising, given the kind of social space they inhabit, that characters deal with people in abstraction rather than in their particularity. For example, the police are less interested in persons than in types of criminals. Ossipon, in addition, appeals often to the work of the Italian criminologist and psychiatrist Cesare Lombrozo (1836–1901), who—influenced by Comte's attempts to apply methods from the natural sciences to the study of humans—attempted to define criminal "types" in the hope of predicting their behavior and taking the mystery out of social deviance. Ossipon predicts that in the coming centuries, science rather than people will rule the world; indeed, science already has begun, he believes, to rule it (*SA*, 233). Sir Ethelred, similarly, looks to the unification of the entire globe by economic means related to the English empire. And Michaelis projects a society defined not by human relationships but as an all-inclusive hospital (*SA*, 95).[15]

It is also not surprising that the principal form of organization is bureaucratic. The structure of the embassy and of the public offices is bureaucratic. Such a structure relates functions to one another in a hierarchy of increasing generalization and abstraction. Offices define their occupants rather than being shaped by them. The bureaucratic form of authority and organization is typical of the whole. It is a form of authority that breeds isolation, anarchy, and nonconformity as its contraries.

Epitomizing the authority of abstraction and the rational, scientific, and mathematical interests that sustain it is the Greenwich Observatory, particularly its position relative to the standardization of time. Built in 1675, the observatory stands as a kind of temple to science and rationality, and it establishes the first meridian for the global time system. Standard time, crucial to the scientific and rationalist orderings of the world as well as to unifying the globe by commerce, transportation, and communication, is the most massively homogenizing and incorporating invention of the modern period. It subsumes heterogeneous, natural, and local bases for time reckoning into a single, abstract, and universal system. Given the utopian, even quasi-religious significance that Comte gave to the unification of human knowledge under scientific laws, it is not surprising that a religious coloration should be granted in the novel to the observatory and to the ordering of time that unifies the world. Vladimir comments: "'the fetish of to-day is neither royalty nor religion. Therefore the palace and the church should be left alone'" (*SA*, 41). "'The sacrosanct fetish of to-day is science'" (*SA*, 42). "'The demonstration must be against learning—science. But not every science will do. The attack must have all the shocking senselessness of gratuitous blasphemy. Since bombs are your means of expression, it would be really telling if one could throw a bomb into pure mathematics'" (*SA*, 43–44). Represented by the first meridian, the standardization of time—which included virtually the entire world by the end of the nineteenth century—coincides with the power and world-inclusiveness of abstraction and provides the means by which economic and social factors can be homogenized and totalized. Standard time, which transcends the vagaries and differences of circadian, lunar, and seasonal time, is essential to actualizing the capacity of social space to become both all-inclusive and drained of content, variety, and physicality. While, by virtue of its transcendence and authority, Greenwich time suggests a sacred presence, it has no physical form that could be acknowledged. It is an idea and only secondarily and conventionally a location.

The rational, abstract relations that constitute and determine urban society find their contraries in unexpected and spontaneous acts of human betrayal, acts marked by the festering desires and frustrations that a diseased social space creates and conceals. The attempted bombing of the conservatory, which Conrad bases on an actual event lest it seem too odd to be credible, contradicts by its pointlessness the rationalism of the environment of abstraction.[16] Unexpected actions of people against one another, especially in situations of intimacy or trust, include Verloc's betrayal by the embassy, the betrayal of Stevie and Winnie by Verloc, Winnie's murder of Verloc, and Ossipon's betrayal of Winnie. Betrayals reveal the lack of mutuality and loyalty between people who are related to one another by means of a formal, abstract structure rather than by physical proximity, mutual work, and trust. These formal relations allow unexpressed emotions to fester and erupt. We read, for example, that when Winnie stabs Verloc she put into the blow "all the inheritance of her immemorial and obscure descent, the simple ferocity of the age of caverns, and the unbalanced nervous fury of the age of bar-rooms" (SA, 203). Unexpected, spontaneous, and brutal acts of betrayal, vengeance, and self-destruction stand as inevitable contraries to, even oddly as human compensations for, the pervasive and determining power of the abstract distinctions and relations that form the structure of a largely mental social space.

Symptomatic of what is wrong with the social space in this narrative is that the characters do little if any actual, especially physical, work. They have positions, offices, and titles, but these, rather than being sites of work, arise from and are sustained by one another. As the professor rightly puts it, "'Revolution, legality—counter moves in the same game; forms of idleness at bottom identical'" (SA, 69).[17] Many of the characters, such as Michaelis and Ossipon, are identified as lazy, and Vladimir accuses Verloc of idleness. Indeed, Verloc is studiously indolent. We are told that he "breakfasted in bed, and remained wallowing there with an air of quiet enjoyment till noon every day—and sometimes even to a later hour" (SA, 24). The narrator tells us that Verloc was "devoted" to idleness "with a sort of inert fanaticism" (SA, 29). He had a "dislike of all kinds of recognized labour—a temperamental defect which he shared with a large proportion of revolutionary reformers of a given social state" (SA, 57). He sees his duty to be the protection of the "whole social order" from "unhygienic labour" (SA, 29). His "habits of mind" were "indolent and secret" (SA, 191). Jacques Berthoud rightly argues that indolence is a key to Verloc's character and reveals his parasitic dependence on the labor of others.[18] Actual, especially physical, work is largely absent from the narrative.

Work appears briefly and strikingly in the horse and cabman scene. The cabman is a worker who has a sense of himself and his job that is, relative to that of others in the novel, credible. People know who he is and have confidence in him. His work, in turn, depends on the physical labor of the horse, which suffers under its burdens and overuse. The scene provokes a response of moral revulsion and compassion. The reader's reaction is voiced by Stevie's outcry: "'Poor Brute, poor people!' was all he could repeat" (*SA*, 139). It is not as though no work gets done in this social world; it is that the characters we deal with ignore or repress it and deny their dependence on it. The cab scene is so powerful because it grants a brief glimpse into the largely concealed underside of derived and abstracted social space, a glimpse that sets off the deceptions and illusions that allow the characters to conspire unconsciously in keeping the truth hidden, namely, that social space arises from and depends on physical labor.

With *The Secret Agent,* we are dealing, consequently, with a negative depiction of social space, and we must infer from it what positive social place-relations would be like. What is the positive contrary to this negative impression? Lacking are mutually accommodating interactions between Verloc and his social context. There are no reciprocal adjustments, for example, between him and the bureaucracy with which he has to deal, and this is true of the entire situation. The social space is also not commodious. It does not allow Verloc to relate his past to his present and future. Although large, even total, the social space is also confining. Efforts toward alternatives are thwarted, and the futures projected by the anarchists offer no viable possibilities. Finally, there is nothing giftlike about the social space and Verloc's relation to it. All the surprises are bad ones. Social space is not a gift or opportunity but a bane, a house of horrors. We can infer, then, that a positive social space would be marked by mutuality, would relate contraries positively, would be liberating, and would offer people opportunities that they could not themselves provide.

II

Conrad embodies more positive marks of social place-relations in some of his sea narratives. But before turning to them, we should look at several novels that stand chronologically on each side of *The Secret Agent.* We shall see in them further exposures of those features of modern social space that erode positive place-relations. The principal cause for this erosion and the rise of negative social space is, for Conrad, abstraction. I begin with *Nostromo* (1904).

Sulaco is a location isolated by high mountains on the one side and by the sea on the other. Isolation from its larger physical context allows Sulaco to be determined by connections with distant commercial centers, especially San Francisco. Despite the many ways in which it differs, Sulaco in its isolation and abstract relations with distant places resembles the London of *The Secret Agent.*

The social change in Sulaco results from developing its silver mine. At first, mining silver is a form of labor that promises to produce a better society. But silver soon begins to determine human behavior and relationships. Charles Gould, who develops the mine to improve the lives of the people, especially the miners, gradually comes under its spell. Emilia, his wife, has loftier goals than Charles; she believes that the mines can be developed to counter the entrenched politics of scarcity. Her English/Italian background relates the vision not only to Giorgio Viola and thereby to Gariboldi but also to the political economist David Ricardo, who theorized the basis of value in labor.[19] Emilia recognizes that the mine becomes a fetish for her husband, and she gradually feels separated from him as though by a wall of silver (N, 221–22). Near the end of the novel, she concludes that the mine's power is "more soulless than any tyrant, more pitiless and autocratic than the worst Government; ready to crush innumerable lives in the expansion of its greatness" (N, 521). Even though she retains a sense of location and of loyalty in human relationships, Emilia appears, in relation to the changes wrought by wealth, naïve. Her moral social values, although not dismissed in themselves, are increasingly divorced from the physical labor upon which they depend (N, 88).

Another measure of silver's effects can be taken from changes in the "incorruptible" Nostromo, a man closely associated with the indigenous people and their traditional values. By virtue of his culture a trusting man, Nostromo is easily exploited by skeptical and manipulative people, and he realizes that Captain Mitchell and Doctor Monyghan betray such "men of the people" as himself.[20] This is because they have no loyalty to the location and workers, and they view the silver as a means of private advantage rather than social construction. Nostromo becomes infected by these attitudes, however important to him inner peace and integrity previously had been. Eventually he "yearned to clasp, embrace, absorb, subjugate in unquestioned possession this treasure, whose tyranny had weighed upon his mind, his actions, his very sleep" (N, 529). Fascination for silver overrides social responsibility and even displaces his feeling for the woman he loves.

Under Western Eyes (1911) allows us to see that the disease of abstraction in social space is not the consequence solely of economic and political factors. In this novel, social abstraction takes a more cultural and linguistic form. The narrator, an educated Englishman living in Geneva, is a student of languages. He has grown to feel that words are cut off from reality. Identified as he is with language, he thinks of himself as standing apart from society as an observer rather than involved in it as a participant.

The narrator identifies his position and attitudes as typically Western, and his view of the Russians that he meets in Geneva are through not his own so much as Western eyes. His impassive, disinterested attitudes typify the West, and, he feels, they stand in sharp contrast to those of "Little Russia" and of Russia itself, in which he takes particular interest.

The society of "Little Russia" reveals three characteristics that set it off from the West. First, authority is charismatic, is based on personal mystery. Social relationships, second, seem to be internal, such as the relation at the end of the narrative of Tekla to Cyril Razumov. Finally, the Russians in Geneva do not allow Western culture to diminish their attachment to their homeland. While it would not do to say that Russia is morally superior to Geneva as a social space, it can be said that Russia is more complex, dynamic, and intriguing than Geneva, and the narrator, among other things, is fascinated by the hold it has on its people despite their distance from it. While the geographical and social size of Russia outstrips its unity and while its society is marked less by diversity than by conflict, the narrator finds Russia more engaging than the static and homogeneous societies of the West, epitomized by Geneva.[21] The social space of Geneva, because of the attitudes of abstraction that sponsor it and that it generates, appears bland and bloodless when compared to Russia.

An aspect of Russian society, in addition to its vitality and extremes, that attracts the narrator is its positive regard for mystery. The Haldin family highly values the Unseen; it motivates political beliefs, as with Victor, and altruistic attitudes, as with Natalia. Russian society seems touched by an otherworldliness that is unlike the empty abstractions of Geneva. However, the spiritual quality of Russian life also seems unrealistic. Natalia carries on her charitable work, upon returning to Russia, out of belief in, as the narrator puts it, "the advent of loving concord springing like a heavenly flower from the soil of men's earth, soaked in blood, torn by struggles, watered with tears" (UWE, 345). Without a firmer social base, "concord" is not likely to spring up, and the charitable qualities of Natalia, however admirable, are not likely to be sustained. Spirituality detaches Natalia and makes her a contrary to the bestial Nikita.

This exchange of religious orientations for forms of detachment and abstraction recurs in Conrad's fiction. We can see it in the relation of the professor in The Secret Agent to his upbringing as the son of an apocalyptic preacher. We find it again in Lord Jim (1900). Jim's identity owes something to his background as the son of a clergyman, a man who had lived with a sure knowledge of the "Unknowable." Unlike his father, however, Jim uses his moral and religious identity to separate himself from other people. His version of belief in the unknowable is his desire for personal peace apart from the complexities of social reality. Because peace is uppermost for Jim, he is never more himself than while luxuriating in isolated calm on the deck of the smoothly sailing *Patna*. When the ship collides with a partially sunken hulk, Jim jumps. He does so more to avoid confusion than to preserve his own life (*LJ*, 71).

Forced into exile, Jim wanders widely, staying in one place only so long as anonymity grants him peace. Settling on Patusan, he works hard to create a separate, tranquil society, but he discounts the political interests of people. When Jim surveys Patusan's peace with a sense of well-being, he places himself in a position not unlike the sense of calm that he mistakenly felt on the deck of the *Patna*. Ship and island support delusions of peace; Jim had felt an "everlasting security" on board the *Patna* and a deeply rooted sense of an "everlasting" quality in life on the island (*LJ*, 19, 185). Discrete settings tempt the imagination to construct peaceful spaces unrelated to society. But social reality presses heavily against the borders of such peace and penetrates them.

Abstraction extends to Conrad's narrator, Marlow. In *Lord Jim* he treats characters as specimens in his collection of human types; he collects types the way Stein collects butterflies. Jim and Brown confirm for Marlow some notions about human types, notions that serve to construct an abstract grid. Marlow's abstraction and Jim's separate peace, though differing, are similar in their standing as contraries to social space.

Abstraction also marks the position of Marlow in *Heart of Darkness* (1902). He stands above the many contraries and exchanges he sets up in the narrative—gloomy London and white Brussels, the Thames and the sea, the sea and the wilderness of Central Africa, Kurtz and his intended, the heart of Africa and the outside world, and his narrative and its hearers. Most provocatively, he stands above the horrendous social space constructed in the Congo by Kurtz.

Whatever else Marlow's story is about—and there is no lack of suggestions as to what that something else is—it is a critique of modern Western culture, primarily its belief, derived from habits of abstraction, that this culture is not particular but universal. It is a story about what happens when a flower of that culture is transplanted into the social space of the African Congo. Marlow's interest in the wilderness of Central Africa yields to an interest in the social and economic space constructed by this epitome of high Western culture. Musician, painter, and writer, Kurtz, removed from his location, runs morally amuck. He becomes a man without "restraint in the gratification of his various lusts" (*HD*, 58). Rather than universally transportable, Kurtz is environmentally lethal when transplanted.

Marlow is as abstracted as are Kurtz and his political and commercial sponsors. His self-elevation above the morally distasteful matters he narrates conceals his actual attitude toward them.[22] By means of abstraction he becomes part of the horror.

The commercial factors in social abstraction are clearer in *Chance* (1913). A banker, de Barral, benefits enormously from the way people trustingly deposit money in his bank, money he squanders on risky and idiosyncratic investments. Marlow describes the imprisonment of de Barral as a mistake that occurs because society thinks it can isolate the cause of its problems. But Marlow's judgment on society does not imply a more positive basis for social space than financial investment. The sea, for example, offers no positive alternative (*C*, 50). Nor can the negative factors of social practices be changed by rational decisions; in fact, intelligence leads people astray as easily as does passion (*C*, 37). Marlow is skeptical about altering human actions and societies, which are as likely to be bad as good (*C*, 23). As the book's title reminds us, so much depends on chance.

There are, however, two factors exposed by the narrative that have potentially positive effects on social space. One is a sense of cooperation between people, which is compared to the loyalty created by a ship's crew working together in the face of shared difficulties. Another factor is the social consequence of strong personal relations, as between Flora and Captain Anthony (*C*, 209).

In *Victory* (1915), we find a further exploration into the possible redemption of social space. The principal character, Alex Heyst, is predisposed to mistrust the world because his father was critical of society. Despite his efforts to maintain a detachment from society, Heyst rescues Lena, a young woman imprisoned within the shady confines of an all-female orchestra that performs for male guests of a hotel. In his relationship with her on the island of Sanburan, Heyst changes. He develops a "greater sense of his own reality than he had ever known in all his life," and he loses some of the defensiveness that social calumnies had produced in him (*V*, 164). But their Edenic existence on the island is broken by the arrival of three men sent to find a treasure they had been told Heyst had gathered. The trio takes on satanic standing when one of them uses the words of Satan from the Book of Job to describe his behavior (*V*, 266). With the help of betrayal by Heyst's servant they destroy the lives of Heyst and Lena. The force of these evils is augmented by eschatological imagery (*V*, 157), and an apocalyptic dichotomy between modern social space and human well-being is recognized (*V*, 151).

III

From narratives that map the abstraction of social spaces and the evils that result we turn now to those depicting more viable and positive social spaces. While his sea narratives continue Conrad's critique of modernity's social spaces, they also give glimpses of positive alternatives, social spaces based on physical labor and consistent with human moral and spiritual well-being. I begin with *The Nigger of the 'Narcissus'* (1898).

The central of its five sections depicts a storm at sea. The storm is extraordinarily fierce, and we are led to conclude that the ship, had it not been "the most magnificent sea-boat ever launched," would not have come through it (*NN*, 40).[23] The open sea and the storm offer the reader a strong sense of comprehensive space. But primary attention is not focused on the wider physical context. Rather, the descriptions of the sea, the horizon, and the storm serve to enhance awareness of the particularity and significance of the social space created on the ship by the mutual work of the crew.

The narrative also provides a strong sense of personal space, which centers on Jim Wait. Because he is ill, Wait is exempted from the work that defines and unifies the crew. In several ways he stands apart from and becomes a mystery to the crew. He is taller than the rest of the men and black. More important, his illness is both controversial (some believe it is feigned) and socially significant (sea lore has it that a dying man delays the return of a ship). The social space of the sailors constructed by their labor stands between the comprehensive and treacherous seascape and the personal space occupied by Jim's closeted and sick body. I take it as a sign of health in Conrad's social spaces that they neither swamp personal space nor occlude comprehensive space.

Another sign of health is that the shipboard society is largely egalitarian; "hierarchy is weak," and the men "feel themselves equal before the unconcerned immensity of the sea and the exacting appeal of the work" (*NN*, 16). True, the crew resent the captain, and they recognize that after they save the ship from the fury of the storm, he and not their labor will get the credit. But the social structure allows for the actualization both of individual efforts and of a viable and flexible society.[24]

After the storm, social cohesion is lost, and social space sours. This loss and shift are identified as modern. Seamen of earlier times were called on to work together and to depend upon one another more constantly and closely, and the elderly Singleton provides a link to former days when men risked more than they now do. Singleton recalls crews who, by their work and mutual trust, "knew how to exist beyond the pale of life and within sight of eternity" and "were the everlasting children of the mysterious sea" (*NN*, 22). Their successors are "children of a discontented earth," "less profane, but perhaps also less believing" (*NN*, 22). The community of the *Narcissus*, although weaker than those of earlier years, is stronger and less dissolute than land-based society.[25] As Michael Taussig argues, Conrad wrote about ships and the sea under the premonition of their disappearance from social awareness. This premonition was justified, given the fact that, while so much of modern life continues to be dependent on the sea and ships, moderns are indifferent to them. Taussig suggests the beneficial effects on social self-understanding produced by an awareness of society's dependence on the sea, ships, and, one would add, the labor of crews.[26]

When we turn to *Typhoon* (1902), we find a clearer depiction of a social space largely built on human labor and characterized by individualities that are communally actualized. Like the situation encountered by the crew of the *Narcissus,* Captain MacWhirr has to deal with two problems. One is external, the typhoon, and the other is internal, the riot among the Chinese workers below decks who scramble to recover their money dislodged during the storm. The storm binds members of the crew together in their efforts individually and collectively to preserve the ship. MacWhirr, Jukes, the chief mate, and Soloman Rout, the chief engineer, are bound together by the tasks of coping with the storm and by their need to communicate. Jukes and the captain "stood clasped thus in the blind night, bracing each other against the wind, cheek to cheek and lip to ear, in the manner of two hulks lashed stem to stern together" (*T,* 164). The social space created by the captain and crew in their common labor seems to enable MacWhirr to act administratively in a Solomon-like way toward the internal conflict below. He distributes the fruits of labor equally among the workers, giving extra to those with greater needs.

While the positive social space that is created on ship by the corporate acts of the captain and crew and that is extended to calm the fighting workers is a social space constructed primarily by physical labor, it has as well a spiritual aspect. The Christmas Eve and Christmas morning when the storm occurred granted the men a "sighting, verily, even the coast of the Great Beyond, whence no ship ever returns to give up her crew to the dust of the earth" (*T,* 196).

The positive social space established on the ship is compromised, however, by its ties to wider economic interests. The crew's work is related to economic initiatives located on land, and the laborers below deck were returning after having left their families to engage in difficult work for meager pay in a distant location.

The narrative reveals the problems in bringing positively depicted social spaces in Conrad's fiction fully into view. One problem is that social spaces, while grounded in the physicality of human labor, are adversely affected by the products of that labor. As *Typhoon* makes clear, human labor produces or is in other ways related to money. While Conrad may be following the argument of David Ricardo that value is based on human labor, he also recognizes, nowhere more fully, perhaps, than in *Nostromo,* that labor produces wealth that quickly takes precedence, even for workers, over labor.[27]

Another problem is that so much work in modern society is not physical but clerical and cerebral. These problems seem to explain why his narrating is given largely to a critique of modern social spaces and why instances of more positive social spaces are located in the past and then, also, often not long-lived.

The Shadow-Line (1917) provides a good example of Conrad's exploration of the distorting effects that economic factors can have on viable social spaces. The two settings of sea and shore are sharply juxtaposed. The narrative ends on shore where it begins, and this shore frame stands in sharp contrast to the larger, middle section that occurs at sea.

The setting on shore is epitomized by the harbor office. The narrator finds there an "atmosphere of officialdom" that would "kill anything that breathes the air of human endeavor, would extinguish hope and fear alike in the supremacy of paper and ink" (*SL*, 29). The harbor-master's "official pen" was "mightier than the sword in making or marring the fortune of simple toiling men" (*SL*, 31). But when the narrator is invited to command a ship, the harbor-master speaks to him in the language of a fellow seaman. There are two languages—the language of economic interests, which has a deadly effect on relationships, and the language of seamen, which creates mutual understanding and support.

The narrative reveals the sharp contrast in Conrad's work between positive and negative social spaces. Modern social spaces, including those constructed on sailing ships at sea, are economically sponsored and produce wealth. This fact means that they cannot be narrated as reliable and constant. The implicit norm is that labor and wealth as well as physical and administrative work must be held together and that there must be a recognition that in the construction of social space, physical labor is primary. Physical labor must be recognized not only as the basis of social space but also as the critique of administrative authority when, as it tends to do, it takes on the air of primacy.

IV

Conrad's fiction advocates the primacy of social space, depicts the diseased conditions of modern social spaces, and retrieves more positive social spaces from the era of sailing ships.[28] The primary marks of diseased social spaces are their suppression and concealment of personal and comprehensive spaces and their abstraction from their reality-granting basis in physical labor.[29] As Donald Benson puts it, "the demands of work honestly done constitute, for Conrad, a reality that sets it quite apart from pretences and principles; it is, in fact, only to skilled and honest work and to elemental nature itself that he applies the word 'reality.'"[30] When social space is abstracted from its physical basis in human labor, it takes on the negative qualities that define the spatiality primarily of the political novels and especially of *The Secret Agent*. Community is not the principal value in Conrad's fiction, as Raymond Williams suggests.[31] The community derives from mutual labor. Wieslaw Krajka has it right, I think, when he refers to the fundamental principle of Conrad's view of community, namely, "unity in work and struggle." Krajka goes on to say that "the heroism and commendable characteristics of the mariners may be attained by every human being. The clear nature and accessibility of these ideals determine the democratic character of the Conradian ethos, the humanism of his canon."[32]

I do not think that the basic, even normative role of work in the construction of social space places Conrad on either side of the political divide suggested by his socially radical, Romantic father and his conservative uncle. Rather, the contrast between them is subverted by Conrad's stress on work because work is both traditional and radical. Work locates persons in ongoing social structures, but it also subverts the putative primacy of political and economic power and management. I also believe that the stress on labor, while primarily having an egalitarian quality in Conrad's fiction, allows for hierarchical structures that, it should be emphasized, need not be bureaucratic. If based on the value of labor, hierarchical structures can serve to organize labor and to attend to other, secondary managerial tasks. The frequently negative depictions of social space in Conrad's fiction, therefore, do not mean that he rejects modern societies totally. By grounding social space in labor, the contrary relation between *Gemeinschaft* (community) and *Gesellschaft* (society) can be undercut. Labor, particularly in the face of common needs and potentials, places all participants in significant roles. And labor always already stands as ground to social space.[33]

Societies formed aboard ships, while they have economic and political ties to land-based interests, are not so vulnerable to disease because crews are always alert to forces outside of social space, especially during storms at sea, and respect personal abilities and relationships. Land-based, especially urban, societies, in their increasing distance from or exclusion of the unpredictable and mysterious potentials of landscape and personal relations, more readily allow social space to be colonized by the abstracting power of results over causes, structure over action, and means over ends, that is, by economic and political factors. There appears to be an irresistible lure in political and economic power to occlude the primacy of physical labor. When powerful members of a society succumb to that temptation, the result is a perversion of social space. Such societies—and they seem to be characteristic if not definitive of Western culture—are marked by the substitution of means for ends and of isolated, often impulsive, self-concerns for communal ones.

So thorough is this distortion, for Conrad, that it even infects his narrators and implied authors. Since the abstraction of people in a society occurs when they establish their identities not in relation to one another and the good of the social whole but in relation to property and personal power, it is important to recognize the lack of relation between his narrators and their constructed readers. The narrators and implied authors of Conrad's fiction, rather than understanding and resisting the effects on them of modern attitudes toward social relationships, create distance not only from the material they narrate but also from the narratee. They retain identity in part by withholding what they consider to be most valuable in their stories. The social space created by the relation of the narrator and narratee in and by his fiction, in other words, is not a space free from the distortions that mark social spaces in Conrad's fictions as a whole.[34]

Conrad's retrievals of positive social spaces on ships are not nostalgic or idealistic but exemplary, expressive of a human potential that has been suppressed and inadequately valued but is still a reality. As Foucault points out, "the ship is the heterotopia *par excellence*," but in Conrad's corpus, ships are not, as Foucault says of ships and heterotopias, places of "dreams."[35] Rather, merchant ships are workplaces upon which modern societies depended and continue to depend. While sailing ships have gone, nothing has radically changed. Society is still dependent on labor, and the sense of common purpose and mutuality in social space arises from labor and from acknowledging its primacy. As Hardy does not expect all of London to move to the heath, so Conrad does not expect office workers to sign up for work at sea or for other forms of physical labor. Rather, social spaces can be rectified if they are particularized, opened to wider contexts, protective of personal interests, and defined primarily by common work. The moral and spiritual potential of social place-relations derives from their primarily physical bases.[36]

We should view *The Secret Agent* in the light of this larger agenda. In a note on the novel that he added after the First World War, Conrad treats it as so extreme as to require justification.[37] He explains that his motivation was to account for the otherwise anomalous behaviors of the actual attack on the Greenwich Observatory and the suicide of the perpetrator's sister. He took these behaviors, then, as having their basis in the felt effects of a social space that was becoming increasingly deficient and distorted. *The Secret Agent* is a novel that exaggerates these effects and their causes in order to retard and perhaps even to reverse them. It is important to remember that he wrote *The Secret Agent* (1906–7) in close proximity to his most personal and often lyrical writings about the sea and ships, *The Mirror of the Sea* (1904–6) and *A Personal Record* (1908–9).

When I return to social space later in this study and to modern cities in the conclusion, I shall look more fully at the ways in which modern, especially urban, social spaces are vulnerable to abstraction. Henri Lefebvre's work will be particularly helpful in understanding such abstraction, what he calls "mental space." We shall see that a rectification of social space is crucial to a more fully human understanding of place-relations and that this rectification is not possible without a reinstatement of the physicality of social space, a physicality closely tied, among other things, to labor. And we shall see in the conclusion that the modern city can and should be rescued not only from the perils of abstraction but also from the negative effects of the cultural construction of the city as profane.

3

E. M. Forster

The Body and the Physicality of Intimate Space

The narrator of *The Return of the Native* begins with a description of Egdon Heath and its "nightly roll into darkness," and the opening paragraphs of *The Secret Agent* describe a street in London and the shop from which Verloc emerges. In contrast to these, the narrator of *Howards End* begins with the description of a house, Howards End, contained in Helen's letter.[1] The shift of attention is crucial. With Forster, we move from a primary attention to comprehensive and social spaces to the primacy of personal space. Houses and other intimate spaces are central to *Howards End* and to all of Forster's fiction.

Wilfred Stone argues, "Houses, for Forster, were living symbols of an emotional and spiritual security that he had only tasted in his half-orphaned experience."[2] But before houses are symbols for Forster, they are specific places, and before being emotional and spiritual, they are physical. Like Hardy and Conrad, Forster moves from the physicality and specificity of places to their potentials and consequences for moral and spiritual well-being. But unlike them, Forster believes that it is first of all in relation to places supportive of personal potentials and relationships that the threats and losses posed by modern attitudes toward space must be addressed. As Forster writes: "Personal relations are despised today. They are regarded as bourgeois luxuries, as products of a time of fair weather which is now past, and we are urged to get rid of them, to dedicate ourselves to some movement or cause instead."[3] To redress this wrong the language of space in his fiction moves *from* personal space *to* the larger social and natural/ontological environments.

It is no small matter, then, that *Howards End* begins with Helen's description of the house, and it is no accident that the house frames the narrative. In addition, the substance of the narrative largely concerns the question of occupancy. Houses, the way people relate to them, and the way people in them relate to one another: these are some of the issues in the novel's treatment of personal space. The locations of personal life are basic in Forster's fiction, and spiritual and moral consequences arise from them.

Intimate space in Forster's fiction, however, is not something that can be taken for granted or that is easily accessible. Indeed, it is severely threatened as well as undervalued. This is due to the consequences of modern attitudes toward intimate spaces, especially attitudes arising from urbanization, mobility, and a money economy. These forces counter the primacy of intimate spaces and diminish their significance. *Howards End,* therefore, not only affirms the primacy of intimate space but also challenges its increasing subservience to, even absorption by, socioeconomically defined space. Although the problem—namely, the shrinking possibilities of intimate space in modern society—is more fully and clearly presented in his fiction than are solutions to it, the narrative retains a firm sense of the primacy of intimate places and of relations to and within them.

I

While *Howards End* opens and ends with the maternal Wilcox home north of London, much of the narrative is placed away from it, largely in London. The two textual spaces are sharply contrasted. While London is contained in the narrative on both sides by Howards End, London should be treated first because it presents the problem to which Howards End and the spatiality it offers are normative alternatives.

London life is marked by two contrary characteristics. One is that social space is determined by a rigid structure that limits personal development and relationships; the other is that social space in London is undergoing rapid change. Both characteristics of urban life—rigid structure and rapid change —have negative consequences for personal locations and relationships. These negative consequences are aggravated by the fact that structure and change are unrelated to one another. Social structure provides the significance of space, but it is unchanging. Social change provides movement, but it is meaningless; indeed, it is chaotic. The social structure, rather than providing meaningful positions in and from which people can relate to one another, separates people and deprives them of relationships within a larger whole. And change, rather than being produced by the dynamics of personal interests and relationships, occurs without regard to them. Indeed, change mainly destroys personal places and replaces them with characterless, impersonal structures.

Social distinctions create separation and confinement because they are determined not by human identity and potentials but by financial and cultural capital. Capital creates two lines of demarcation that define the social space. The first runs between the social location of Leonard Bast and the social world that the Schlegels and the Wilcoxes share. The second runs between the culturally contrasted Schlegels and Wilcoxes. The action of the novel is given over primarily to the clarification of these distinctions and the challenge to them posed by personal initiatives and relations and the places that house them.

Leonard Bast wants very badly to change his social location. His private space is determined by the class structure, and it is confining. There is nothing personal about it. The food he eats is artificial. The furniture in his flat is not his own. His relation to Jacky is defined by the social expectation of marriage. Bast, confined, deprived, and burdened, wants to improve both his financial position and his share of cultural capital. His main attempts to change location—attending a concert and changing his position from one firm to another—are precipitating events in the narrative. The problem is that the power to change his location lies wholly outside him. Change, rather than a result of personal development, is resisted and determined by social and economic boundaries, and his attempts to improve his position by crossing those boundaries weaken and finally destroy him.

Bast attends concerts and reads Ruskin because the social class of which he is a part lacks a culture. Unlike the underclass in the countryside, which, as we see in the neighbors of Howards End, has a culture, the urban underclass has none. The underclass in the countryside also has a physical location directly related to their occupations and livelihood. The urban underclass does not. Bast, who was raised in the countryside, works as a clerk in a financial system that he does not understand and that is subject to vagaries he cannot track. The cultural and financial power to support self-improvement and enrich personal relations is not a part of his location, and his attempts to gain such power are haphazard and counterproductive.

Forster's depiction of Bast's location as lacking integrity and content is provocative. It counters the belief, recently explicated so convincingly by Pierre Bourdieu, that people of every class inhabit their locations in such a way as to impute meaning, even moral superiority, to them.[4] Also, it counters beliefs that workers form a potential social location from which a morally infused challenge to the dominant class can arise. Bast's location has little if any significance, and there seem to be no others similarly situated with whom he can make common cause.

The second major line of distinction, one that divides the dominating class, runs between the Wilcoxes and the Schlegels. The two families represent the two kinds of capital held by the dominant class: financial and cultural. The families conflict with one another over which of the two kinds is primary. For the Schlegels, cultural capital is more important than financial capital; for the Wilcoxes, economic capital is the more important. The conflict between the two groups is complicated by the fact that, as Bourdieu makes clear, those in the dominant class who have their place more by cultural than by financial capital are likely to side with workers and members of the petit bourgeois against the financially dominant group. In the novel, the Schlegels, especially Helen, have a far more accommodating attitude toward Leonard Bast than do the Wilcoxes. The Wilcox/Schlegel conflict is expanded by the fact that it takes on a national status: Which of the two, cultural or financial capital, is the more important in defining the present and future power and significance of England?[5] This question gathers force in the novel from the contrasts and relations drawn between English and German national power and prestige.

The social structure depicted by the novel, then, resists the potential of personal development and relationships by exclusion, confinement, and conflict. Resolutions are attempted, however, by the Schlegel sisters. In response to Bast's fruitless attempts to cross the lines that exclude him from a higher economic and cultural level, Helen, mostly because of her impulsive nature and her anger with the Wilcox family, becomes personally involved with him. Their relationship finds its contrast in the affair that earlier had occurred between Henry Wilcox and Jacky, a relationship that, by being financially determined, confirms rather than challenges the boundaries separating the classes.

A more successful resolution to the negative consequences of the social structure is achieved by the marriage of Margaret and Henry. The marriage is based on the personal magnanimity of Margaret, who is able to look beyond Henry's offenses. The primary role given to Margaret in the marriage and her handling of the personal and social crisis created by Helen suggest that while culture and money require one another, culture is, of the two, the more significant in overcoming the tensions or conflicts between them.

Despite the initiatives of the Schlegel women, gender distinctions and roles largely conform to the boundaries set by the social structure. Cultural capital and interests are primarily feminine, and financial power is primarily masculine. Howards End is the family home of Mrs. Wilcox, and Margaret and Helen occupy it at the end. London is the location of Henry Wilcox's economic power, and it is extended both into the countryside, by his ownership of houses, and into the world, by his position in a large, imperial corporation. What seems to have happened is that masculinity has emerged as a power that is brutal for want of integrity and moral purpose. The Wilcox men, particularly Henry and Charles, because they lack culture and treat places as commodities, are unlocated. The moral vacuity, even the exploitive and violent character, of power unenclosed by culture creates a lack of moral strength for which the Schlegel women, particularly Margaret, partially compensate.

The economically determined structure of English society, then, is depicted as negative because it is deficient in culture and resists change. The overwhelming result of its demarcations is to entrench people in their locations and to discourage, if not prevent, movement across lines. People occupy their positions primarily not in terms of positive attitudes toward one another but negatively, in terms of difference, disdain, envy, and pity. While the effects of this structure are partially overcome, the structure itself is not significantly altered.

In contrast to the social structure and perhaps contributing to its static character are the changes that occur in London. Social structure and social change occurring in London have no real relation to one another, and the changes are no less negative for personal places and relations than is the structure.

Changes are forced by an expanding population that puts physical pressure on space. More and more people are crowded into less and less space: "These [that is, houses of the kind in which the Schlegels live], too, would be swept away in time, and another promontory would arise upon their site, as humanity piled itself higher and higher on the precious soil of London" (*HE,* 8).[6] These effects are so impersonal and pervasive that water and other images of dissolution and chaos are used by the narrator and characters in their descriptions of and reactions to London. To Mrs. Wilcox, London is even satanic, and it raises in Margaret thoughts of hell. Older residences like Wickham Place are swept away, and the architecture of "hurry" matches, Margaret notices, "the language of hurry on the mouths of its inhabitants" (*HE,* 132–33). The narrator shares her evaluations: "month by month the roads smelt more strongly of petrol, and were more difficult to cross, and human beings heard each other speak with greater difficulty, breathed less of the air, and saw less of the sky" (*HE,* 131). The changes that mark social life in London are not improvements because what compels them is not cultural value but brute force.[7]

Other social changes in modern life are, if not destructive, at least ambiguous in their effects on personal life. Increasing travel opportunities, for example, promote wider contacts between people and exposure to diverse sites. But newer forms of travel also produce dislocation and indifference to place. Margaret, while riding in the motor-car, loses "all sense of space" (*HE,* 241–42). We are told later that she was able to recover her orientation because "she recaptured the sense of space, which is the basis of all earthly beauty, and, starting from Howards End, she attempted to realize England" (*HE,* 249). While the Schlegels stress the cultural benefits of travel, transportation for the Wilcox family is related to acquisition and violence. In addition, the possibilities for social change suggested by the women's rights movement seem dim. Rather than expand and enrich human potentials and relations, the opening of society to a greater influence from women is resisted and even ridiculed by the Wilcox men. Schlegel women, despite their cultural capital and personal gifts, do not effectively challenge the social boundaries of women's space and are confined to domestically, sexually, and procreatively defined roles. One could surmise that Forster, in his concern for the viability and future of intimate places and in his assumption that women are more sensitive than men to the force and importance of such places and the life possibilities they grant, was not ready to risk the results for personal or intimate space of narrating meaningful ventures by women into more public social space.

Since social space in the narrative neither responds to personal interests nor promotes human relationships, characters in the novel explore the relation of personal to comprehensive space, a space, in other words, that transcends London. Margaret sees London for what it is, "a caricature of infinity," falsely comprehensive (*HE,* 343). This stimulates her desire for a comprehensive space that is steady and spiritual, and railroad stations seem to her like portals to it.

Attempts to access comprehensive space are made difficult by the fact that in several ways social space becomes comprehensive. The economy, for example, forms the common background upon which classes are distinguished from and related to one another. Money also extends London's space out into the world, through such agencies as the Imperial and West African Rubber Company, with which Henry Wilcox is identified. Money not only plays powerful roles in establishing social space and creating distinctions within it; it also has a kind of spiritual authority or presence. Helen thinks of it as a means of grace by which Leonard can be helped. And at Christmas the religious qualities of the season blend with the economic. But money, while a necessary support for personal spaces, separates people more than it unifies them, and possession of too much money seems to complicate personal identity negatively and to compromise human relationships. Margaret is puzzled by the Wilcox desire for more than enough money, and she increases her sense of personal worth by divesting herself of some of her financial assets.

Another form of comprehensive space is the nation, particularly because of England's island identity. Its natural, specific boundaries make it a physical as well as a political entity. It also has an appropriate size, capacious and varied yet not so big as to intimidate the imagination. But it does not provide an adequate horizon because it lacks meaning, a vital mythology. Its underdeveloped sense of the ancient and the spiritual becomes all the more significant given the failure of Christianity to fill that lack. In the form of St. Paul's Cathedral and Oxford, for example, Christianity and Christian culture, while pervasive, seem too abstract or formal to provide a vital, comprehensive support for personal integrity and relationships. Finally, England also seems compromised by its competition with German culture, its identity as a financial power, and its imperialistic ventures.

A comprehensive space that is distinguishable from social space and seems supportive of personal space is identified as the "unseen." The Schlegel sisters believe in it. It is the transcendent, the spiritual, the More. A question arises about the unseen's relation to the material and specific. Helen separates the unseen from the material and specific and, according to Margaret, broods too much on it. Margaret wants continuity between the unseen and the seen. She stands, one could say, between Helen and Henry in this regard, trying to connect the two—Henry with his preoccupation with the seen and Helen with her orientation to the unseen.[8] The narrator tells us that Margaret distinguishes herself from both: "The business man who assumes that this life is everything, and the mystic who asserts that it is nothing, fail, on this side and on that, to hit the truth" (*HE*, 236–37). Among the many contraries posed by the novel, either by the narrator or by the characters—the inner and outer, the particular and the inclusive, the steady and the whole, the cultural and the financial, the prose and the passion—the contraries of seen and unseen seem most important and inclusive. Margaret's view of their relation and the narrator's close identification with Margaret's view give her position authority. She recognizes continuities between the physical and the spiritual, the particular and the transcendent.

Death amplifies the sense of a comprehensive spiritual space. It has, as Helen says, a genuine power; it is, she says, "'really Imperial'" (*HE*, 291). Behind coffins and skeletons stands, she believes, something immense to which all that is great in us responds. While death itself destroys, awareness of death, the idea of it, creates a container for personal life. "'Death destroys a man: the idea of Death saves him'" (*HE, 291*). Death forms an inclusive horizon for human identity and relationships, but it does not overpower them. Mr. Schlegel and Mrs. Wilcox, though dead, continue to influence.

Intimate space, particularly Howards End, allows for continuity to be recognized between the unseen and the seen, death and living, past and future. The intimate physical place created by Howards End for the two women and the child has healing potential because it contains contraries, sponsors potentials, and challenges the dominance of both social and comprehensive space. It provides a life-enhancing environment in which relationships between differing people and interests can evolve. We are told of Margaret that "her only ally was the power of Home. The loss of Wickham Place had taught her more than its possession" (*HE,* 270). Howards End has the authority of the past, and it accommodates the new. It makes place for the Schlegel furniture. It shelters what society is unable to accept. It is open to the surrounding countryside. And the correspondence between the house's name and the book's title suggests a close relation between personal places and narratives of developing personal identity and relationships. The relationship between Margaret and Helen that Howards End accommodates physically has moral force. Personal space counters the mores of society in the name of more charitable and humane values.

However, Howards End, while invaluable, is vulnerable to the threats of a rapidly growing urban space. Margaret muses, "London was but a foretaste of this nomadic civilization which is altering human nature so profoundly, and throws upon personal relations a stress greater than they have ever borne before" (*HE,* 319). The question arises whether Howards End can withstand the pressure and material force of urban space. The potentials for moral identity and relationships that reside in Howards End are vulnerable to the power behind the expanding metropolis and to the identification of people with that power, people such as the Wilcox men, especially Charles.

Prospects for the future are dimmed by the fact that scions of cultural capital, like Tibby Schlegel, seem increasingly to be precious and detached. The future seems to be threatened by the sharply articulated division between the brutal Charles Wilcox and his opposite, the feckless Tibby.[9] The principal problem is that money and culture, rather than being subordinate to the nurture of personal integrity and relationships, have become ends in themselves and, by providing contrary forms of identity, are increasingly detached from one another and reduced.

What seems to hold out a positive alternative is personal, intimate space, such as is provided by Howards End, where material power can be culturally infused and morally directed. It is intimate space and its potentials that are normative for the novel and not as much the attitudes and behaviors of the characters, including Margaret. As the narrator says, "the world would be a grey, bloodless place were it entirely composed of Miss Schlegels" (*HE,* 32). Even less is Mrs. Wilcox normative; her deficient understandings of intimate space are pointed out by Margaret when Margaret rebukes Mrs. Wilcox for the lack of intellectual discussions at Howards End. Margaret contends:

"'Discussion keeps a house alive. It cannot stand by brick and mortar alone'" (*HE*, 92). Personal space, while it has a physical basis, a particularity, also can and should have a moral and spiritual content. Margaret's "conclusion was that any human being lies nearer to the unseen than any organisation, and from this she never varied" (*HE*, 35). Personal integrity and relations require, are created and sustained in and by, intimate space, and from the primacy of personal space, changes can be effected in social values, structures, and goals. Personal relationships and identity should alter social space rather than be determined by it.[10]

This does not mean that Forster collapses social relations and dynamics into personal ones or fails to see them as related. Wilfred Stone, for example, takes Forster to task in this regard, chiding him for positing "personal relations as antithetical to social relations" and failing to "recognize their close dependency on each other."[11] Forster neither confuses social with personal locations and relations nor sets the two in opposition. It is a question of primacy. For this novel and for Forster's work as a whole, personal potential and relationships and the intimate spaces in which they can develop are primary, and society should defer to and be altered by them. As the narrator puts it early on, the Schlegel sisters "cared deeply about politics, though not as politicians would have us care; they desired that public life should mirror whatever is good in the life within" (*HE*, 32). Personal space has a powerfully redemptive potential that accounts for the religious language of the novel, a language that describes the primary role that intimate space should have in securing the moral and spiritual potential of the human environment.

We can summarize the characteristics of positive personal place-relations at the conclusion of *Howards End* by recognizing, first, that there is a mutual adjustment between Margaret and Helen and the house. The house accommodates changes, suggested by Helen's pregnancy and the Schlegel furniture. And the women, however different in their backgrounds they may be to the legacy that the house represents, adjust themselves to it as well. Second, the house is a commodious personal space. It joins past to future and the physical to the moral and spiritual. Margaret, by taking in Helen and her child, betokens a future that will mark departures, but the spiritual inheritance of Mrs. Wilcox is a part of the house and its significance. This spiritual legacy is joined by the strong realities embodied in Helen by her break with traditional class determinants. Third, the house, while affording security, is not confining. Helen and her child are not fully identified with the house, and they will not be constrained and retained by it. Finally, the house is very much a gift, a bequest, and Helen's inclusion in it is a gift to her from her sister. The giftlike qualities of the house stand in sharp contrast to the Wilcox control of it and the unsuccessful attempt made in the name of ownership to thwart the potentials of personal space for grace.

II

The primary and normative position of personal, intimate space in *Howards End* is the principal issue of Forster's narrative art more generally. The locations that persons and their relationships require and create are continually stressed. A pattern emerges by which personal interests and relationships, accommodated and stimulated by particular places, often challenge social settings. England unfortunately seems increasingly to construct spaces that are unaccommodating to personal interests. The question is whether other, non-English locations are more supportive of personal integrity and intimacy.

In *Where Angels Fear to Tread* (1905), England, particularly the town of Sawston, is contrasted to Italy, particularly the town of Monteriano. The English location is marked by a social space that sharply limits personal behavior, distances neighbors from one another, and encourages judgmental attitudes. Monteriano, in contrast, fosters freer personal behavior and regards liveliness of personal style more highly than the boundaries and mores of social space.[12] A major reason for the difference between the two sites is that Monteriano's cultural history is mythologically richer than its English counterpart. This makes it more accommodating to human emotions and interactions by suggesting models of expansive identities and dramatic relationships.

Philip Herriton knows both places. Italy, he believes, "'purifies and ennobles'" a person; it is "'the school as well as the playground of the world'" (*WA*, 15). But despite his fascination for Italy, his English background has so conditioned him that he recoils from Italian culture. He disdains Gino, whom his in-law had married and who fathered her child, because Gino is the son of a dentist (*WA*, 41). However, he also recognizes that Sawston suppresses personal vigor and that Gino possesses a liveliness that transcends class standing: "'He's got a country behind him that's upset people from the beginning of the world'" (*WA*, 130). However, Philip's sister, Harriet, does not share his assessment of Italy. When she goes there to fetch the child of the family's in-law, Lilian, who died while giving birth, Harriet thinks it is to rescue the child from all that Italy represents: excess, uncleanliness, and immorality.

Caroline Abbott, a companion of Lilian and a friend of the family, has an even more affirmative attitude toward Italy than Philip. She had encouraged

Lilian's relationship with Gino, and she later admits her own love for him. But in England she is swayed again by English norms: "Sawston . . . was certainly petty and dull; at times she found it even contemptible. But it was not a place of sin" (*WA*, 124). But when in Italy she affirms its "beauty, evil, charm, vulgarity, mystery" (*WA*, 158).

England, because it defines personal life primarily by socially located moral distinctions, is, compared to Italy, confining and even deadening. The English social structure separates people while the culture of Italy brings people together, as the music at the opera encompasses the audience. Italy provides and fosters locations for actualizing the physical exuberance of persons and their relations to one another. It is a culture that does not allow social boundaries and mores to determine and define intimate, personal space.

The variety of personal, intimate spaces becomes clear in *The Longest Journey* (1907). Rickie Elliot, the principal character, has a strong sense of place. We are told: "He was extremely sensitive to the inside of a house, holding it as an organism that expressed the thoughts, conscious or subconscious, of its inmates. He was equally sensitive to places. He would compare Cambridge with Sawston, and either with a third type of existence" (*LJ*, 179). At times he loves his room more than he does other people (*LJ*, 72). He recognizes that his belongings take on unique qualities in his new dwelling in Sawston and that it is a very different place from that offered by his Cambridge rooms. The narrator confirms Rickie's sense of place by naming the three sections of the narrative after the three locations that Rickie often compares with one another.

Intimate places are not limited to the interiors of buildings. Rickie also forms a strong attachment to a dell on the outskirts of Cambridge. This dell "became for him a kind of church—a church where indeed you could do anything you liked, but where anything you did would be transfigured" (*LJ*, 28). He connects this location to an ancient stone circle, where he learns for the first time that he has a half-brother.[13]

Despite the stature that his strong sense of place gives Rickie, he reveals some limiting attitudes toward place. For example, he is nationalistic and shares the imperialist attitudes of his brother-in-law. "'Thank God I'm English,'" Rickie says, and he places the cultures of Greece, Italy, and France below that of England (*LJ*, 57–58). His chauvinism is challenged by Stewart Ansell, the young philosopher from Cambridge, who argues that the earth is filled with little societies and that none of them is great. Greatness has become confused with goodness, but goodness is always particular (*LJ*, 77).

The value of intimate spaces in the narrative is heightened by the fact that social spaces determine and limit people. Stewart Ansell will not receive an academic position because of his social class and ethnic identity; the suburban Pembrokes allow considerations of wealth to determine place; Rickie's parents hold a higher social position than the Pembrokes, while the Failings, with their older, larger house, stand above the rest.

The power of social space to determine personal identity and relationships is countered not only by the value of intimate spaces but also by a philosophical question. The question that opens the narrative and that returns again like a refrain is whether something exists when nobody is present to observe it. It queries the relation of human perception to the force and meaning of physical places and events. Places have a force of their own, but they also acquire qualities from the relations people have with them.

Rickie's half-brother Stephen brings out the primacy of intimate space most fully. He has always been irreverent toward social placements and their ideological and monumental warrants: "Stephen overthrew the Mosaic cosmogony. He pointed out the discrepancies in the Gospels. He leveled his wit against the most beautiful spire in the world [Salisbury], now rising against the Southern sky" (*LJ*, 128). What gives him a sense of place and identity is not social, religious, or national placement but a sense of life as personal, as "a personal combat or a personal truce" (*LJ*, 278). This sense of location as founded by personal behavior and relations grants the narrative its center and culmination.

A Room with a View (1908) extends the thesis that Italian culture is more supportive than English culture of personal potentials while also adding dimensions to Forster's narrating of personal space. The title suggests not so much a juxtaposition of indoor and outdoor or of the cultural and the natural aspects of human experience but rather the complex character of intimate space. Intimate space provides both particular boundaries or seclusion and, at the same time, access to something larger, something beyond the familiar in life.

These two qualities of intimate space often are sundered from one another. This can be seen in the experience of Lucy Honeychurch. Conditioned by a sheltered background, she is intrigued by larger perspectives and prospects of adventure, and when she plays the piano she feels transported to a more expanded world. But the two dimensions of particularity and expansion are disconnected. Particularity has become confinement, and larger possibilities are only vague aspirations. This split affects her relations to two potential lovers. Cecil is a person her mother would be proud to have her marry because he represents a society structured by the dominance of males. George, a man with unorthodox ideas, is unpredictable and holds views of gender equality. The two men, in other words, are related to the spatial sides of Lucy's identity, her contrary orientations both to confinement and to open possibility. Personal space, one is led to conclude, should contain both specificity and potentiality, both room and view.

The contrast between room and view, between the defining and expanding qualities of intimate space, conditions the contrast between English and Italian cultures. English intimate spaces restrict view; windows in the drawing room of Windy Corner are covered by draperies, and English tourists to Italy confine their views to sites dictated by their Baedekers. Florence, in contrast, fosters breadth, a sense of unpredictability, and varieties of behavior that stimulate and expand personal life. The effect of the flowing river on Lucy as she talks with George Emerson, the fight in the Piazza Signoria, the sexual sport of the carriage driver and his girlfriend, and the violet-covered terrace—"the well-head, the primal source whence beauty gushed out to water the earth" (*RV,* 110)—where George kisses Lucy for the first time: Italian places sponsor vitality and unpredictability in personal behavior and relations. However, while they have the effect of stimulating and enlarging personal awareness and intimacy, they also suggest a disconcerting lack of stability, in other words, more view than room.

The question arises here, as in *Howards End,* as to whether a balance between the contraries of room and view, a balance that is optimal for personal space, requires an orientation to natural or comprehensive space. Mr. Emerson, George's father, is a strong proponent of nature and of natural impulses, and he proposes a relation to the natural not so much as a return to something humans once had, since humans may never have enjoyed full rapport with nature in the past, but as something that can be created in the future, a new relation to natural space that awaits human experience. We have, he contends, yet to enter the Garden of Eden; "'We shall enter it when we no longer despise our bodies'" (*RV,* 194). The recreating power and significance of nature and the body are reinforced by the characters' responses to the seasons of the year, especially the spring. And the naked swim of George, Freddy, and Mr. Beebe transforms them into uninhibited and joyful advocates of body, water, and woods. The narrative, in other words, sutures personal and natural space by means of physicality.

The tie between personal and comprehensive space is also reinforced by the many allusions to mythology. We are told this of the piazza Signoria: "Here, not only in the solitude of Nature, might a hero meet a goddess, or a heroine a god" (*RV,* 93–94). The young Italians in their sexual sporting take on mythic size: "he was Phaethon in Tuscany driving the cab. And it was Persephone whom he asked leave to pick up on the way" (*RV,* 95). A lively mythology provides Italian culture with a repertoire of personal gestures and relations having a size, force, and significance that can be drawn on or imparted during their reenactment by persons in the present. Mythology grants to Italian culture a transcendent gallery of gods and goddesses who, by the vigor of their personal styles and by the intensity of their relationships, provide stimulus and models for actualizing and transforming personal potential and relations.

These several aspects of personal space are gathered and tested by Forster's *Passage to India* (1924). In this novel we are given an image of India unlike the Romantic construction of India as a culture that, by virtue of its simplicity and spirituality, nurtures personal potentials and relationships. The city of Chandrapore, described at the opening of the novel, for example, is monotonous and uninviting, and Indian society contains much that resists the development of human integrity and relationships. The Indians are not themselves a unified people, and Moslems and Hindus often do not understand one another or intermix. The British and the Indians also stand in relations of distrust and disdain. And the landscapes of India resist personal interests. "There is," we are told, "something hostile in that soil" (*PI*, 18).

It is to this larger, quite negative setting that the three dominant locations of the novel—the mosque, the caves, and the temple—are contrasted. They provide conditions that foster and challenge personal potentials and relationships.

When Aziz enters the mosque he enters Islam, which is for him not so much a faith as a placement "where his body and his thoughts found their home" (*PI*, 19). The mosque occasions and sponsors the unusually close friendship that grows between Aziz and Mrs. Moore. They happen to meet during an evening when Aziz retired to the mosque as an alternative to the natural terrain and Mrs. Moore comes upon it as an alternative to the social space of the British colonial club. The two are bound by common interests—both have lost their spouses, and both have children; by an ability immediately to recognize and to appreciate friendliness in a stranger; and by a willingness to transcend social, cultural, and religious compartments.

The caves in the second part occasion dissonance in human relationships. Aziz realizes that he runs risks with this expedition because "he had challenged the spirit of the Indian earth, which tries to keep men in compartments" (*PI*, 127). Miss Quested, the young woman who has accompanied Mrs. Moore to India and who may marry her son, stands in a contrary relation to Aziz. She lacks appreciation for the mysteries of the caves ("'I do so hate mysteries'") (*PI*, 69); she underestimates the force of Indian social distinctions; and she assumes that differences between people can be dissolved by some vaguely human universality (*PI*, 145). Her fragility cannot survive the disorienting force of the caves, and she feels so vulnerable that she believes she has been molested in the cave. By disorienting bodily location, the caves create dissonance in personal space and relations. This dissonance spreads outward to affect the social relations of English and Indian people.

The third section, "Temple," provides a setting for the partial resolution to the conflicts created in the second. The setting is the festival of Gokul Ashtami, the Hindu celebration at the time of the rains, the quickening of the earth, and Krishna's rebirth.[14] While the setting of the festival and the soaking in the water do not dissolve the differences between them, Fielding and Aziz develop a stronger and more complex relationship than their earlier friendship. Aziz will also seek a rapprochement with Miss Quested, and Fielding has a better sense of relation with his wife: "There seemed a link between them at last—that link outside either participant that is necessary to every relationship. In the language of theology, their union had been blessed" (*PI*, 318).

Although not all the gaps and barriers between people are overcome—so much militates against unity (*PI*, 322)—the Hindu festival, combining some aspects of both the mosque and the caves, provides a setting for increased and more complicated understandings and rapport. And Aziz projects a time when he and Fielding will be friends. The present sociopolitical situation, especially as it affects the relations between English and Indian people, contains too many negative factors, and the final words of the novel, in reference to the possibilities of personal space and intimate relationships, are "not yet" and "not there."

Forster's narrative that most fully affirms the authority and primacy of personal space is his posthumously published *Maurice* (begun in 1913). It clearly establishes the moral superiority of personal, intimate space over a social space structured by class and cultural boundaries.

Maurice, a London resident, lives in a rigid and confining rather than a mobile, open, or responsive social world. As a child he was taught that personal intimacy is ontologically grounded and determined by divine decree: "male and female, created by God in the beginning" (*M*, 13). This grounding is socially confirmed. Maurice, therefore, accepts a rigid and religiously sanctioned structure of personal intimacy without question.

His reaction to this determination is not to challenge it but to try to grow beyond it, "to ascend, to stretch a hand up the mountainside until a hand catches it" (*M*, 41). And he finds this higher space in friendship with Clive Durham. Clive differs from Maurice because he both denies Christian faith and inhabits a higher social class. When Maurice moves away from a Christian orientation through his relation with Clive, he recognizes that "he loved men and always had loved them. He longed to embrace them and mingle his being with theirs" (*M*, 62).

Maurice's sense of conflict between his own desires and social space is two-sided, then. First, he recognizes the limits imposed on him by his class identity; Clive's family treats him as though they were "conferring a favour on him" (M, 94). Second, his sexuality conflicts with the heterosexuality mandated by both the society and the Christian theology that validates it. Although he wishes that his personal interests would conform to social space and its laws, he recognizes that to actualize his own integrity he must move outside social convention into an unknown place (M, 161).

He finds that place with Alec, a worker on the Durham estate. The two men, despite initial uncertainties and fears and despite their cultural and economic differences, join against "the world" and its "majorities" (M, 201). They get no support, not even from Clive, who finds their relationship distasteful for both social and moral reasons.

The intimate space that Maurice and Alec create is contrary to the society, but rather than feel isolated by their move, they consider England's future as affected by it. The human possibility developed in intimate space has a force and integrity that is bound to affect the future of English society. That future lies not in the perpetuation of existing social structures but in the new identities and relationships that can develop in intimate places. "Her air and sky were theirs, not the timorous millions' who own stuffy little boxes, but never their own souls" (M, 239). Personal, especially physically secured, space holds redemptive possibilities for the larger social structure.

What the novel celebrates in its conclusion is not first of all homosexual love, although it is presented in a very positive way. What is advocated is an exchange in place-evaluation. Rather than determined by social categories and ideological prescriptions, intimate space becomes primary. Its primacy rests on its physicality, on the resources of the body for creative relations and intimacy. Projected outward from personal space are the possibilities of a new society, one that recognizes the continuity between personal realities and England's future.

III

Maurice stands as a subtext of Forster's entire corpus because it clearly presents the potentials in personal, physical relations for challenging the prevailing structures and ideologies of English social space. By excluding homosexual identity and relations, English social space limits the actualization of human potentials. Human, particularly physical, potentials are nurtured by and in places that constitute real and recognizable challenges to the dominance of social space over personal potentials. The primacy of intimate spaces, their contrary relation to social space, is thereby clarified. Homosexual intimacy occasions the recovery of intimate space from the colonization of the personal by a commercially driven and religiously sanctioned social tyranny.

The space defined by homosexual interests stands, in the fiction, then, not as an anomaly but as a beachhead. From it a campaign can begin for affirming the realities of intimate space as primary. Homosexuality illuminates personal space and its potential for reforming the society and subverting its domination.

There is, in other words, a social and political agenda implicit in the position given by Forster's fiction to intimate space. It is neither that he isolates personal space from social and political considerations nor that he has "faith only in the individual and in personal relationships—and in the love and loyalty that make them vital."[15] No, personal identity and relationships require and create particular locations where they can emerge and grow. Without a place of their own, physical human relations become secondary relative to society's norms. Since personal identity and relationships are primary for Forster, the physical places where they are nurtured and by which they are supported have an intrinsic value not determined by social space. While the personal is also spiritual, it is first of all bodily, and the personal requires physical location. Once established, intimate places have potentials for altering and improving social space.

While homosexuality provides Forster a particular strategy for clarifying the distinctive character of personal space and its primacy relative to social space, the high evaluation of personal space is also part of his personal heritage. That heritage can be traced from the Clapham Sect, of which his great-grandfather was a member, to the Cambridge Apostles, and to the Bloomsbury group, several members of which were former Apostles. While that historical line is marked by many, even radical, changes and differences, it also carries a continuity relevant to Forster's beliefs concerning the relation of personal to social and political interests and actions. All in that tradition, from Henry Thornton to his great-grandson, put a premium on the personal, both individual and relational. Particular persons and small gatherings of the like-minded carry a moral sensitivity that the society in general lacks. The person and the like-minded, especially when they have the material and political means to influence the public, can effect morally beneficial changes in social attitudes and policy. However different Forster may be from Henry Thornton, there is also a line that connects them, and it is a moral or spiritual line as well as a physical and material line, namely, the connection to the Clapham Sect that Forster's great-aunt provided him.

While *Maurice* reveals the role of homosexuality as a human potential that Forster could use to clarify both the difference between the personal and social and the primacy of the personal relative to the social, the larger contrast between the two kinds of locations and identities is established by his biography of Marianne Thornton. The role of the family home, named for the street, Battersea Rise, as a location defining the family's personal integrity and as a gathering place for enacting morally directed social, political change is very much at the center of Forster's narrative. The act of retrieving that earlier site is not simple nostalgia or an attempt to reinstate an earlier culture. Forster admits, "There will never be another Battersea Rise" (*MT,* 5). But he does feel continuity between himself and the past with which his great-aunt formed so visible a link. For the home was not only a refuge but also a launching site. The character of the household and of the gatherings there was moral and spiritual. As he says of his great-aunt: "Like her parents, Marianne was but little concerned with ritual or dogma. . . . What she cared for was the Christian life, rooted in the family and flowering in action, and she desired to see that life growing all over the world" (*MT,* 130). The personal is primary relative to the social because it is the place where conscience and moral insight have their principal play. As Christopher Tolley puts it, the Clapham Sect "stood for a more confident and outgoing relationship between religion and politics, and their journal, *The Christian Observer* . . . took an informed interest in the whole spectrum of public affairs."[16] The results were a sense of the moral quality of personal identity and the positive potential of personal conviction and action for the larger social world. "The Clapham education developed a sense of obligation which was closely bound up with the kindred ideal of personal integrity and proved as durable an inheritance."[17] At the end of his biography, Forster draws a direct line between the Thorntons' attachment to Battersea Rise and his own relation to the family home in Herfordshire from which as a teenager he was dislodged and which provided the model for Howards End. As he confesses, "The impressions received there remained and still glow—not always distinguishably, always inextinguishably—and have given me a slant upon society and history" (*MT,* 301). While the houses that located and supported these values are not retrievable, the sense of personal location and of places that will give physical specificity to personal moral and spiritual potentials continues to count.

As *Howards End* makes clear, Forster saw his own experience of dislodgment and its consequences for personal identity and relationships as representative of a turn in English culture from respect for the sanctity of personal spaces to a disregard for them under the pressure of increasingly impersonal social and economic power.[18] Forster's particular interest in homosexual identity and relationships should not be thought of as simply concealed beneath his public attention to personal relations that are heterosexual. The heterosexual intimacy of the room George and Lucy occupy at the end of *A*

Room with a View, for example, is valid, is integral to the narrative, and is comprehended by Forster's sense of the human. Heterosexual relationships in Forster's novels are not simply substitutes or metaphors for homosexual relations.[19] Rather, he is interested primarily in personal and relational potentials and their dependence on a physically grounding location. As to sexuality, I agree with the editors of *Queer Forster,* who say that eros, as a bodily force, is for Forster "powerful and disruptive" and that the heterosexual elements in his fiction present, along with homosexual relations, "a potentially destabilizing force that undermines class and convention."[20]

Personal spaces, such as Howards End or the Schlegel home in London, not only acquire qualities from the persons who inhabit them but also bring out those qualities. Mutuality is created between a dwelling and its inhabitants that, while it has first of all a physical character, is spiritual as well. By implication, people who have no sense of attachment to place, who use location only to signify social or economic standing, damage the potential for a real interdependence between personal potential and place that long attachment can provide. So also a society that encroaches on such spaces, that discounts the importance of such attachments, must be viewed as morally antagonistic. The role of social space, rather than to threaten or destroy intimate spaces, should be to encourage and protect them.

What also seems required is a narrative setting for personal life that informs it with incipient or recovered mythologies—ties, that is, between personal gestures or relations and transcendent and enabling models, models that will inspire and validate expansion and innovation in personal behavior and relationships. The appeal to the deities and heroes of classical myths, to Italian settings, and to the mosques and temples of Indian Islam and Hinduism suggest that English culture and English Christianity do not support the primacy of personal life despite the legacy of the Clapham Sect. Christianity seems to draw the drapes on personal space, restricting the wider view. It seems to have fallen into a simple approbation of social structure and repression. Personal spontaneity, complexity, and mystery are intimidated by such a context. There are occasional exceptions, as when some Englishmen throw off restraints and frolic in natural settings. But English Christian culture places too high a value on decorum and restraint, order and conformity, to allow such moments to become anything more than ineffective exceptions.

Although not specifically or even recognizably Christian, the beliefs that support the role of intimate space in Forster's fiction are religious. Rukun Advani tries to distinguish them from Christian beliefs this way: "While the orthodox believer reveres the unseen beauty of God, a humanist considers earthly beauty the only firm evidence of spirit."[21] But this distinction is not only between Christian and non-Christian but also between kinds of Christians. Some Christians eschew the mundane and particular for the sake of the spiritual, and some believe that the spiritual is mediated through the temporal, personal, and carnal. I think that Advani is closer to the center of Forster's beliefs when he comments on Forster's admiration for Hebrew wisdom literature.[22] Biblical wisdom gives ample textual warrant to Forster's attention to everyday and bodily life as the locus of the moral and spiritual. In any event, I think that the relation of the body and its space to the spiritual in Forster must be kept in view, kept, that is, from becoming transparent either to a homosexual ideology or to psychological and purely individual issues. This is because intimate space in Forster's fiction is crucial for the redemption of social spaces.[23] Establishing the primacy and moral authority of intimate space will not, given the dominant social attitudes, be easy. But that change is critical. For Forster's work, the future not only of intimate space but also of all human spatiality is at stake.

When we turn more directly later on to theories of human spatiality, we shall see that Forster's view is not idiosyncratic or unrealistic. It has solid supports and valid warrants. For example, Gaston Bachelard's descriptions of the structuring of childhood memories by personal spaces reveal that people take into their spatial orientations needs and potentials that can only be understood by taking the effects of personal, intimate space on them seriously. Forster will be crucial, then, for our later attempts to secure a stable and resonant understanding of personal, intimate space in a general theory of human place-relations.

Part Two

Later Modernists and the Teleology of Place-Relations

4

Graham Greene

Mystery and the Space Between

The early modernism that provides the background of the first part of this study developed from an accumulating awareness of the costs of a history of "progress" and expansion, especially its costs for places, place-relations, and spatial orientation. Later modernism, due primarily to the First World War, reveals, on top of that accumulation, the consequences of more abrupt and traumatic cultural changes. It registers a sharper discontinuity with, and a more negative appraisal of, the recent past. Prewar culture is frequently perceived as holding few resources for rectifying place-relations. This lack gives to writers and their fiction a greater sense of abandonment, of having to narrativize from more improvised resources. Their orientation is more to the future than to the past, and creative work becomes more a matter of discovery than of recovery. Finally, the spatial language of later modernism draws more attention to the spiritual than to the physical aspects of place-relations.

Graham Greene shows all the signs of this shift. His work assumes a separation from, even a negative attitude toward, the prewar culture. This takes a noticeable form in the caustic account that he gives of his upbringing and schooling. This appraisal should not be viewed as merely a personal, domestic reaction.[1] It is part of his sense of the culture as betrayed by and disconnected from a past that was unable to prepare people for World War I, postwar dislocations, and, later, the violence of World War II.

The principal spokesperson for this change in attitude in the period after the First World War was T. S. Eliot, to whom Greene, in many explicit ways, defers.[2] It is not as though Greene developed his attitudes and craft from reading Eliot's *The Waste Land,* "The Love Song of J. Alfred Prufrock," and "The Hollow Men." Rather, Eliot articulated the mood and style that pervaded the period, one of which Greene was wholly a part. This does not mean that all writers at that time participated in this spirit. For example, several of Virginia Woolf's novels make at least partial reconnections with prewar culture, and D. H. Lawrence's fiction, somewhat like Hardy's, recovers a sense of the physicality of places and their ties to the pre-Christian past.[3] Jay Winter, working at a broad cultural level, argues convincingly that the people who grieved the fallen of the war, as did a large portion of the population, did so in mainly traditional ways.[4]

Greene's judgment on the immediate cultural past as inadequate to present conditions and even as having concealed basic truths about the human condition does not lead to cynicism for two reasons. The first is that his fiction is motivated by a rigorous desire for and confidence in truthfulness. The fictional worlds that Greene creates are not personal or willful—he disliked the notion that he had created a private "Greeneland."[5] Rather than a private world, his fiction reveals what he took to be true about the present state of human affairs. Similar to Hardy, Greene believed that present conditions, traumatic as they may be, disclose truth about human beings and the world they inhabit. Like Hardy, too, Greene sees taking refuge and finding certainty in religious or political institutions or ideologies as tantamount to avoiding truth and losing moral integrity. His principal characters are placed in a primary relation to what is perceived as real, as that which, because the real is also elusive and painful, institutions tend to exclude. The second belief that keeps Greene's project from cynicism is that the present cultural situation stimulates a need and search for comprehensive space. The inability of human constructions to contain or to account for human experience, need, and desire drive the disciplined mind and imagination to seek completion in something on or beyond the borders of a world that is constructed and increasingly controlled by human beings.

Greene resembles Hardy, then, both in his understanding that cultural change exposes truths heretofore concealed and in his primary attention to comprehensive space.[6] However, he is unlike Hardy not only in that he looks to the future rather than the past, to discovery rather than retrieval, and to the spiritual more than to the physical aspects of place-relations but also because he is, unlike Hardy, urban in orientation and deeply influenced by the culture of images, especially cinema.[7] The normative figures in his fiction, then, are not people who, like Gabriel Oak, are rooted and sturdy but rather people who are rootless and resemble the religious ascetics who separated themselves from the world and deprived themselves of its supports. Indeed, "Greene presents us with some terrifying images of twentieth-century homelessness." His characters abandon domestic security and choose a state of "hopeless exile."[8]

Being abandoned by society and culture and eschewing their comforts and securities become, in the fiction, occasions for spiritual disciplines. Cultural and social rejection and exile frequently take on the features of a religious *via negativa* or asceticism. Greene's characters often practice extreme and negative religious disciplines. This does not mean that his work should be categorized as "religious fiction"; indeed, he resisted such labeling. But it does mean that negative conditions in his fiction often have spiritual associations, and when they do they direct the attention of characters to realities that lie beyond human construction and control. What comprehends or transcends human constructions and control in Greene's fiction is, while not without negative aspects, alluring and fulfilling.

The places where, in his narratives, one is most likely to encounter what lies beyond human constructions and control are transitions or gaps between human constructions. His characters are drawn to interstices within the culture or to its edges. The fascination that his fiction reveals for these in-between and marginal places is even greater than Hardy's and could almost be called an obsession. Greene would not have minded that label; he says, in *The Lost Childhood*, "Every creative writer worth our consideration, every writer who can be called in the wide eighteenth-century use of the term a poet, is a victim: a man given over to an obsession" (*LC*, 79).[9] Despite the variety of locations in his work, many of them exotic, a recurring place is privileged, namely, one clarified by its noninclusion within human structures. By being unconstructed and uncontrolled, these negatively defined locations provide positive access to comprehensive space and gather an alluring spiritual significance and force.

However, in Greene's fiction, Western culture has extended its control almost over the entire globe. His characters, therefore, must travel far in their quest for locations relatively free from its determinations. These travels and the situations to which they lead are often taxing and hazardous. The quest for distance from the dominant culture causes lack of certainty, subversion of identity, and even loss of life. While distant and dangerous, these locations, by being exceptions to the dominating structures of modern culture, grant these exiles a new sense of moral and spiritual possibilities. These possibilities are not projected by characters onto places but are revealed in and by the places themselves. This potential in places arises from the access they grant to a reality that comprehends and transcends human constructions and that Greene refers to as "mystery." Indeed, if one is to call Greene in some sense a religious writer, it is exactly here that the designation makes sense. His fictional, cultural, and spiritual interests converge in narrating locations that give those who venture into them access to "mystery."[10]

The principal unconstructed places exposed by Greene's fiction stand between religious institutions and their secular, usually political, contraries. The provocative implications of this constant in Greene's fiction is that Christian and secular institutions depend on one another. Each would lack identity were it not for its contrary. And unwittingly they conspire to create, by their mutual opposition, a gap through which another possibility can be detected. This gap, a place between them coopted by neither side, becomes, however difficult to enter, enticing to his principal characters. They recognize these spaces betwixt and between as more real and truthful than human constructions, spaces where unanswered needs and desires can look for something other or more. The difficulty of entering such places is exacerbated by the fact that people identified with existing institutions react strongly to such seekers by condemning them and imposing their own or their institution-serving interpretations on them.

Interstitial places, although defined and entered negatively as alternatives to identifiable options, have positive consequences. They grant a person the possibility of confronting reality and achieving personal integrity. The confines and comforts of institutions foster a false sense of reality, distorted self-understandings, and injurious human relations. Relations to in-between places may produce few certainties, but they validate the search. Greene's fiction, therefore, commends what Hardy called "dubiousness," an uncertainty that is morally and spiritually healthy.[11]

Attention to these difficult places is supported by the settings of his fictions, which are often exotic and produce almost palpably forceful atmospheres. These locations range from England, especially urban settings, to places in South Asia, Africa, South America, and the Caribbean. The principal characters are positioned in these locations as outsiders. This means that they are usually lonely and rootless. In addition, they are often under external pressures, most of the time as objects of pursuit.[12]

It is not as though Greene's narratives, due to an interest in the spiritual qualities and moral potentials of places touched by mystery, neglect the physical aspect of place altogether. Interstitial places are concrete locations that, by their particularity, make settings defined by institutions and ideologies less real. It is not the case that characters project onto places their internal needs or desires; they are attracted by something in them not of their own making.

Finally, these spaces gather moral and spiritual force and significance and grant a sense of access to transcendence not because characters bring religious beliefs or theological ideas to them. Indeed, characters, even if they once had such convictions, have lost them. They are not in search of confirmations of beliefs they already have. Unconstructed places, in their life-renewing potential, are mysterious primarily because they are exceptions to the prevailing cultural obsessions with convictions and certainties. The intellectual yield of the search for spiritual places undertaken by his characters is, therefore, elusive. Neither mystery nor what is received from contact with it can be clearly formulated.

In order more fully to understand these desired or discovered places, their location, spiritual significance, and moral effects, I shall look first at *A Burnt-Out Case* (1961), a novel that is particularly helpful for this topic. I shall then go backward in the corpus to discuss the role of interstitial places in earlier work and forward to more recent efforts. It will then be possible to draw some general conclusions.

I

Like Conrad's Kurtz—*Heart of Darkness* is a subtext for *A Burnt-Out Case*—Querry is a symptom or flower of modern Western culture.[13] As an architect he prosecuted its most characteristic and space-affecting interests. In addition, Querry's style was formalist; his interests were confined to "space, light, proportion" (*BOC*, 50). He took a strictly abstract and instrumental attitude toward materials, and he gave little if any thought to the uses of his buildings, their particular locations, or the people who would enter them. His most noteworthy churches grew in popularity when they were modified by use, his plain windows replaced by stained glass, and his interiors altered to suit the needs of worship. Like many modern artists, Querry held a disdainful, even adversarial relation to the tastes and values of ordinary people and to traditional culture.

In addition, he was an abstract expressionist, and he understood his artistic work as arising from self-generated projections. As he says later: "'Self-expression is a hard and selfish thing. It eats everything, even the self. At the end you find you haven't even got a self to express. I have no interest in anything any more, doctor'" (*BOC*, 52). By assuming a professional disinterest in people and conceiving his vocation as a transaction between his own interior potentials and the abstractions of light and geometric proportion, Querry not only felt increasingly alienated from actual places but also increasingly depleted of personal resources.

His vocational identity and practice corresponded to patterns in his personal relations. He has been estranged from his wife, and he has had several mistresses, one of whom committed suicide. He also no longer keeps in touch with the children he has fathered (*BOC*, 52).[14] His personal relations were as much marked by domination, distance, and self-interest as his aesthetic and professional life. Indeed, he relates the two: "'I don't want to sleep with a woman nor design a building'" (*BOC*, 52).[15]

Querry's religious beliefs also evaporated. One could say that his belief in

God was undermined by his self-deification, the elevation of himself above the circumstances of his immediate context, and his imposition of abstract forms on places. The loss of faith and the crisis in his vocation are linked in his mind as well: "'To build a church when you don't believe in a god seems a little indecent, doesn't it?'" (*BOC*, 143). This does not mean that Querry moved from religious belief to secular—for example, political—convictions. He also lost the capacity to believe in the meaning and importance of politics: "'I accepted a commission for a city hall, but I didn't believe in politics either. You never saw such an absurd box of concrete and glass as I landed on the poor city square'" (*BOC*, 143).

Querry's rejection of his former life and of the modernist culture of which it provides an epitome constitutes a strong, though indirect, critique of that culture and an attempt to get out from under its domination and the habits of domination that it nurtures and rewards. The exchange of Western Europe for Central Africa is the occasion for that attempt.

Querry quickly learns that the heart of Africa has not escaped the constructions and controls of modernity. The reach of Western colonialism extends to it. Indeed, the violent and coercive habits of modern culture become, in this climate, more blatant. The priest who captains the boat, for example, shoots at animals because he has "a passion for slaughtering any living creature, as though only man had a right to a natural death" (*BOC*, 8). Querry's stay in the Congo is taken up by his attempts to negotiate around and between the coercion and interpretations directed toward him by colonial representatives of modern culture's religious and political institutions and ideologies.[16]

The Europeans Querry encounters in Africa are people who persist in their loyalty to Western culture, particularly the habit it sponsors of imposing their own beliefs, constructions, and convictions on other people. Querry, a well-known Catholic architect who has suddenly and inexplicably exchanged fame for obscurity and European culture for the heart of Africa, becomes a question to which such people are quick to provide answers that serve their own institutional or ideological locations.

Rycker, one of them, has a seminary background that he uses to elevate himself above other people, including clergy and his wife. He constructs Querry as the culturally significant Catholic whom he deserves as a worthy interlocutor. Rycker is a particularly offensive religious person. He assumes a righteousness and an interest in theology that thinly disguise his self-centeredness and arrogance. And his relations with others are manipulative and disdainful. This is clear in his attitudes toward Marie, his young wife, whom he intimidates and controls under the validating ideology of a Christian marriage.

Although not so distasteful as Rycker, some of the clergy share his need to construct Querry as the cultured Catholic or Christian saint. Father Thomas, who also thinks of himself as a cut above his fellows, interprets Querry's distance from the church as the sign of a deeper and purer kind of faith and constructs Querry as the sort of exceptional Catholic he fancies himself to be.

These religious interpretations find their secular counterpart in the figure of Montague Parkinson, the English journalist who has lost a sense of his work's integrity and whose size suggests his capacity to consume. He pursues Querry because he needs a story, and he is willing to create out of Querry whatever will sell. The result, an article with the title "An Architect of Souls: The Hermit of the Congo," is the first in a projected series on Querry as popular hero and saint.

Of his two tormentors, Rycker and Parkinson, Querry prefers Parkinson. Parkinson is motivated by a cynicism that Querry understands. Like Querry, Parkinson once had a sense of vocation, but he lost it by exchanging the search for truth for the construction of what will sell. As the narrator speaking for Querry says: "If he had to have a tormentor how gladly he would have chosen the cynical Parkinson. There were interstices in that cracked character where the truth might occasionally seed. But Rycker was like a wall so plastered over with church-announcements that you couldn't even see the brickwork behind" (BOC, 180).

Querry's relations to and observations of the native patients of the leproserie form a significant elaboration of his reaction to modern culture and its colonial representatives. He sees that they not only suffer from their various diseases but also feel the effects of Western imperialism. Querry learns that the Africans judge the technologies of healing as intrusions that have disrupted their lives. Dr. Colin tells him that Africans may be so easily infected by the disease because of other illnesses that have been brought to them by Europeans (BOC, 69). Colin is also aware of the construction placed on the lepers by the Catholic cult of suffering, and he believes that the religious workers may be more interested in leprosy than in the lepers. They certainly seem more interested in the lepers than in healthy native people and their culture (BOC, 20).[17]

The search of Querry for some place outside or between the religious and secular structures and ideologies of modern culture is refined by Greene's creation of two representatives and spokespersons who are, compared to Rycker and Parkinson, attractive. Querry finds the Superior and Dr. Colin as easily distinguishable from Rycker and Parkinson as they are from one another. The three men are on friendly terms and respect one another. But however attractive Colin and the Superior are, they still represent ideas and assumptions that Querry ends up rejecting. By rejecting them both, Querry reveals that they differ, by their contrary identities as religious and secular, less than they resemble one another.

Dr. Colin is a modest and dedicated man. He is aware of the suffering around him, particularly the fact that lepers are as much hurt by Europeans as healed by them. His own suffering and his awareness of the suffering of others do not defeat him. He is engaged in a battle with disease, and he works willingly with the Superior in their common cause. Querry finds it not only possible but increasingly easy to communicate with Colin. Both stand apart from the religious life of the community; both are candid and appreciate honesty in others; and both are more aware of problems than of solutions. Querry seems positively affected by Colin's moral integrity and dedication. But with all that is attractive about him, Colin thinks in terms of metanarratives and universals. He tells Querry that suffering puts a person "'in touch with the whole human condition'" (*BOC*, 157). And he goes on to give Querry not only his views on the struggle against such enemies as disease but also the larger program of which that struggle is a part—"'We are riding a great ninth evolutionary wave'" (*BOC*, 160). Colin represents, in a word, a substantial continuity with the nineteenth century. He tells Querry: "'The nineteenth century wasn't as far wrong as we like to believe. We have become cynical about progress because of the terrible things we have seen men do during the last forty years'" (*BOC*, 160). This is a direct challenge not only to Querry but, as we saw, to Greene's views of the past and its disconnection from late modern culture. It is not surprising that Colin's beliefs strike Querry as being "'every bit as superstitious as what the fathers believe'" (*BOC*, 160).

As Querry prefers Parkinson to Rycker, the Superior is not as close a companion to Querry as Colin. But the Superior is favorably presented, and both Colin and Querry respect him. True, he is naïve while Colin and Querry are not, but he does not have the compulsions and distortions that mark the other Catholic colonists. One indication of the Superior's generosity is his nonexclusiveness. He does not, as do others, require that persons be Catholic before taking them seriously. He works closely with Colin and does not disdain him, as does Rycker, for his atheism. Indeed, he consistently practices what could be called a doctrine of the anonymous Christian, a position most closely associated in recent Catholic theology with the work of Karl Rahner. This theology of inclusion means that the Superior can evaluate non-Christians and their acts of charity positively, as actually Christian. He clearly announces this policy in the sermon that Colin and Querry overhear: "'When you make a song you are in the song, when you bake bread you are in the bread, when you make a baby you are in the baby, and because Yezu made you, he is in you. When you love it is Yezu who loves, when you are

merciful it is Yezu who is merciful. . . . Everybody in the world has something
Yezu made. Everybody in the world is that much a Klistian. . . . There is no
man so wicked he never once in his life show in his heart something that God
made'" (BOC, 101–2). Querry assumes that the Superior's sermon is an
answer to Querry's earlier challenge to him. When the Superior identified
Querry's remorse as a kind of belief, Querry resists: "'You try to draw everything into the net of your faith, father, but you can't steal all the virtues.
Gentleness isn't Christian, self-sacrifice isn't Christian, charity isn't, remorse
isn't'" (BOC, 93). The Superior's sermon amplifies the theology of inclusiveness to affirm that whatever there is that is good in the world is Christian.
Querry sees this theology as coercive, and he does not want to be included in
its universal net.

The positions represented by Colin and the Superior are institutional as
well as personal. The leproserie is operated by church and state funds; "The
support of the leproserie was the responsibility of the Order; the doctor's
salary and the cost of medicine were paid by the State" (BOC, 17). They
represent religious and political ideologies that Greene has put in their best,
most charitable and constructive, light. But they are also continuous with
the more manipulative and violent attitudes of Rycker and Parkinson.

Since the social space of Querry's world is so dominated by the institutions and ideologies of Western modernity, Querry is drawn to personal
alternatives. Deo Gratias, a native leper whose disease has run its course,
leads Querry into one of them by his search in the forest for Pendélé, a
felicitous place associated by Deo Gratias with water, his mother, singing,
dancing, games, and prayers (BOC, 68). Querry's night in the forest with
Deo Gratias is as close as he can come to such a place, but he is even less
likely to reach it than is Deo Gratias.

The value of Deo Gratias stands out in comparison with Marie Rycker,
whose innocence also offers an exception to the dominant social space.
Querry spends a night with her, too. But Marie's personal place is more
romantic and even less accessible to Querry than the Pendélé of Deo Gratias;
hers is "a dance at a friend's house, a young man with a shiny simple face,
going to Mass on Sunday with the family, falling asleep in a single bed'"
(BOC, 93). Both Deo Gratias and Marie are appealing because they offer
alternatives to the coercions of Western culture and reveal a pervasive longing within it for the personal places of simplicity and innocence. But their
longings are unrealistic and, by so being, dangerous. Both give Querry's
antagonists reasons to impose their self-serving constructions on him.

The final reality that attracts Querry is death. He is drawn to it by his
dreams. Not only is death not colonized by Western imperialism, it is also
a source of modern anxiety, its silent adversary. Rather than fear death,
Querry moves steadily toward it, carried by the kind of careless certainty

that brought him to the Congo. Death is a place that, because it is fugitive in modern culture, gathers an unspecific significance to which the ellipsis at the terminal point of Querry's life seems to point.

The question arises, finally, as to whether Querry's search for some place that has not been constructed or occupied by modern Western interests can be related to the forest and the natural space it represents. The first thing to note is that the forest is a forceful presence. Indeed, it advances to the very thresholds of houses. Consequently, it marks a limit that resists Western secular and religious pressure and seems impenetrable. In addition, its constant noise calls one's attention to it, and the heat and humidity, along with the odors of the forest, make one always aware of natural conditions. No less undeniable is the constant presence of mosquitoes, flies, and cockroaches. Furthermore, unlike what stands in for nature in Europe, this forest has not been textualized in Romantic terms. "It had never been humanized, like the woods of Europe, with witches and charcoal-burners and cottages of marzipan; no one had ever walked under those trees lamenting lost love, nor had anyone listened to the silence and communed like a lake-poet with his heart" (BOC, 63). Indeed, the forest is cognitively unmapped; "These woods and spaces would remain unexplored, it seemed likely now, for longer than the planets. The craters of the moon were already better known than the forest at the door that one could enter any day on foot" (BOC, 63). The forest leads Querry to wonder, "wasn't it just as possible for a god to exist in this empty region as in the empty spaces of the sky where men had once located him?" (BOC, 63). The forest, forbidding and resistive to colonization, is forceful and potentially meaningful. And it is closely associated with what I have been calling comprehensive space.

However, the alterity of the forest is itself partially a construct. Projected on it are typically modern notions of the unexplored, the exotic, and the primitive. In addition, it is not simply natural space; it is the home of an indigenous people who relate to the forest in ways very different from those of the outsiders.[18] Furthermore, although not romanticized, Africa and its dark forests have been textualized by the Stanleys, Schweitzers, and Conrads of modern political, religious, and aesthetic culture, as allusions in Greene's novel make clear.

Yet, with all of these qualifications, it can be said that the forest contributes to Querry's modest and gradual recovery. And the point is worth making because in all of Greene's fiction the truthfulness, integrity, and sense of reality for which his characters search and that has shown up as missing in the culture of Western modernity is not only spiritual but also physical. Place is tangible, and its physical qualities are important for Querry's recovery. The forest also locates the extremities of modernity, and it exposes, in the representatives of the culture who elect or are consigned to such a place, the obsessive, even addicted attachment of the colonists to Western culture. The boundary between the forest and the limit of colonial penetration is a significant place betwixt and between. Furthermore, the forest reveals where the fabric of imperialism has, by being stretched, grown so thin and frayed that one can see through it. It reveals the Western project to be as much an illusion as are the constructions placed on Querry by people who need to use him as though he were a blank page on which their own identities could be inscribed. The forest suggests a space that antedates and resists human constructions. Querry finds himself placed, consequently, between a culture with which he has little in common and to which he cannot return and a natural environment that he does not know and cannot enter.

However bizarre his death may be, Querry seems to have allowed death to regain associations both with the natural and with prospects for spiritual advance. Rather than something alien and problematic, as it is in Western culture, death becomes for Querry associated with comprehensive space and transcendent meaning. He does not seek or pursue death, but he approaches it as to something further, something more.

During the narrative, then, Querry divests himself of modern culture, resists the constructions of him produced by others, and slowly relates to the widest spatial context of human life. He realizes, then, a positive relation to comprehensive space, and that relation has at least four ingredients. First, there is a mutuality between Querry and the site. The heart of Africa evokes something from him, and he contributes something to it. That is, he, among other things, is able to retrieve at least some of his architectural skills and is able to alter the place. Also, he finds the location commodious. It not only allows him to relate his past to his present, but it also relates physical to moral and spiritual realities. The forest and the bodies of the ill are tied closely for him to the possibilities, especially in contrast to other people he encounters, of moral and spiritual integrity and a lack of anxiety and fear in relation to his own dying. This does not mean that the place has a kind of finality to it. Indeed, Querry is always also moving on. Being there is not permanent. Finally, the location is giftlike. Comprehensive space grants Querry more than he intended. He drifted there, and the place has an effect on him that he does not himself cause. By accepting the gift of this location, including his relation to death, he has access to a way of being in the world that is an alternative to the confinement and control exerted by secular and religious institutions, their ideologies, and their adherents.

II

By looking at some of Greene's other major work we will be able more fully to understand how his obsession with places located between contrasting modernist constructions, especially between the church and nonreligious, often political, institutions, works itself out. We will also, then, have a clearer understanding both of why that place is associated with "mystery" and to what degree Greene allows mystery to take on more specifically religious qualities.

In *Brighton Rock* (1938), interstitial, unconstructed space is only partially clarified because its occupant is not the principal character Pinkie but Rose. Despite her lack of centrality, however, she holds a clearly marked and painful position between the materialistic Pinkie, whose child she is carrying, and the church. Rejected by the church, she turns to Pinkie, but from him she will receive, as we know, only the injuries of his recorded message. Rose's position, then, exposes a place between institutions and their ideologies, especially between the church and the secular world, a place that constitutes a constant in Greene's fiction.

This place is more fully exposed in *The Power and the Glory* (1940). Its occupant is an immoral priest who stands between secular political authority, which wants to rout religion from the district in Mexico, and the church, which generates a "stifling atmosphere of intimacy and respect" (*PG*, 29). The priest moves in a no-man's land between a churchless society, represented by the lieutenant who prosecutes the goals of the secular government, and a worldless church, represented by a past the priest has left behind. The institutional conflict between the church and political secularism finds its personal counterpart in the priest. Unchaste and intemperate, he is both a channel of, and an obstacle to, grace. He is "a damned man putting God into the mouths of men" (*PG*, 83).

The attitudes and program of the lieutenant are to a degree validated by the fact that he views the church as concealing people from the truth of their conditions and sapping their ability to confront it. In this regard, he resembles the priest, who also thinks of the church as creating a deceptive isolation. Indeed, when he works outside of the lieutenant's jurisdiction, "he could feel the old life hardening round him like a habit" (*PG*, 226). "Life," he concludes, "didn't contain churches" (*PG*, 244). While both agree that the church obscures the truth about human life and relationships, they disagree as to where the truth lies. The priest recognizes that the lieutenant, like all political leaders, locates the truth in abstractions "like the state, the republic." For the priest, the truth lies in particular realities such as a single child, who is "more important than a whole continent" (*PG*, 111). The problem with the priest—and I think it is important not to overplay the authority of his attitude—is that he takes his own way of accessing truth, that is, by means of deprivation and hardship, as a definitive pattern of life. He takes the squalid conditions of the prison, for example, as revealing what life is really like (*PG*, 169). His harshly negative assessment of life's possibilities, while consistent with many of Greene's own attitudes, should not be taken as final in the novel.

The Power and the Glory, by presenting the place between as both taxing and revealing, has the meaning-effect of exposing the mutual resistance of the church and its secular alternatives to the potential of unconstructed places for revealing the transcendent. The sacramental acts of confession and Eucharist in the narrative enlarge and reinforce the meaning of those places and their relation to mystery. Real presence is found between or beyond human constructions in places that, by being exceptional, grant access to the power and significance of comprehensive space.

The principal character of *The Heart of the Matter* (1948), like the whiskey priest and Querry, also lives under strongly negative conditions. The heat in the African colony is unrelenting and overbearing. The colonial community is marked by jealousy and suspicion. The Syrians and the natives are perceived by the colonists as menacing and untrustworthy. War intensifies the oppressively negative qualities of these social conditions. And the principal character's behavior, like that of the whiskey priest in *The Power and the Glory*, contradicts his office.

Henry Scobie, a police officer, has decided that protecting needy people and ministering to their unhappiness are more important than the laws that he is expected to enforce. In situations of increasing complexity, he chooses to neglect and finally to defy both secular law and Christian morality in his improvised attempts to help people in distress. He is drawn to human situations that stand outside secular and religious jurisdiction because he doubts the adequacy and flexibility of those institutions. He finds human needs more real and truthful than social, political, and ecclesiastical responses to them. The question raised by the narrative is whether Scobie's behavior arises from genuine compassion or from self-indulgence. It seems appropriate to say that the narrative puts the reader in a position like that of the reader of many of Hardy's novels, that is, betwixt and between contrary judgments.

Sarah Miles finds herself similarly situated in *The End of the Affair* (1951). She loves both Maurice, her paramour, and God, and she is unable to reject one of them for the other. By affirming both, she suffers in obscurity. Her vow to God that she would end her affair if Maurice's life would be saved during an air raid and her inability to disavow her love for Maurice create contrary loyalties. Sarah tries to get relief by eliminating one of the two sides. When she goes to church to be reconciled to God, the condition is that she give up Maurice, which she has not been able to do. To free herself from God, she visits a rationalist in the hope that he will prove God to be an illusion, but Sarah is unconvinced by arguments for God's nonexistence. Unable to free herself from either side, she neglects her decaying health and finally dies. At the end Maurice finds himself similarly situated. He is faced with judging events as either miracles or coincidences. But Maurice, lacking Sarah's commitment, cannot recognize the potentials for transcendence in that in-between place.

The question of miracle as creating fruitful uncertainty is more fully explored in Greene's play *The Potting Shed* (1957). The Callifer family, staunchly rationalistic, has begun to doubt its convictions when the possibility arises that James Callifer, at the age of fourteen, had been raised from the dead by the prayers of his uncle William, a recently converted Catholic. The boy had been driven to suicide because he could not resolve the conflict between instruction in Christianity given him by his uncle and a debunking of the faith by his rationalist father. Memories of that conflict and of his "resurrection" work on James during the ensuing thirty years, but he re-presses them. At the start of the play, he is what Greene in the preface calls a "hollow man," but he is brought out of this state by the idea that the prayers of William Callifer had raised him from the dead. While the family cannot share this conviction, they are at least stimulated by the problem and the uncertainty it creates. The play affirms Greene's contention that uncertainty is more life-giving than certainty and that, as faith should not exclude doubt, doubt should not exclude faith.

The novels that follow *A Burnt-Out Case* explore more fully both the reality available in places between or at the edges of cultural constructions and the potential of those places for access to comprehensive space. However elusive it may at times be, interstitial, exceptional space holds spiritual and transcendent possibilities.

In *The Comedians* (1966), the inability of the principal character, Brown, to identify himself with any ideology or institution is supported by the socio-political environment of Haiti. Everything and everyone seem drained of vitality and purpose by the oppressive political atmosphere. Characters have jejune names—Brown, Jones, and Smith, for example. Haiti is a "land of terror" (*C*, 239), deprivations, and public ineptitude. Electrical power is arbitrarily interrupted; roads lie uncompleted or are impassable; beggars are everywhere. Each day reminds an inhabitant that social and political institutions retain and exert power despite their irrelevance to actual human needs. Brown treats Haiti not as "an exception in a sane world: it was a small slice of everyday taken at random" (*C*, 137). It epitomizes the larger world in which "'violent deaths are natural deaths,'" as Doctor Magiot puts it. Brown is drawn to Haiti, then, because of the unconcealed truth he finds there about the inability of Western institutions to address actual human needs and potentials. He relates his reading of Haiti to the fact that he was brought up by priests in Monte Carlo. He was more influenced by the location than by Catholic doctrine. Monte Carlo, "a city of transients," conditioned him: "transience was my pigmentation; my roots would never go deep enough anywhere to make me a home or make me secure with love" (C, 239). Although tempted by the certainties of the priests, he fought them off "as other boys fought with the demon of masturbation" (C, 59). The clear alternatives that confront Brown are the church with its doctrines and the "nowhere" of modern culture epitomized by Monte Carlo.[19] Unwilling to identify with either the church or modern culture, Brown is left without a place. The reality he finally locates is signaled by the miniature brass casket that serves as his paperweight. Death here, as in *A Burnt-Out Case*, becomes an extension of cultural divestment and gathers to itself the force and significance of reality, truthfulness, and transcendence.

Travels with My Aunt (1969) treats transience, too; Henry Pullen's aunt is physically and morally unsettled: "'The point is the journey,'" she tells him; "'I enjoy the traveling not the sitting still'" (TA, 55). Pullen leaves his settled life as a retired banker to travel with her to such places as Istanbul and Paraguay. In addition, his aunt has had many affairs and adventures, often with disreputable men. However, she remains Roman Catholic, even though she does not "'believe in all the things they believe in'" (TA, 135). Her religious identity is noninstitutional, and her moral attitudes are nondogmatic. The difference between Pullen's transience and his aunt's and that of Brown in *The Comedians* is that they are oriented to the unpredictability and mystery not of death, as is Brown, but of life. Movement in the context of modern culture becomes productive because it exposes the unexpected, especially in unaccustomed places, and the unexpected is what modern culture with its habits of containment and control undervalues.

Placement between institutions and the access to reality and mystery it provides are more religiously articulated in *The Honorary Consul* (1973). Set in a small house on the Paraguayan border of Argentina, the action is created by insurgents who hold the honorary consul as hostage in the hope of winning the freedom of comrades in Paraguay. The house has been surrounded by police, and a deadline has been given to those inside, putting heavy and increasing pressure on the situation.

The principal characters in the house have complex identities. Dr. Plarr, whose English father worked in Paraguay against the government on behalf of the poor, has a Paraguayan mother. His exposure to illness and poverty has made him capable of little feeling or hope, and he is a man with no political or religious identity. As he says: "'I feel no more interested in the Church now than I feel in Marxism. The Bible is as unreadable to me as *Das Kapital*'" (HC, 261). Father León Rivas, a schoolboy friend of Plarr, is more ideological, having moved in his interests from law, to theology, and finally to Marx. Although ordained, he is a married man estranged from the church but not from the faith. He defines the church not as fixed but as movable. Indeed, "'The Church is this *barrio,* this room'" (*HC,* 238). Moreover, he believes that God is closely implicated in human lives and is not limited only to the good: "'He made us in His image—and so our evil is His evil too. How could I love God if He were not like me? Divided like me. Tempted like me'" (*HC,* 269). By being the honorary consul's potential executioner and confessor, he relates to him as well as to others in ambiguous ways, as he believes God relates to humans. In the closing minutes before the deadline given by the police, he celebrates the mass. Thereby the border house becomes a real and spiritually significant place. This effect is intensified by secular and religious institutions, their negative relations to the house, and their complicity with one another. Though closely tied to death and under pressures from without, the house provides a setting for the real presence of the transcendent in the sacrament.

While the reality of interstitial places gives them sacramental potential, they also are related by Greene to moral integrity. In *The Human Factor* (1978), for example, Maurice Castle, a sixty-two-year-old English secret agent, becomes an agent for the Russians not for political reasons or financial gain but because of gratitude. He is indebted to the communist Carson for helping him and his family to leave South Africa despite his illegal marriage. With obvious reference to Conrad's *The Secret Agent,* we are told that "a man in love walks through the world like an anarchist, carrying a time bomb" (*HF,* 185). This allusion to the professor in *The Secret Agent,* along with the shady bookshop, the relations between secret service and colonial administration, and the bureaucratic character of government agencies, tie Greene closely to Conrad, but there is an important difference. It is the human factor. Castle's cover is blown not by accident or by political plot— as he says, "I have no politics" (*HF,* 20). Rather, it is blown by his feelings of gratitude and his desire for increased honesty in human relationships. We read that "he felt an irresistible desire to communicate directly by word of mouth, without the intervention of safe drops and book codes and elaborate signals on public telephones" (*HF,* 237). This desire increases under conditions of evasion and secrecy.[20] "He was tired to death of secrecy and of errors which had to be covered up and not admitted" (*HF,* 277). Gratitude, a need for human contact, and a desire for honesty have a potential both to subvert the authorities and putative totalities of religious and political institutions and to point beyond them.

Geneva, in Greene's *Doctor Fischer of Geneva* (1980), plays at least two roles. It epitomizes Western, especially financial, abstraction, and it is a location of cross-cultural interaction. Jones, the narrator, holds a critical stance toward modern culture, and he has that stance because of his war experience, scars, and personal losses. Rather than having negative consequences for him, adversity and uncertainty have put Jones in a truthful and real location. This makes him the contrary of Doctor Fisher, who loves wealth and power, despises other people, and holds a "contempt of all the world" (*DF,* 16). Fischer even has no feeling for his daughter, Anna-Louise, whom Jones loves. Their differing attitudes make Fischer and Jones antagonists. During a party that Fischer hosts in order to exhibit his power over people by exploiting their greed, Jones resists Fischer's temptations because Jones shares neither the greed of the others nor their fear of death. The struggle between Jones and Fischer takes on theological importance because Fischer's power is compared to God's. Jones tells Anna-Louise that when she speaks of her father she does so as though he were "'Our Father in Heaven,'" and she replies that "'that about describes him'" (*DF,* 31). Fischer asserts that God, like Fischer himself, desires human humiliation (*DF,* 71). Jones, because of his concern for truth, his care for others, and his lack of fear toward dying, separates himself from such a God, from Fischer, and from the culture of greed and anxiety represented by Genevan society.

The sacramental potential of the unconstructed space between institutional alternatives appears conclusively in *Monsignor Quixote* (1982). Father Quixote, positioned between the clear alternatives of the Spanish ecclesiastical structure and the political convictions of his communist companion, develops a modus operandi that, while clarified negatively by its detachment from both alternatives, has sacramental potential by being real. Before turning to that content, the rejection of the alternative locations should be made clear.

Although generally depicted unattractively by Greene, the church is treated particularly harshly in this novel. The bishop dislikes and distrusts Father Quixote and is eager to believe distorted reports about him. The church administration in Spain is allied with the government and its repressive police force. The procession of the money-covered virgin becomes a symbol of the church's attachment to wealth, and newly rich members of the church seek its social legitimacy more than its sanctity. The depiction of the church as sorely compromised finds its only counterweight in the recommendation made by a visiting bishop favoring Father Quixote, a recommendation that initiates the action of the narrative.

On Quixote's other side stands the secular mayor who forms a friendly bond with the priest because they are both maligned and discounted. The mayor, as communist and politician, differs from other secularists, such as Professor Pilbeam, in that the mayor appreciates possibilities of fiction while the professor, wedded to facts, does not. It is this quality in the mayor that seems to attract Father Quixote, who develops in response to the mayor a genuine interest in Marx; he reads some standard texts and points out aspects of Marxist theory that place it in a more favorable relation to religion than normally supposed. But the convictions of the mayor, although they engage the interest of Father Quixote, strike him as finally too clear-cut.

Father Quixote's position, therefore, is clearly identifiable by its location between the church and secular political ideology. It is a position of uncertainty, and, for Father Quixote, doubt is definitive of the life of integrity; without doubt there can be no faith: "'Oh, Sancho, Sancho,'" he says, "'it's an awful thing not to have doubts'" (MQ, 73–74). He says further: "'I am riddled by doubts. I am sure of nothing, not even of the existence of God, but doubt is not treachery as you Communists seem to think. Doubt is human'" (MQ, 180). For Father Quixote, the lives of saints and the tradition of church doctrine and practice operate in his life in a way similar to the role of medieval chivalry in the life of his namesake. They represent ideas, goals, and codes out of place in the present, not defensible or even credible in modern contexts. But by his interest in them, Father Quixote takes exception from the modern world, although by doubting them he also avoids the temptation of constructing out of them an alternative certainty. The position he occupies is marked by reality and risk. At the end it becomes sacramental. In the mass that he celebrates although forbidden to do so, God becomes tangible even when the sacramental elements are absent.

III

I do not think that the sacramental qualities of the places Greene's characters discover between conflicting ideological and institutional structures bring his novels through the back door of the church even while they stand so clearly distant from, and even disdainful of, the front.[21] Such surreptitious entry could be argued. When interstitial space is associated with reality, when it produces honesty, humility, and charity in characters, and when it suggests mystery, transcendence, and the sacramental presence of God, one would think that Greene has led the reader by a route that avoids much of church structure and authority but ends before its altar. Although such a case could be argued, I think his fiction should be read in terms of their rejections of religious as well as secular answers to the modern quest for certainty and the power that certainty grants. The pretension and complicity of religious and secular institutions and the culture of modernity they represent have served to conceal and militate against a sense of the real. The religious language and behaviors he associates with locations of the real serve to secure and enhance their importance and not to relocate them in the church. The religious language serves the language of comprehensive space and not the other way around. The interstitial sites exposed by Greene's fiction make clear that there can be no transcendence if there are no real, that is, unconstructed, places.

Greene's fictions separate truth and reality from the institutions and ideologies that claim them as their own and relocate them in places aside from human construction and control. Modern institutions, by subsuming the actual and truthful under their own coherences and by competing with one another for totality and authority, become estranged from, even antagonistic toward, the truth and reality that comprehends ordinary life. The force and meaning of the spatiality that comprehends human life defies institutionalization and is available only to persons in their suffering particularity. These persons provide critical points from which to measure the confident self-deception of modern institutions and ideologies, and they thereby gather moral and spiritual weight. They reveal reality in the midst of illusion, truth in the midst of pretension, and particularity in the midst of abstraction. The church and its secular counterparts should defer to out of the way or in-between places in modern human experiences that are entered by disciplines of suffering, exile, and divestment. Those places are primary in their critical effects and in their positive potential. If the church is to look for the real presence of divinity in its own sacramental life, it must look first of all for the true and real when they are revealed in the interstices, on the borders, and at the overextended edges of human control.

While Greene's project should be seen, at the end, in a positive light, as revealing places where reality and the comprehensive space again become available, we should not dismiss the negative aspects of his project lightly. Greene's work has been faulted for its attention to deviance and perversity as modes of exception that bear positive moral and spiritual fruit. That critique has taken its most pointed form in a recent biography. Greene along with his work are depicted as deceptive, perverse, and destructive.[22] The evidence gathered from Greene's life, from the testimony of others, and from his own admissions may be enough, especially if concentrated and underscored, to give some support to such an opinion.[23]

Greene, in his writing and in his life, pursued negative disciplines, that is, strategies of deception, divestment, and diversion, with unrelenting rigor. He did not want to be categorized or, perhaps, even understood. His path was one defined in a primarily negative way. And that negativity was not always benign.[24] One has to concede, however, its consistency. More, I think that one should recognize that it was productive not only of a set of powerfully effective fictions but also of a sense of the inadequacies, distortions, and repressions of modern social spaces in even their most commendable forms. What is most powerful in his fiction is that Greene did not take the condition of social space as an occasion to indulge only in private escapes. A more difficult path needed to be taken. And that path led to countersites marked both by divestment and by a placement where the comprehensive and transcendent could again be encountered. It was a path created by someone with, I believe, a firm sense that the social and personal in human life needed to be placed in relation to a spatiality that transcends and comprehends them both.

What Greene liked about the narratives of Hardy and James is that they place characters in relation to the transcendent. This is what Greene means by "the religious sense." (LC, 36). As he says, "It was as if the world of fiction had lost a dimension; the characters of such distinguished writers as Mrs. Virginia Woolf and Mr. E. M. Forster wandered like cardboard symbols through a world that was paper thin" (LC, 69). The dimension that Greene restores is one that is not possible except when human beings are understood in relation not first of all to intimate or social but to comprehensive space, a space that, while having tangible features, has for him a primarily spiritual force and significance.

The means for locating comprehensive space are improvised. They include questionable and objectionable behavior and attitudes, such as Michael Shelden catalogues. If Greene and his fiction avoid the worst, it is because they prosecute their goals in a way that is not finally or basically negative. There is always the confidence that there will be something real and true discovered by relentless exposure and attention, something that has a positive, integrity-granting potential. That positive yield is visible at the point of relation to comprehensive space. And it is the potential and reality of that kind of place-relation that intimates the reality of a narrowly accessible power and glory.

Greene's comprehensive place-relations make his contribution to a theory of human spatiality invaluable. In addition, his attention to "natural" sites, to sites unincorporated by Western constructions, especially the forest in A Burnt-Out Case, makes him particularly relevant to our discussion later of the relation of comprehensive space to the ambiguous role of the natural in modern culture. Finally, Greene, more than any of our other writers, anticipates the question, important for an adequate theory of human spatiality, about the relation of movement and mobility to placement. Greene helps us to recognize that mobility is not simply a contrary to place-relations but also their necessary accompaniment.

5

William Golding

Vision and the Spirit of Social Space

Like Greene, Golding considered his cultural location to have been so altered by war as to sever it from its immediate past. Also, like Greene, this
separation could be registered most effectively in regard to space and place-
relations. However, unlike Greene but like Conrad, Golding tries to redress
the losses felt in place-relations by affirming the primacy of social space. But
unlike Conrad's, Golding's fiction does not direct our attention to normative
models of social space located in the past and associated primarily with
physicality but to models that direct attention to the future and to the spiritual aspects of social space. When we move from Conrad to Golding, we
move from the primacy of social spaces built on labor to the primacy of
social spaces directed by vision.

One of the ways in which Golding acted out a sense of break between his
own situation and that of the immediate past was to alter or invert the thrust
of earlier fictions. Most notably, *Lord of the Flies* is a contrary text for *Coral
Island*. In addition, Golding pointedly commented on his contrary relation
to the rationalist culture of his home, which he describes as the "scientific
humanism" of H. G. Wells and against which he posed *The Inheritors*. He
says, "during the formative years of my boyhood I did feel myself to be in a
sort of rationalist atmosphere against which I kicked."[1]

However, Golding is most explicit about the break between the cultural
present and immediate past when he comments on war. The two wars fused
and formed, he writes, "a foundation on which all our assumptions are
based." While on the surface life goes on as ordinary, "frivolous, worried,
cynical, anxious, amused," "beneath, in some deep cavern of the soul, we

are stunned" (MT, 99).[2] In the First World War, the "irrelevance of the Geor-gian poetasters was burned away." The Second War "came near to demol-ishing all the assumptions of the first one and uncovered entirely different areas of indescribability" (MT, 101, 102). He says of the traumas of the Second World War: "The experience of Hamburg, Belsen, Hiroshima and Dachau cannot be imagined. . . . Those experiences are like black holes in space" (MT, 102). Here is an even more pointed comment, one that also is directed toward social space:

> Before the second world war I believed in the perfectibility of social man; that a correct structure of society would produce goodwill; and that therefore you could remove all social ills by a reorganization of society. It is possible that today I believe something of the same again; but after the war I did not because I was unable to. I had discovered what one man could do to another. I am not talking of one man killing another with a gun, or dropping a bomb on him or blowing him up or torpedoing him. I am thinking of the vileness beyond all words that went on, year after year, in the totalitarian states. It is bad enough to say that so many Jews were exterminated in this way and that, so many people liquidated—lovely, elegant word—but there were things done during that period from which I still have to avert my mind lest I should be physically sick. (HG, 86–87)

Golding implies that the present-day attitudes of people toward society, at-titudes of cynicism and suspicion, are largely justified and were formed by war experiences. People were drawn into events as though "conned into the mincing machine" (HG, 100). As in Greene, then, we find in Golding not only a break with the immediate past but a sense of betrayal and a burning need to tell the truth about things, to address the present situation honestly, and to keep fiction from being a false comfort or distraction.[3]

Another characteristic of Golding's writing is the remarkable awareness it creates of the force and significance of places. While not as widely traveled as Greene, Golding's accounts of such diverse places as Greece, Holland, and Egypt are convincing evocations of their spirits. But it is particularly his comments on the south of England that suggest his attention and attachment to place. Place-attachment centers on Wiltshire in general and on Salisbury in particular and is augmented by the layered human history of the area and its remarkable monuments, especially the cathedrals. I take the difference between Greene and Golding in their spatial interests as consistent with their contrasting orientations. Greene eschewed attachment to social locations, I think, as a means toward a more comprehensive spatiality. For Greene as for Hardy, human constructions, social, political, and religious, need to be

placed in critical relation to a context that outstrips them. Golding's attention is on human constructions, and his sense of space is far more social.
That is clear when he talks about the effects of Salisbury cathedral on the
town: "So it stands, a perpetual delight, a perpetual wonder, with the whole
of our little body politic shrugged into shape about it" (MT, 17). Basic to this
sense of space is the identification of people with the places that they create
together and with the consequences of those creations for their sense of
community. His fictions are attentive to the construction of social spaces.
Even when a fiction focuses on an individual life, that life is displayed in its
social character. And when attention is given to a more comprehending spatiality, as suggested by the sea, that larger context, as with Conrad, provides
background for the construction of social space.[4] Social space is formed
from and by the needs and potentials within people, but it is also a response
to shared threats.[5]

It may seem that Golding, no less than Conrad, harks back to earlier
social models; in several of his fictions we find ourselves in past time: *The
Inheritors, The Scorpion God, The Spire,* and the sea trilogy, for example.
But the uses of the past for Golding are designed to recover the potential for
confidence in creativity and the future. And as there is in his work a going
back in time in order to find the resources for creating the future, so there is
in his work a going down into what is concrete and physical as preparation
for an upward, spiritual direction.

The principal strategy Golding employs to enact these interests is the
construction of social and political microcosms and of individuals who
epitomize the effects and potentials of social space. These models and representative characters expose the problems in modern social space and the
potentials and prospects for creating social spaces that more fully will actualize the moral and spiritual possibilities of corporate human life.

The model of social space that seems to stand as a norm has three general
characteristics. It is inclusive, with various kinds of people interacting with
and mutually appreciative of one another. It is functionally hierarchical,
with levels defined in relation to the whole and to a goal. And it is oriented
to possibility, dynamic and productive of innovations that produce new
forms of inclusiveness and social identity.

This norm of positive social space as well as the other characteristics of
Golding's work—an emphasis on social space as oriented to the future and
the transcendent and the use of microcosmic and representative locations
and figures—can all be found in *The Spire* (1964). After giving attention to
this pivotal novel, I shall point out other aspects of narrated social space as
revealed by his novels. I then can end by suggesting some of the ties between
Golding's fiction and the spatial theory developed by the last part of this
study.

I

The setting of *The Spire* in late-thirteenth-century Salisbury allows the reader to compare and contrast medieval and modern societies. One finds that Golding's use of medieval culture is not Romantic. He is deliberate in describing the evils of medieval society: the selling of ecclesiastical offices, the incompetence and competitiveness of clergy, the corruption of politics at the highest levels, and the violence and pain that people are able to perpetrate on others and to which they are themselves subject.

Despite these harsh qualities, however, medieval society as epitomized in Salisbury cathedral possesses a number of features that appear attractive because they support, or at least allow for, the relation of creative vision to the construction of social space, features that, one can infer, are lacking in the construction of modern social spaces. These features include a sense of societal wholeness or inclusiveness, the use of particulars as microcosms, the primacy of vision, and an orientation to the transcendent.

The wholeness or inclusiveness of medieval society is indicated in several ways. One is the subordination of identity and social position to vocation. There is no antagonism or even gap between one's work, social position, and personal identity. So, Jocelyn is quite consistent with the world he represents when he assumes that his sudden, precipitous rise to the office of dean of the cathedral holds some potential public meaning, that something equal to the extraordinary nature of his calling should result from his occupancy of the office. The vision recorded in his brief autobiographical account, which Father Adam reads during the last part of the narrative, describes how Jocelyn discovered the answer to the question raised by his unexpected appointment as dean.

Wholeness is also suggested by the combination of inorganic and organic as well as material and spiritual elements within an inclusive world. Like social positions and their significance, the physical and the spiritual are not opposed or even separated from one another. Correspondingly, there is no compartmentalizing of aspects of human life—internal/external, emotional/intellectual, religious/secular.

Finally, while Christianity supersedes pagan beliefs and rites, there is no gap or conflict between the two. Salisbury and Stonehenge are close enough for transactions between them to occur, and the resources of the pagan, embodied in the boldness and energy of the workers, despite resistance by some of the cathedral's clergy and caretakers, are taken in and imprinted onto the spire. Implied is the notion, it seems, that for a significant creative achievement to occur there must be an inclusive attitude toward all aspects and possibilities of a society, its various cultural strata, its emotions and drives, its intellect and skills, and its spiritual visions and aspirations. Implied as well is that if something spiritual is to arise it must do so not by repressing the carnal, the painful, or even the shameful in human life but by incorporating those factors in the act of transcending and unifying them. The criticism of modernist societies that can be inferred is that they tend to separate and compartmentalize aspects of human interest and potential, to be selective rather than integrative, and to clarify human potential by exclusion rather than by incorporation.

Another characteristic of medieval England is the capacity to interpret particulars as microcosms. In Golding's fiction, islands, towns, enclosures, ships, and, here, a cathedral become epitomes of social space. Golding seems to use this trope not only as a narrative strategy but as a way of affirming the social standing of particular creative acts. He has no difficulty drawing that point from this material, because the cathedral for medieval Christianity was a microcosm. The image of the cathedral as Noah's ark, of the clergy as representative of humanity, and of the church as a continuation of the incarnation all go into the production of the cathedral's space as a social microcosm. In addition, the human body, viewed also at the time as a microcosm and as containing all of the ingredients found scattered throughout the cosmos, is frequently tied in the novel to the image of the cathedral as microcosm. Finally, while the cathedral's similarities to the human body are drawn primarily in male terms, due to the emphasis on the spire, the cathedral, named for the Virgin, is female as well.

The final characteristic of the thirteenth and fourteenth centuries that Golding seems to emphasize in contrast to modernity is the primacy of vision. Goals outstrip and transcend means. While building the spire requires remarkable, even incredible, technological skill, daring, and creativity, and while it depends on much heavy labor, there would be no spire without the vision. This primacy of the spiritual, of the transcendent and the visionary, creates a hierarchy of functions and, while inclusive and affirmative of the whole, clarifies distinct levels. At the bottom are the energy and courage of the laborers; above them are the technological and organizational skills of the master builder, Roger Mason, and his assistant, Jehan. And above them, giving occasion, goal, and meaning to the whole, is the visionary. In this case it is Jocelyn, whose vision, while inclusive of many motives and needs, particularly erotic ones, is recorded in the autobiography as a relatively convincing determinant.

The setting of the novel in late-thirteenth- and early-fourteenth-century southwestern England and the action of adding the tower and spire to Salisbury Cathedral, then, bring into focus the relations between the construction of social space and human creative vision. The events of the narrative relate the mobilization of the people toward the erection of a structure that reorients and confers identity on the society. It suggests that the potential of social space is most fully actualized when people are unified in and by the construction of something monumental, something that grants visibility and dignity to the otherwise invisible structures and aspirations by which social space is constituted.

While the narrative is dominated by the language of social space, it has other remarkable features. The point of view, with few exceptions, is first and limited third person, and it grants the reader participation in the process of construction. In this, as in all of his novels, Golding does not construct the typically modernist effect of establishing a relationship between the narrator and the narratee.[6] The absence of a narrator who is trying to create a relationship with the reader would distract attention from the primacy of the setting, and it would suggest a rhetorical effect more needed in the modern period than in the premodern. Also, a narrator who sorts things out for the reader would give a primacy in human values to distinction and rationality, a primacy that Golding wants to avoid. Nor are Jocelyn, his vision, and the construction subjected to a narrator's evaluation. The reader experiences the process, hears the judgments of others, recognizes the larger picture of which Jocelyn at the end becomes aware, and is left to make his or her own judgment.

The point of view also gives the reader jolts of recognition that coincide with those of the characters, especially Jocelyn. For example, the reader learns that the cathedral has no firm grounding, that the pillars bend, that a height is reached that surpasses anything previously achieved, that the capstone is very large and heavy, that Roger fears heights, that the tower sways, and that the angel at Jocelyn's back is only (or is also) consumption of the spine. The point of view, in other words, serves very well the emphasis of the narrative on the process of constructing social space, the dependence of that process on vision, and the ways by which monumental space affects the community.

The primacy of the cathedral as setting does not repress the importance of the novel's plot, either. It is neatly segmented into three parts. The first four chapters give the "problem" section of the plot. It becomes increasingly clear that Jocelyn is the only one in favor of the construction. Others resist and ridicule the project. Grave warnings are offered by the open pit and the lack of foundations. The financial sources are tainted, especially by the intentions of Jocelyn's aunt to gain burial in the cathedral and by Ivo's father, who donates timber to gain an ecclesiastical office for his son. The lineage of loyalty to the cathedral that Pangall represents is broken. And the venture has clear and complex erotic entanglements. At the end of the first part,

Jocelyn realizes that he is and will be the only support for building the spire, and Roger Mason, who is the only builder capable of doing the job, is locked into the project by Jocelyn.

The second part, the next four chapters, is the "passion" section. It includes the disruption of the cathedral's life, the delivery and death of Goody Pangall, and the increasing strain both on the four pillars of the church and on the four characters on whom the burden of consequence for the project is imposed. Central to the last of these is Jocelyn's exploitation of his pastoral knowledge of the tensions within the two marriages and of the sexual needs and potential attraction of Roger and Goody for one another. Golding employs, with this play on the physical and human pillars, a narrative strategy that he takes to be characteristic of the period, an exchangeable or interpenetrating relation between the nonhuman and human, the inorganic and organic. In this part as well, other difficulties are encountered and other transitions are negotiated. The workers realize that the building now exceeds in height what anyone else has done. Ranulf, a skilled stonemason, defects. Jocelyn sees the capstone. And the pillars of the cathedral bend.

The growing strain on the pillars is also related to the tensions the project creates in Jocelyn. For as the work continues, it requires more and more faith. Risk and faith, while contraries, depend on and support one another. The person of faith is willing to take risks, and risks require more faith. This is also true of the guilt and the joy that Jocelyn experiences in the mounting spire. Golding reveals an interest in the medieval motif of the *felix culpa* to support this tension. The joy of forgiveness and grace is not a joy one can feel without first having sinned, and the greater the guilt the greater the possible exhilaration and recognition of grace and forgiveness. So, the guilt produced by building so high, of defying the caution of experts, of harming the relationships and lives of other people, and of suspending normal responsibilities for the life of the cathedral is in productive tension with the exhilaration of being lifted above the confusions and entanglements below.

The final part of the plot gives the recognition and reversal of fortune. Jocelyn faces the depositions that have been submitted against him, including one by Father Anselm, the Cathedral's sacrist, and he is examined and judged by the visitor and the panel of seven. In a conversation with his aunt, he learns that his calling, his sudden elevation to the position of dean, was a result of the postcoital whim of his aunt's royal lover. His visit to Roger Mason exposes to him the cost that the spire has exacted from Roger's physical and emotional health and the cost of the death of Pangall, killed with "a sliver of mistletoe between his ribs" and, apparently, cast into the pit (*S*, 204).[7] And he learns that his comforting angel is really, or is also, consumption of the spine. But Jocelyn, in response to the fright of the people during a horrific storm, climbs into the spire and secures the relic nail. Despite the storm, the spire stands.

The plot is strongly classical. Like the Oedipus of Sophocles, Jocelyn was driven to act on the basis of what he knew and believed, but he did not have crucial information which, when he learns it later, calls his entire program into question. It is also a plot that, as Aristotle notes of *Oedipus* and commends in his treatise on tragedy, allows the recognition and reversal to occur together.[8] Finally, it is classical in its humanism, for there is, it seems to me, a strongly, even religiously, humanistic issue produced by the plot. Human creativity, however conflicted, marked by violence, pain, and desire it may be, and however inclusive it may be of what stinks as well as what edifies, can produce something so magnificent, self-justifying, and world-orienting as this spire. The novel, in other words, is not limited to the terms of its medieval and religious setting. As Golding says of *The Spire*, "I would have thought it's more about art than *Free Fall* is."[9]

The microcosm offered by the setting of this novel, then, is a social space that is organized by and able to defer to vision, to a sense of the transcendent as future possibility in which present and past find their fulfillment and justification. This is a society able to pierce beyond the prudent and precedented and to break through to the new. It is a society that assumes continuity and interdependence between the physical and spiritual, the repulsive and the edifying, the pagan and Christian. It is a society that looks for its significance and justification in what lies ahead, what is yet unachieved. This something ahead or above is what mobilizes, unifies, and makes productive the potentials in past and present. This nonrational, undetermined new is more important than reason or the skills and labor by which the new is to be achieved. Without the visionary, socially reordering creative enterprises would not occur; vision gives place, direction, and significance to mind, labor, and material.

Social space is hierarchical, but the hierarchy is dynamic, its levels being connected and indispensable to one another. Golding's models of social space have, consequently, a pyramid shape. The vision at the apex, since it mobilizes and directs the whole, is given, by its function, an inherent authority. The result of this configuration of social components may, however, be the mystification of the ministerium, that is, the sanctification of individual authority. One thinks, for example, of Marshall Berman's critique of visionaries, which he sees as a crucial ingredient in the negative tradition of Faust figures.[10] The question to ask is whether Golding's model for the rectification of social space should also be read as a blueprint for a specific political agenda. Let us postpone this question until we have looked at his other major work.

Before leaving *The Spire,* let us be reminded of some of the qualities that serve to constitute the relation of Jocelyn to the social space provided by the cathedral. For one thing, there is a mutuality between them. While not by any means without pain and injury to others, the cathedral does evoke from him the aspiration to build the spire, and the spire is completed largely because it draws so much from him. Social space is changed by the contributions of persons, and their potentials are actualized by the roles provided to them by the principal project in the social space, namely, the erection of the spire. Also, the social space is capacious. It allows for a relation between past and future and between the physical and spiritual aspects of people's lives. The narrative makes clear the role that social place and relations to it can play in confirming the interdependence of past and future and of the physical and spiritual to one another. Finally, the social space is giftlike. Jocelyn receives his position gratuitously, and the spire, despite the storm, stands. While planning, human effort, and skills go into its construction, the spire is also unprecedented and improvised. Its effects, such as reconfiguring the town, are surprising. There is a language of grace interwoven throughout the novel with a language of fault and judgment. Finally, it could be said that the social space is liberating in that it inspires creativity. However, this potential in social space is severely curtailed by the fact that Jocelyn must imprison people in order to press them into the service of his vision. The principal cause of damage in the narrative lies precisely here, namely, that while Jocelyn's dedication to the project is an act of his own, the continued involvement of others in it is largely due to his manipulations. The liberating and enabling potentials of positive social place-relations are thereby sharply reduced.

II

Golding's most widely read novel, *Lord of the Flies* (1954), clearly reveals his major interest in the construction of social space, why that construction is both difficult and necessary, and what happens when it fails. The need for social structure is created both by the external conditions in which the boys find themselves and by the potential conflicts internal to the group. The island's isolation, the heat, the dense jungle, the storms, the oppressive silences, the blinding light of the lagoon, the atmosphere of war in the outer world, and the fearful "beast" all put pressure on the boys. In addition, their lives together reveal increasingly sharp differences between them, differences that become fractures and hostilities and eventually produce deaths. Threats come, then, both from outside the group and from conflicts within it. For both reasons, a social order is needed.

The principal impediment to social order is the conflict between Ralph and Jack. It arises from their differing but legitimate emphases on structure and spontaneity, responsibility and pleasure. Ralph wants to secure a future by building shelters and keeping a signal fire burning, and Jack wants to use their freedom to hunt and eat pigs. The reader can infer that a healthy or viable social-political construction avoids splits of this kind by relating energy and desire to organization and future possibilities. It would be a mistake, then, to distinguish Ralph and Jack from one another as good and evil forces in society. True, Jack initiates the break and increasingly turns on Ralph. But Ralph works with a notion of how social space should be constructed that is limited. He longs for peace, and his model of peace is the home he loved as a young boy. He visualizes it more than once (*LF*, 139, 203). By projecting a model of personal space onto a social and political situation, Ralph minimizes the complexities and dynamics of that larger arena and is incapable of incorporating adequately the interests and potentials represented by the other boys. His model also allows him too fully to favor Piggy, the scientifically oriented, critical rationalist and nonworker or nonplayer. He is drawn by Piggy's influence into a managerial role, moving more and more from a visionary to an autocratic leader.

What most clearly indicates Ralph's valid role in the social structure, however, is his desire to maintain the fire signal. He identifies it with the future, with hope. It is as close in the potential structure of social space on the island as we get to "vision," without which—the allusion to Proverbs 29:18 seems unmistakable—the people perish: "'Without the smoke signal we'll die here'" (*LF*, 172). "'We've got to make smoke up there—or die'" (*LF*, 101). His stress on the fire as a link to the future, a hope for delivery, and the highest goal of their efforts is, however, too private to be shared by the others because it rests on faith in his father, a commander in the navy, and in his belief in the omniscience of the queen (*LF*, 49). Because Ralph cannot convey to the others the personal faith and hope that fuel his vision, they are not socially productive.[11] Finally, Ralph's model of space—where "Everything was all right; everybody was good-humored and friendly" (*LF*, 139)—excludes human instincts, such as the hunger, fear, and energies of the group. These are mobilized by Jack, who assumes an alternative and finally dominant position. But Jack's interests, undirected by a vision, produce fright, fits of insanity, and death.

We do not do justice to the novel, it seems to me, if we think of it primarily as a depiction of social evil, of the threat to social well-being posed by despots, or the dependence of society on the officialdom suggested by the rescue at the end. The principal issue of the novel is the failure of the boys to retain a vital, though uneasy, continuity between energies or material resources and aspirations or spiritual vision. While societies are threatened from without, they are threatened more constantly from within, from an inability to hold contraries in productive relation within an inclusive sociopolitical order. This sociopolitical order is not natural; it must be constructed, and it cannot be constructed without vision.

In *The Inheritors* (1955), Golding reveals his interest in the construction of social space by turning to the very origins of human societies. The novel inverts the view of Neanderthals expressed by H. G. Wells and epitomized in the book's epigraph. Golding's inversion presents Neanderthals not as ogres but as gentle and communal. Homo sapiens, in contrast, are hostile and unpredictable.[12] Golding exposed his intentions for the narrative during an interview with John Carey. Speaking of his father, Golding admits to living in the shadow of a "Wellsian rationalist" that he came to reject. He goes on to say: "But I think that the root of our sin is there, in the child. As soon as it has any capacity for acting on the world outside, it will be selfish. . . . That is, they learn unselfishness through this extra-ordinary nexus between people—maybe between parents and children, nurses and children."[13] Social space is not necessarily evil; it's a moral arena.

The narrative is also a critique of modern societies. The technological advancements of the new people, their voraciousness, domineering attitudes, penchant for internal strife, xenophobia, and fear of what they do not understand or control seem descriptive not so much of homo sapiens in general as of Western rationalists, particularly of the imperialistic, bellicose, and technological societies of the late-nineteenth- and twentieth-century West. If this is so, if the new people resemble modern Western societies, then the Neanderthals are similar to the Romantics.[14] As an antidote to modernist preoccupation with technology and control, some characteristics of Romanticism should be reevaluated and reappropriated: appreciation for the past and the foreign, rapport with the earth and with emotions, and communal and cooperative rather than competitively individualist attitudes. This does not mean that the novel is nostalgic. As the Neanderthal community dies off in the novel, so also Romanticism belongs to the past. In addition, not all in Romanticism is good. Innocence is often simply ignorance, and emphasis on the past and on unity can detract from advancement, creativity, and an upward direction for social life. Lacking vision, the Neanderthals perish. Homo sapiens fill a vacuum, but while doing so they fail to acquire those qualities of the Neanderthals that they lack. Without a more thorough sense of inclusiveness, especially of the unknown and the preconscious, human societies become unstable, fragmented, and violent.

It could be argued that *Pincher Martin* (1956) and *Free Fall* (1959) are departures from Golding's focus on social space. But the two narratives, while they deal with individuals, present them as social beings. Because the center of attention in *Pincher Martin* is a dying man alone on a rock at sea, Kinkead-Weekes and Ian Gregor read it as "a single, simple image of a Being reacting to Non-Being."[15] But there is more social analysis and criticism in the novel than such existentialist readings admit. Martin is a product and epitome of a society that, among other things, separates imagination from reality, is driven by greed, is haunted by repressed violence, and is narcissistic. First a writer and then an actor (Golding was first an actor and than a writer), Martin joined the navy (Golding served in the navy during the Second World War) because it would offer contact with "reality" in contrast to the imaginary culture of his former life. The separation of imagination from reality is revealed as harmful because it produces in Martin a terrible nemesis, namely, a free-play of both. Martin also exhibits the consumerism sponsored by the society. Teeth, mouths, and acts of devouring are recurring images, and Martin's memories depict him as voracious. He is a man who has had many women, including the wives of friends and acquaintances. By his own admission he has made his way over the bodies of others toward some sense of individual self-fulfillment. In addition, Martin has established his identity by repressing a recurring mental picture of an old woman in a cellar surrounded by coffins. It is an image suggestive of Golding's comment, cited above, that postwar society has constructed a surface that conceals that "in some deep cavern of the soul, we are stunned." Martin is also a representative of modern society in his narcissism. He regrets the lack of a mirror, and as an actor he liked to observe himself performing not only on stage but also in society. Finally, Martin as modernist has a high opinion of power. He recalls a toy he once had, a jar covered by a membrane with a figure inside. By applying pressure to the membrane he could make the figure move. The toy let him feel like God; now he feels like the figure, toyed with by a force he does not control. In anger he defies heaven (*PM,* 167, 178). What we have in Pincher Martin, then, is an epitome of modern society. It is not a pretty sight. A victim of violence—his ship was torpedoed by a U-boat—he is also a perpetrator. A consumer, he is likely to be eaten by hovering gulls. An artist, he is hounded by hallucinations. A narcissist and manipulator, he is toyed with by forces he defies. His death seems insignificant.

The confessional *Free Fall,* while personal, is no less oriented by social space. Sammy Mountjoy remembers images primarily of social places. Primarily he locates himself between contraries: his mother, whom he associates with the earth, and Evie, who has unrealistic dreams; Johnny, who is good at technical things, and Philip, who understands people; his teachers, Miss Pringle, who taught Scripture, and his science teacher, Nick Shales (*FF,* 214); and two women, Beatrice, who is sexually passive, and Taffy, who loves vigorously.

Sammy's recurring question concerns the loss of freedom, and it surfaces critical events in his life: the death of the lodger, trespasses that he and his friends commit, and conquering Beatrice. These events lead him to conclude that living implicates people in mutual harm; "'our imperfections force us to torture each other'" he concludes. "'We are the guilty. We fall down. We crawl on hands and knees. We weep and tear each other'" (FF, 251). The narrative reveals that a person's life is lived not in isolation but in social spaces where injuries as well as favors are given and received. Sammy's confession, then, reveals the unavoidably social character of human life (FF, 184).

This story of the artist as a young man locates artistic identity not in individuation, as with James Joyce, but in socialization. Sammy recognizes that art's discoveries are public as well as private. Art reveals the mysteries in life, delivers people from fear and darkness, and renews things (FF, 191). The artist is a social agent who creates images of social unity that, unlike the utopias of others in the story, from Evie to the Socialists, are inclusive and attainable.

In The Pyramid (1967), Golding turns his analysis and criticism of modern society to the small town of Stilbourne. The title suggests the shape and rigidity of the town's social structure and compares it ironically with the social constructions of the Egyptians.[16] Stilbourne's static structure may be especially noticeable to Oliver because he narrates from a transitional point, his departure for Oxford. He presents Stilbourne as shaped by a rigid hierarchy of social and economic distinctions, a structure that the town is determined to maintain. Resources for change exist. Music, for example, carries heavenly suggestions to Miss Dawlish and her father, and illicit sex carries suggestions of hell. But Stilbourne is unaffected by these extensions, and the transcendent lacks social relevance. This means that Oliver's critical insights will have no effect on the pyramid of social order.

By being closed to what transcends it, Stilbourne is vulnerable to takeover by hostile social-economic forces, even by industrial and financial development. Its future looks grim indeed. Stilbourne, then, pays the price of a lack of social vision. That price is the loss of its most gifted youth, the shrinking of its own significance, and its vulnerability to incorporation in futures imposed on it by others.

Golding's bleak assessment of social space moves from small town to London in Darkness Visible (1978). The picture is even darker, and the tone and atmosphere are apocalyptic. The narrative is framed by fire. The characters are products of a terribly inadequate and objectionable social situation. Matthew Windgrove, however, is an exception. A marred survivor of the war, he becomes a savior of children. Due to his disfigurement, Matty holds a marginal social position. Shunned by people, he is visited by angels, and these visitations are elaborated by biblical texts that he has taken from apocalyptic scenes in the books of Revelation and Ezekiel and memorized. Though disfigured and ostracized, Matty has both a positive attitude toward other people and a transcendent vision from which his judgment on postwar society gone to seed in extremism and obsession derives. Since the society makes no room for charity and vision, the most that can be hoped for is a future society more inclusive and more directed by vision than this one is.

In *The Paper Man* (1984), we return to a view of society by means of the artist's role. The aging and successful writer Wilfred Townsend Barclay is trying to distinguish himself from the social construction of him as the "artist." Because he has put so much of himself into his writing and because his identity is dominated by his reputation, he feels caught like a fly in flypaper. To free himself from social determinations, he travels, and, in an Italian church before a statue of Christ, he has an emancipating experience that is both religious and caused by a minor stroke.

The narrative reveals the perversion of the social role of art and the artist by society's commodification and consumption of them. Art and the artist must struggle against such absorption. "But in a society that is more concerned with . . . image rather than reality, a society whose sacred speakers have become scarcely more than so many gas-filled balloons, it is hard to retain individuality and integrity."[17] One way to resist absorption is to forego fame. Release grants the writer freedom to envision counter social possibilities, thereby clarifying the role of the artist as social visionary.

Given Golding's interests in social spaces, it is not surprising that he constructs a ship as social microcosm in his sea trilogy. The emphasis is on both the structure of social space and on the forces of creativity and destruction within that structure. As Golding says of the novel: "It's making some urgent statements about class. Unless we can get rid of it or at least blunt the pyramid or make it a little less monumental, we're done, we're finished, and it had better happen quickly."[18]

Rites of Passage (1979) gives us a ship sailing from the south of England to the Antipodes sometime in the early decades of the nineteenth century. The narrative is constituted by two documents, a journal kept by Edmund Talbot for the sake of his godfather and a letter sent by a young clergyman, Robert James Colley, to his sister. These texts reveal the contrasts between their authors' social positions. Talbot is secular while Colley is spiritual, and they differ in their response to conditions on the ship. These conditions are generally unpleasant. It is a time of warfare, and the ship has been pressed into service for general passenger and transport duties despite its age and questionable condition. The ballast of the ship stinks; people have confining and meager quarters; and the heat intensifies as the ship travels southward.

Colley is spiritually minded and tenderhearted.[19] Talbot, in contrast, is politically connected and moves well in the social space of the ship. He keeps Captain Anderson's authority over him in check because Anderson knows that Talbot is writing his journal for an important political personage.

It would appear that the heart of the narrative lies in the rite celebrated as the ship passes over the equator. The rite allows the social structure of the ship, which is normally rigid and jealously guarded, to be ridiculed and compromised. But it is primarily the rite's effects on Colley and Talbot to which attention should be given. Both men relate the social structure of the ship to interests that transcend it. Talbot maintains contact with his godfather who, by virtue of sociopolitical position and benevolent wisdom, gives Talbot a perspective from which to evaluate behaviors and events, and Colley defers to the religiously transcendent. Because Colley is detached from social realities, he lacks resources for dealing with the event; he retreats to his room and dies of shame. Talbot's orientation seems preferred. The novel thereby endorses a social space that can include disruption as well as stability because it is oriented by a benevolent political wisdom.

In *Close Quarters* (1987), Talbot emerges more fully as a representative social being. Still backed by his wise and influential godfather, he has no doubt about the strength and worth of English political identity. His social theory places responsibility in the hands of worthy people; "'the more civilized a country is, the smaller is the number of people fitted to understand the complexities of its society!'" (*CQ*, 11). "'The civilized nations,'" he tells Mr. Summers, "'will more and more take over the administration of the backward parts of the world'" (*CQ*, 9).

In addition, Talbot gives textuality a strong social significance. His written record provides the voyage a coherence and significance that it otherwise would not have. The voyage becomes increasingly risky and questionable, but Talbot's journals will make the journey known and remembered. The combination of social interaction and writing serves to provide a "habit of dignity" that "asserts the positive necessity of proclaiming to a world of blind force and material something like—*I am a man. I am more than blind nature!*" (*CQ*, 259). Adversity clarifies the significance of responsible social action, and when the war with France ends, a question arises about maintaining human dignity and social identity in times of peace (*CQ*, 55). Talbot feels emptiness rather than elation at the prospect of war's ending. It appears, however, that during times of peace, letters supply the social unity and goal that otherwise war provides. Writing continues to hold potential for social cohesion, identity, and change.

Fire Down Below (1989) completes the trilogy by securing positive changes in people's lives effected by social interactions. Principal among them are changes in the relationships of Edmund Talbot with Mr. Prettiman and Charles Summers. Summers and Prettiman are unlike one another politically, and association with them stretches Talbot in contrary directions. Summers, both practical and religious, is politically conservative. Prettiman holds, in contrast, strongly negative opinions about the social and political structures and practices of England, and he is setting out to attempt a new social order in Australia.

Talbot's relation to these men is complicated by his contacts with Benét, a refugee from the French Revolution. Inventive, poetic, and romantic, he is responsible for jeopardizing the ship because his attempt to remove growth from the ship's bottom creates leaks. Now he wants to secure the mast, and to do so he needs to introduce intense heat to its base, a fire that Summers rightly fears and that finally destroys the ship, although only after its arrival in Australia.

What we end with, then, is the formation of Talbot as a social man, a formation that brings his earlier abilities and orientations into positive relations with the practical, religious character of Summers, the utopian goals of Prettiman, and the impulsive actions of Benét. His formation coincides with the death of his patron, for whom his journal had been kept. Emerging with a social identity of his own, Talbot, writing from a point in his life years after both the voyage and a successful political career as a member of Parliament, gives us this autobiography as a journey toward that formation. Although placed by Golding in the past, Talbot emerges, as well, as Golding's projection of social beings sufficiently directed and capacious to secure and direct society in a postwar period.

Talbot's authoritative position as social being seems compromised by his national loyalty. He says of himself, "'when I search my heart, among all the prejudices of my nature and upbringing, among all the new ideas, the acceptance of necessary change, the people, writers and artists, philosophers and politicians—even wild-eyed *social philosophers*—the deepest note of my heartstrings sounds now as it will to my dying day—"England for ever!"'" (*FDB*, 261). Earlier he describes himself as "'a political animal'" who wants "'to exercise power for the betterment of my country: which of course, and fortunately in the case of England, is for the benefit of the world in general'" (*FDB*, 221). The role of God in Summers's view of things, of Nature in Benét's, and of the Absolute in Prettiman's is taken over by "England" in Talbot's social theory. Although he is not of a mind to subscribe to "'my country right or wrong,'" (*FDB*, 261), he affirms "England" as an incorporating social structure and project. The question is whether a social vision loses its critical and transforming potential when it is so closely tied to national identity.

III

Golding's novels advocate a theory of social space that requires social formation in relation to goals and direction. This is implicit in the ship analogue. While goal or direction has a practical side, it is spiritual, too. A society needs its visionaries. This theory of social space refutes prevailing social structures because they are too rigid, are closed to what lies below and above them, and lack direction. A society led by its visionaries will move in a creative way toward actualizing human potential for the betterment and expansion of individual and communal life.

A society that is both practical and spiritual and that is directed toward a goal must be inclusive. This means cooperation between people and the ordering of diverse abilities and interests in relation to the inclusive goal. It takes into account both the most ordinary and base of human interests, desires, and instincts and the most elevated and edifying. The adumbrated social space is one in which there is a place for everyone. This placement has a functional justification, for there are many skills and many interests, all of which can and should be included within and directed toward social goals. Just as Talbot can move among various kinds of people—passengers, seamen, philosophers, and politicians—these kinds of people must be related to, and not separate from or disdainful of, one another. However, social location is also important. Functions carry authority and responsibility, and there cannot, with all of the continuity among differing people, be a breakdown in social differences and structure.

A mobile, forward-moving social structure reveals a functional hierarchy. In a noticeably elevated position stands the artist, who takes on roles traditionally ascribed to religious offices, especially of prophet and seer. The artist criticizes society and sets before it suitable visions. The artist recovers the repressed and marginalized, relates disparate parts of the society to one another, and represents in artistic work the society as a whole. The position of the artist not only displaces that of the religious prophet and seer but also stands above the positions of scientist, technician, and manager. These find their direction and correction in the work of the visionary. But the office of the artist, placed in social primacy, is borne not by the artist but by the artist's works and their effects. The artist, while sharply individuated, is the "social animal" par excellence.

Golding's implicit model or theory of social space can be read as politically conservative. However, the principal effect of his fiction, I believe, is not to advance a particular political agenda but to attack stasis, the lack of ideals and purpose, and the fragmentation of contemporary social life, along with the exclusiveness, repression, and rigidity that mark the English social class system. The social space of Golding's fiction, while vulnerable to appropriation by a conservative agenda, need not be. His social space does not necessarily represent, as S. J. Boyd suggests, an apology for the Thatcher era.[20] Golding is as hard on the individualism, competitiveness, and consumerism of that option as he is on the utopian social models of the political left. But the language of social space in his fiction does leave open the question of social goal and purpose. The future toward which a society is oriented and by which it is always being changed and challenged derives its authority not so much from below as from above, by means of vision. Without vision, apparently, a people will perish. However, without knowing what those visions are and where they will lead, many may demur.

In response, three things should be said. First, Golding's model advocates change as a constant factor in social life. We can see this in two ways. One way is in his consistent and biting critique of social rigidity, fragmentation, exclusivity, and superficiality[21] and, even more, the schizophrenic, narcissistic, greedy, and violent natures of modern societies. Golding's diagnoses are radical. Rather than blame this condition on certain people, he takes it as the result of a loss of faith. He implicates everyone in this loss, since it seems to have been produced by the consequences of and reactions to the world wars. People cling to what is stable, distrust one another, and have little concern for the corporate good. This is due to the grand betrayals that mark the period. As he writes, "Our leery and cynical suspicions that the system will do you down if you don't watch it all the time derive from the attitude of frontline troops, who having been conned into the mincing machine and astonishingly escaped with their lives and at least part of their bodies and wits, are too fly to let themselves ever be deceived again" (MT, 100). What is required is a restored affirmation of the social future and of the importance of visionaries to provide a social orientation to possibility. Crucial to vision are creative artists, who are able to stimulate, unify, and edify a society by making creative possibilities public.

The second thing that must be said is that Golding thought of artistic work as countering the preoccupation of modern societies with means. The artist is attentive primarily to ends, to the idea, possibility, or goal. The artist starts with the end and then tries to figure out how to bring it into being. A sense of the future, a vision, is received. As he says: "The writer does not choose his themes at all. The themes choose the writer" (MT, 168). This means that the writer does not take in the idea but is taken in by it, does not possess but is possessed.[22] The idea, possibility, or vision, is discontinuous with, transcends, the present. What the artist then does is to create a continuity between vision and reality, between possibility and reader. The artist pontificates, builds bridges, that is, between there and here, the future and now, possibility and reality. The transcendent cannot wholly be articulated; "Words can only bring us to the point where something either becomes 'visible' in the 'opening' between them, in the space beyond—or does not."[23] The goal is always moving ahead, and it is always elusive. The visionary follows it, as do also, in their turn, those engineers, planners, managers, workers, and other citizens who have their minds not only on the present and themselves but on the future and the whole.

The third characteristic of the social theory implicit in Golding's fiction concerns the nationalistic emphasis especially expressed by Talbot toward the end of the sea trilogy. This should be read, I think, primarily as Golding's sense of attachment to particular places, and a social vision should be shaped with particular locations in mind. Social identity cannot be formed in abstraction from or in defiance of one's particular social, political context. To put it another way, national loyalty is a responsible and positive stance toward the potentials within a political, social situation for its renewal and redirection. Persons are, for Golding, social beings, and the social is always specific and concrete. But the social also has faults and lacks, and national loyalty includes both a granted identity and a restless urgency to challenge the past and the present with viable visions of a more just and humane social future.

What commends Golding's work for a theory of human place-relations is his orientation to social space and, even more, his belief that social spaces not only must be but also can be radically altered. We shall see later that social, particularly urban, spaces need rectification. While agreement as to how they can be positively altered may elude us, attention to the reimagining and reconstruction of social, urban space is not something that an adequate spatial theory can ignore. We shall have to probe the prospects for allowing urban spaces also to become what David Harvey calls spaces of hope. His call is not one that a responsible spatial theory can avoid.

6

Taking Exception

Muriel Spark and the Spiritual Disciplines of Personal Space

There is much that relates the work of Muriel Spark to that of Greene and Golding. With them, she posits war and other shared traumas as occasioning truthfulness and reality. She shares, too, their belief that the lacks and faults of the present outstrip the resources of the previous culture. Her project is related, then, more to the future than to the past. As with Greene and Golding, as well, Spark looks to spiritual resources to redress present locations. Identifying and benefiting from those possibilities require rigorous attention, personal sacrifice, and alienation from the prevailing cultural context. However, the sites of these tasks for Spark, unlike for Greene and Golding, are located, as with Forster, in personal or intimate places.

As we move along the course of the century with these three writers and even when we move within the corpus of Spark's own work, we find increasing critical exposure of the cultural power of the media in general and of image making in particular. The identity constructed for and imposed on Querry by Rycker and Parkinson and the power of images in Golding's *Pincher Martin* and *The Paper Man* become, when we turn to Spark's fiction, no longer exceptional. Her fictional worlds, especially in her later work, are marked increasingly by the power of social constructions to determine human identity and to compromise particularity and integrity. Indeed, it is largely because the culture is so controlled by the image-making industries that her characters have trouble finding personal space, places free from social coercion.

The best way to describe how personal or intimate spaces are located and secured in her fiction is through the discipline of taking exception. In an article on her youth, Spark explains the use and force of the word "nevertheless." She says that she is "indoctrinated by the habit of thought which calls for this word" and that much of her "literary composition is based on the nevertheless." Indeed, she goes so far as to say, "It was on the nevertheless principle that I turned Catholic."[1] The vivid example she uses to convey the force and significance of "nevertheless" is Castle Rock, which rises abruptly in Edinburgh between the New Town and the Old. "To have a great primitive black crag rising up in the middle of populated streets of commerce, stately squares and winding closes, is like the statement of an unmitigated fact preceded by 'nevertheless.'"[2] This locution, this intervention of "nevertheless," is crucial, I think, to what she means by personal space, to what constitutes an exception. Despite the coercions and homogenizing effects of the culture, of the media in their various forms, and of the image industries, there is always the human possibility of taking exception. But that possibility requires courage, integrity, and spiritual discipline. It also both requires and produces personal, intimate places.

There are two principal strategies that mark Spark's search for personal places that actually or potentially are exceptions to the culture. The first is that she constructs locations and conditions for her characters that from the outset already lie beyond the main lines of social interest or that rank low on the scale of social value. Old age, artistic vocations, poverty, a remote island, being unmarried, having been betrayed or abandoned, caring for a baby: these are some of the conditions with which her characters start or some of the situations into which they are thrust that provide at least some discontinuity with the dominant culture. While one would expect that her second strategy would be avoiding the image-making power of social space by finding locations free from images, that path seems for her not possible. We are asked to infer from her work that, unlike with Greene and, to some degree, Golding, there are no places free from texts and images. Rather, she places her characters in situations that have potential for being exceptional because that potential is opened by the texts and images of exception. In other words, Spark responds to the culture of textuality by retrieving and projecting textual exceptions, marginal potentials for deconstructing social power with the gesture of "nevertheless."

To expose these strategies and their effects, I begin with *The Only Problem* (1984). I shall then go on to point out in her other novels similar attempts to secure intimate spaces by taking exception, by avoidance and divestment. We shall have a basis then to see how the spiritual disciplines that secure intimate spaces are distinguished from their counterfeits.

I

It is important to comment, first, on the force of the title. It does not only mean that the novel deals with a problem in human life that, by virtue of its size and difficulty, makes claim to be the *only* problem, namely, the problem of suffering, especially undeserved or innocent suffering. It also registers a demurral, part of a phrase we use when, having been treated to a totally adequate solution to some situation, we reply, "Yes, that's fine. The only problem is . . ." In other words, the title is also an instance of Spark's principle of "nevertheless." It is the moment of exception, of recognizing a loose end, something overlooked. And it has the added force that what has been overlooked may be the most important thing of all. This locution, this intervention of "nevertheless," is, as suggested, crucial to what she means by personal space, to constituting an exception to the control of our lives by the media and the image industries. The "only problem" response to social space grants possible access to a space that is an exception.

It is also important to begin with some comments on the painting *Job and His Wife* by George de La Tour (1593–1652) because it is pivotal to the novel. It provides the imaginary upon which resistance to the power of social constructions is based. One stands before the painting almost as a voyeur of an intimate space occupied by a suffering man and his wife. They are caught in a moment of intense interaction. Intimate space is created, among other ways, by the eye contact of the two, their lack of awareness not only of us but of everything else. They do not appear as types of people, either as religious figures (the painting was for some time not taken as biblical but mistakenly as the visit by a woman to a prisoner) or as sufferers. We have first of all an ordinary, tightly knit couple in a space structured by personal relationship. The viewer is also aware of the light, which comes from within the scene and not from a source outside it. Indeed, we assume that the man has been, until a moment ago, sitting alone in darkness.

The intimacy of the space between and around the couple is not achieved by strong similarities between the figures. Indeed, they are strikingly unlike one another. He, almost naked, his aged skin hanging on a visible skeleton, sits on what looks like a block of stone, with a broken bowl his only possession. She, younger, stands richly robed, the long sleeves of her under-dress pleated and embroidered at the cuff in gold, her earring dangling and reflecting the light that comes from the candle that she holds. The man's mortality is evident in his weakness and vulnerability (de La Tour often includes reminders of mortality in his paintings, such as those of St. Jerome and of Mary Magdalene, of which there are several), while the wife carries within her broad dress what seems to be an ample, life-bearing body. Her intent and caring gaze contrasts, however faintly, with the strong gesture of her left hand. The look on Job's face is one both of puzzlement and of pain, a man totally at a loss, who looks in expectation at a familiar person with whom already much of life has been shared. She seems to come both to comfort and to goad. The space created by and between them is complex, therefore, and resonant. It is a remarkably arresting and provocative painting.

I begin with this painting because it is crucial to the novel. Harvey Gotham, the principal character, has become a puzzle to other characters because of his interest in this painting, in the biblical Book of Job, and in interpretations of Job's suffering. Indeed, Harvey has taken up residence in the northeast of France in order to be within reach of this painting, which hangs in a museum in Epinal. He is fascinated by its presentation of a lonely, exiled man in an intimate exchange with his wife, a man who tenaciously pursues, despite the cost, the quest for truthfulness and reality. Harvey has sequestered himself in a country house in order to write a monograph on Job. Indeed, as the novel opens we approach this house, this isolated space to which Harvey has retreated.

It should not surprise or bother us, given Spark's interests, that Harvey is not an engaging character. Very few of her characters are. The culture of late modernism, which I take to be a matter of principal interest in her work, does not give rise to complex and resourceful personalities. Indeed, many of her characters are not even likable. The personal depth and complications that make for engaging characters have become the lack that her fictions address. She cannot deploy interesting characters and still depict a social space in which persons are deprived of particularity and of places and resources by which arresting and meaningful particularity could be cultivated. Harvey, by not being very interesting and even likable is, then, no exception.

We learn some incidental, though helpful things about Harvey, however: he is marginal, having been born in Canada and having come to England as a teenager; he is wealthy; and he is thirty-five years old. Although married, he is separated from his wife and prefers to be alone, and his friends seem to have cause to be put off by him. He separated from his wife when her long-standing antisocial attitudes and actions reached what he takes to be a sufficiently annoying point. He seeks solitude to pursue his obsessive interest in the figure of Job, an interest piqued and sustained by the painting of Georges de La Tour.

The painting seems to be arresting to Harvey not only because of the figure of Job, his suffering, and his quest for truth and reality but also because it is an image of intimate or personal space. The painting, then, offers a sharp contrast to the socially determined life that Harvey has known and to the socially determined antisocial attitudes of Effie, his wife. The long-standing and deep intimacy between Job and his wife, despite their differences, counters the distance and indifference between himself and Effie. The space depicted so fascinates him because it stands as a contrast both to the world around him, which he tries, during the course of the narrative, to elude and resist, and to his own marriage. We should add that Harvey does not pursue his interest in Job and in this painting because he is a religious person, a connoisseur of art, or a scholar. Other characters in the novel are more substantially tied to religion, the arts, or the scholarly life than he. Indeed, he is the only one of the major characters without a religious background.

One of these other characters, Edward Jansen, brings to the fore the power of a social space governed by images, roles, and representations, a power so strong as to absorb not only individuals and their potentials but the church. Edward is an actor, having earlier been a cleric. As the story progresses, Edward is increasingly identified with his profession. He is so successful as an actor because he can easily project himself into prescribed roles, an ability, it is suggested, that marked his earlier life as a clergyman, too.

Harvey's wife, Effie, who is beautiful, impulsive, and unpredictable, is a clergyman's daughter. She testifies to the power of social space by having had a sociological vocation and, finally, by divorcing herself from society through antisocial, even terrorist, acts. She enters a life of revolutionary activity, although we have access to her actions only through the images of mass media. Why she suddenly turns against and attacks society is not completely clear, although it may be related to the fact that her father was a clergyman. If so, her move suggests a theologically grounded form of social protest and radical politics, options that had currency in the postwar decades. However, Harvey seems to relate her behavior less to these reasons than to the social whole from which he tries to remove himself.

Effie's sister, Ruth, who comes to live with Harvey, cultivates a quietist attitude toward the world around her. She carries a degree of credibility and integrity by her adoption of maternal and domestic roles.

We have seen before that in narratives shaped by a dominant language of space, characters often represent types of responses to their location. That seems to be the case here. If the three responses of these characters are to be ranked—and Muriel Spark often includes responses or attitudes that can be arranged from more to less preferable—Edward's capitulation is lowest, Effie's active resistance seems to stand next, and Ruth's quietism and care seem, of the three, most highly commended.

The problematic conditions that surround these characters and to which they are responding are not conditions that they fully understand. Indeed, the resistance posed by society to the cultivation of personal life is not fully explicated in the novel. This tends to make the behaviors of some of the characters, especially those of Harvey and Effie, appear puzzling and even bizarre. The characters and their behaviors are primarily symptoms of a culture totalized by media and driven by economic and political interests. Edward's absorption, Effie's resistance, Ruth's quietism, and Harvey's concentration on the possibility of suffering as an entry to personal space all indirectly testify to the subtle but powerful and pervasive effects of the culture.

The exceptional, even transcendent possibilities that Harvey pursues are textual and activate potentials within the culture for its own undoing. The de La Tour painting not only is arresting in and by itself but also because it opens up a range of related texts that deal with being—or taking—an exception. What Harvey does, in attempting to secure a personal space as an exception to the culture, is not to establish a position free from texts but to align himself with countertexts, with de La Tour's painting, with the Prometheus of Aeschylus, with the Philoctetes of Sophocles, and with the biblical text of Job, the figure of undeserved suffering. By doing that he aligns himself with the exceptions posed for society by these texts, primarily with problems for which the society has no answer.

This alignment does not relate Harvey to an ontological transcendent. God is, for him, a character in a story, a figure in a text. Harvey does not become a believer. Indeed, he comes to these texts neither by way of personal suffering nor by way of belief in the transcendent. He is drawn to them by their exceptional qualities, their potential as indicators of a countersite to the prevailing culture of answers. They oppose the culture because they take exception to the surface quality of social space in their depiction of radical, alienated, and suppressed questions in human life.

Harvey's actions produce suffering in three ways. First, by means of a self-exile that is dedicated to the study of Job, Harvey takes on the problem that the society avoids, namely, the problem of insoluble problems. Second, his form of exile alienates him from a society that, dedicated to answers and security, is threatened as much by insoluble problems and enigmatic behavior as by acts of terrorism. Third, he himself becomes a victim of intrusion, surveillance, and interrogation not only because of Effie's actions but also because his own behavior has no social credibility. His antagonist becomes not, as with Job, God but the society against which both he and Effie, in contrary ways, have set themselves.

It is fascinating to see how forms of social power attempt to absorb or discount Harvey's attempts to take exception. If he were cultivating private space to write a pornographic book, for example, his privacy would be understandable and its results digested by the economic system. But his solitude is not explainable in social and economic terms. Indeed, the personal space he tries to create for his writing is not so much for the sake of the writing; the writing serves the attempt to establish personal space. This act not only puzzles others; it also offends them and arouses their suspicions. In this way Harvey resembles Effie, whose actions also seem to be unrelated to some larger cause and reveal no traceable pattern. However, she cannot avoid so well as does Harvey already established images of nonconformity and insurrection. For this reason and not primarily from a condemnation of violence, it seems, the actions of Harvey are preferred in the novel to those of Effie.

The effect of all this is that in a secular world of coherence and comfort, the problem of suffering, rather than holding its traditional position as a threat to religion, becomes a threat to secular culture and an entry to personal freedom. But to have these consequences, the problem of suffering must be one for which no answer can be found. "Nevertheless," or taking exception to the culture, becomes possible in the place created by suffering, particularly suffering in the form of a question to which no answer can be found. The lack of answers marks a space apart from the social space of answers and solutions. Once a space has been clarified by uncertainty and discomfort, it can be enlarged. If there is no answer to the problem of suffering, then there may be other problems and questions that society cannot answer. Indeed, are any of the answers that go into constituting the society of comfort and security free from being questioned when basic questions in human life go unanswered? Indeed, rather than being an exception, the unanswered question begins to permeate and corrode the fabric of social space.

Unlike the spire that is open to the view of characters and readers at the end of Golding's novel, the book that Harvey writes on Job and the response it provides to the problem of suffering are not shown either to the reader or to other characters. The irresolution of the problem of suffering at the end, the withholding of Harvey's work from fictional and actual readers, keeps the space he has secured both closed and open. It is closed because characters, other than Ruth and the children, as well as readers cannot share a sense of that discovered place. However, the place of exception is held open because by remaining hidden it is not subject to appropriation by social and economic interests. Intimate or personal space in relation to social space becomes viable to the degree that it remains hidden or problematic.

The ending marks change. Harvey turns from his preoccupation with Job and from its antisocial consequences to Clara, and his subsequent life is dedicated to daughters and to the tasks of edification and nurture. This move can be related to other moments in Spark's fiction when characters seem to secure some sense of personal space by relating intensely to actual particulars, such as babies.

Harvey's actions, in other words, embody Spark's principle of "nevertheless." He becomes an exception by recognizing a loose end, something overlooked. And it has the added force that what has been overlooked may be the most important thing of all. The "only problem" response to social space coincides with the opening of a personal alternative. The move allows problem to become a cause of suffering and suffering to be a form of taking exception. We have Harvey's thoughts on the matter: "How can you deal with the problem of suffering if everybody conspires to estrange you from suffering? He felt like the rich man in the parable: it is easier for a camel to go through the eye of a needle than for him to enter the Kingdom of Heaven" (OP, 65).[3] Squeezing out of the society in order to find a discomforting place that, by being exceptional, is personal, that is free from the controlled surfaces of society, relates personal space to uncertainty and transcendence.

It is not too much to say, I believe, that in Spark's novel texts that pose problems that cannot be solved hold redemptive potential in a society committed to the comforts and protections of certainty. The fact that puzzling and impenetrable texts can also be fascinating and life-changing suggests that the pervasive power of the culture of answers, of answers that are possessions, is finally vulnerable and unsatisfying. A text that stands as an exception to the culture draws attention to itself because the viewer or reader is led to recognize that not all questions have answers and that not all problems have solutions. The culture tries to dissolve the problems that Harvey and Effie present or have become because the culture is impatient with unanswered questions, particularly those posed by people who cannot be fitted into some category, even if only in some category of deviance. And unanswered questions or problems have a kind of transcendent status in a world identified with and enclosed by the securities of its own solutions and certainties. Such questions are threats because they carry the implication that if there is a question for which the culture has no answer or category, there may be other things that also fall outside its control.

The novel also leads us to read the Book of Job not for the answers it may offer but for the question or puzzle that it can become. And this way of reading Job is worth taking seriously. It may be a mistake to read the text as though it offered answers to a question or even to read it as dealing primarily with a problem. The narrative is first of all about a man who suffers and is exiled, about the man's response to his suffering, and about the responses of others to both his suffering and his response to it. The reading of Job that can be inferred from Harvey's comments and from de La Tour's painting is defensible, then. The Job texts create desire in Harvey because they open up the human possibility of intimate space, albeit at the price of divestment of social identity and its assurances. Harvey begins with the painting, but he then goes further, as though into the poetic section of the Book of Job with its laments and attempted consolations. That extension leads Harvey to what he seeks, namely, a place where a person can be relatively free from the constructions of society, including its constructions of the religious or suffering person. Job also resists the culture of answers, and when Yahweh speaks to him, what he gets is not answers but more questions. What is surprising is that these questions seem to grant Job relief. He prefers Yahweh's questions to the answers of his comforters. Culture, including its religious language, deals primarily in answers. Exiting the culture means finding a place where questions are alive and well.

The end of the narrative is not the resolution of the problem it exposes. While there is an ending, the reader is left with the unanswered question of Harvey's reading of Job, the question of what it was to which that reading led him. Spark's novel suggests that texts like the Book of Job, de La Tour's painting, and, perhaps, *The Only Problem* bring their readers and viewers to the edge of social space and to an exit into a personal space opened up by unanswered questions.

Despite the ambiguities of its ending, Spark's narrative gives us a largely positive depiction of personal place-relations. At the end, Harvey seems to have discovered a place at least partially outside of and free from the determinations of social categories and identity constructions. The effects on him of this place are registered by the caring roles he assumes. In addition, the place relates his past, primarily his long-standing interest in Job, to his future, particularly his relation to children. Child-caring points toward growth and change. No less, the place joins a physical location to a personal freedom and integrity. This does not mean that the place is final and complete. It is bound to be temporary, if for no other reason than because the care of children is temporary. But it also seems that such personal spaces, given the force and pervasiveness of social pressures, must be won over and over again. Finally, the personal space is not only the result of Harvey's efforts; it is also a gift. While pursuing the possibility of taking or being an exception, Harvey did not know beforehand of what personal space would consist. Indeed, by definition, personal space cannot be scripted. If it were, it would become part of the culture of duplication and prescription. The possibility of taking or being an exception arises every so often and even, perhaps, anywhere.

In a culture of coercion and certainty, personal space, while freeing, is not comfortable. Exiting society is, as Harvey puts it, like squeezing through a needle's eye. And it lands one in a place that is hidden and problematic.

However, the possibility of and the need for personal spaces lure and haunt Spark's characters. Such places offer freedom from the controlling, self-reflecting surfaces of society. Personal spaces and squeezing into them recur, then, in many ways in her other fiction.

II

In the late modernist, economically unified, and image-determined world that shapes Muriel Spark's fiction, personal space is not easily achieved, even, as in Forster, when the personal takes on antisocial characteristics, such as defiance of the society's strictures against homosexuality. Indeed, some of Spark's characters are homosexual, but this forms no clear alternative to a society that seems inexhaustibly able to absorb resistance and cancel particularity. Nor does money secure personal space, as in Virginia Woolf's prescription for a room of one's own. Many of Spark's female characters live independently, but the spaces available to them are affected by their social contexts. Before looking at some of the situations that pose possibilities for intimate or personal space and at attitudes and behaviors requisite for it, we should detail characteristics of late modern society that, in her fiction, militate against personal space.

One characteristic of that society is, as we saw in *The Only Problem,* its general impatience with problems and mysteries. The society is geared to solve problems and maintain comfort. We see it in its religious form in her first novel, *The Comforters* (1957), which alludes in its title to the attempts of Job's friends to give explanations for his problematic condition. Chief among the "comforters" is Georgina Hogg, who has a "terrifying" zest for faith and for converts to it that is indistinguishable from self-interest. For all her corpulence and zeal, she is insubstantial and has "no private life whatsoever" (*C,* 171). She drowns trying to save herself by clutching frantically to Caroline Rose, whom she almost pulls down with her. The oppressive, self-serving effects of religious answers in late modernity could not, it seems to me, be more forcefully presented. Addiction to answers takes a secular form in the character of Tom Wells in *Robinson* (1958), who invades people's privacy in order to gain power over them. In his need to know, he not only violates personal space; he also wants to penetrate the mysteries of the universe and to predict the future. When placed in contrast to Robinson, the owner of the island, who identifies uncertainty and mystery with personal space, the reader can recognize Wells as consistent with a culture that it is Robinson's intention to resist.

A second characteristic of late modern society is the power of its images and roles over personal identity. In *The Public Image* (1968), Spark turns to the Italian movie industry and to the life of an actress, Annabel Christopher, who is undergoing another in a series of image-formations. She and her husband, also an actor, are being made over for public consumption into people who are formal by day and intensely erotic at night, an image that seems to reinforce Italian preconceptions of English people. Their lives are determined by images, and Annabel's husband avenges himself by attacking her public image.

Images have such social power because, among other reasons, they dissolve the mystery of personal space. For example, in *Not to Disturb* (1971), the Baron and Baroness Kopstock, during a stormy night, have secluded themselves in the library of their home with their secretary, the baroness's lover, and have asked not to be disturbed. The action of the novel is carried on by the staff and others in and around the house outside the library. While the emphasis is on the library—"not to disturb"—personal space is overshadowed by the image making of the people outside of it. The house staff and others project their various interpretations of what is going on in the library. Fabrication dominates the personal space of intimacy, love, and death, and, as it turns out, it epitomizes the larger context of Geneva outside. However comical its style, the novel is a pessimistic depiction of personal life exploited by social fabrications.

The power of social images is also due to the insubstantiality of reality. In *The Hothouse by the East River* (1973), Elsa Hazlett cannot distinguish real from imagined people. People in New York City seem specterlike. In contrast, the play her son produces, a version of "Peter Pan," gives her a sense of the real presence of someone she had known in the war. She calls her preference "persevering in a pretense," and it amounts to exchanging a bland reality for forceful images (*H,* 38).

The preference for pretense is characteristic of the whole society in *The Takeover* (1976). It bewilders the principal character, Maggie Radcliffe, because she is unable to distinguish authentic art from fakes, guests from thieves, or antiques from reproductions. It is a society that operates on the dictum of Hubert Mallindaine that "'appearances *are* reality'" and that "'reality is subjective'" (*T,* 102).

Social images, representations, and fabrications also dominate personal identity because people are unrelated to one another. The characters of *The Bachelors* (1960) live in London, that "great city" (the epithet alludes to the description of Nineveh in the Book of Jonah) (*B,* 9), and their lives, rather than personal and intimate, are simply lonely. London is a city of unattached people whose relations are determined by sexual, financial, and legal alignments. The reader is left to infer that the city creates a social space that dissolves attachments between people and between people and places. Personal times and spaces, such as Sunday afternoons at home, become empty and dreary.

Spark's most extreme depiction of a personal life drained of content is *The Driver's Seat* (1970). The principal character, Lise, who has been working as an accountant in a London bureaucracy, travels, like Thomas Mann's Aschenbach, to Italy, dressing brightly and hoping to meet someone exciting. The man she meets, Richard, attracts her as someone who may be willing not only to love her but to kill her, and with her help he does, cutting her throat during sex. There is nothing in Lise that the society has not been able already to colonize or discredit. The story testifies to a society powerful enough to control and finally to destroy personal identity.

A third characteristic of late modern society, in addition to its repression of questions in favor of answers and its power to absorb personal identity and particularity, is its ambivalent relation to the Second World War. For example, the integrity of characters in *Territorial Rights* (1979) is compromised by unacknowledged pasts, especially the history of Italians and Bulgarians during the Second World War. Lina Pancev, who is there to find the body of her father, who was murdered during the war, cannot locate it and cannot gather reliable information about the war. The characters in Venice, whether English, American, or Italian, have pasts they repress. The repressed past is often related, by Spark, to the Second World War, which lies concealed, like the bomb in *The Girls of Slender Means,* waiting to go off. However, along with repression of the war one also finds in her fiction a nostalgia for it. The culture of warfare seems preferable to the present because during the war people were unified by shared problems. This is the situation in *The Girls of Slender Means* and in *The Hothouse by the East River,* in which characters and events of the war have a reality that those in the postwar period lack. So also the environment of Jerusalem, which is unsettled by conflict, matches the complexities of Barbara Vaughn's personal identity in *The Mandelbaum Gate* (1965). But the postwar period in England, its relative prosperity and security, primarily diminishes personal identity and relationships.

Indeed, when persons or groups take on more positive characteristics in Spark's fiction, it is often because their positions in life resemble those of war. The old people in *Memento Mori,* for example, are not understood or appreciated by the society around them, and their families, eager for inheritances, wish they would die. They also live in fear of burglary and physical harm. As Miss Taylor puts it: "'Being over seventy is like being engaged in a war. All our friends are going or gone and we survive amongst the dead and the dying as on a battlefield'" (*MM,* 37). While characters under these conditions do not all achieve personal integrity and a sense of community, some of them do, especially those who are able to hear the telephone calls reminding them of mortality. Aged people living alone can take on battlelike qualities, too, as does Lady Edwinia, who is so much liked by Fleur Talbot, the principal character of *Loitering with Intent*.

Perhaps it is the warlike qualities marking the lives of criminals and political radicals that grant them positive evaluation in Spark's fiction. We saw this in the role of Effie in *The Only Problem*. Robert and Anna in *Territorial Rights* take up a Bonnie and Clyde life of crime and end as trainees in a Middle Eastern terrorist camp. Such drastic behaviors, in addition to their warlike qualities, may also play the kind of role that homosexuality plays in the fiction of Forster, namely, to expose a personal space by means of socially unacceptable or threatening acts. Terrorism still holds that potential, although it holds it in a way that is highly ambiguous and potentially too destructive to be advocated. The outlaw activity of Helena's mother in *The Comforters*, her involvement with diamond smugglers, by being less violent and by using sacred places as drop-off points, is more productive of a personal style. However, not all social deviance is productive of personal space, as can be seen by the forgeries and deceptions perpetrated by Hubert Mallindaine in *The Takeover*.

Late modern societies, then, by their impatience with uncertainty, preference for image over personal identity, and ambivalence toward war, threaten personal space. The question is whether that threat is met in the role and work of artists. The answer is mixed. Artists are often agents of social pressure. For example, Nicholas Farrington in *The Girls of Slender Means* (1963) tries to establish personal relations with single women in the May of Teck Club, but his motivations are exploitive. He desires the beautiful Selina Redwood, and he believes that another woman, Jane Wright, who works in publishing, can help him place his book manuscript. Nicholas makes headway toward integrity when he gives up his social ambitions and enters a religious order doing missionary work of some kind in Haiti.

The question of art's relation to personal integrity also arises in *Memento Mori* (1959). A rather full catalog of artistic interests is given, but art does not secure personal spaces. Guy Leet, a critic, is a parasite on art, and he seems more interested in the sexual contacts art provides than in art itself. Charmain Colston's fiction lacks particularization, and the realism of Eric Colston arises more from a bitterness he holds toward life than from an appreciation of particular realities. Art and the vocation of the artist do not form clear alternatives to society's power to absorb the personal and particular. This is true of all art forms, from architecture in *The Takeover* to the dinner parties given by the artist Hurly Reed in *Symposium*. When art plays a positive role in Spark's fiction, as it does, for example, by means of the poetry of Hopkins in *The Girls of Slender Means,* it is because of the attention art can draw to the details of life. Particulars give art its value; art does not necessarily confer particularity on things or on the artists.

Some of Spark's characters seek an alternative to social space in small communities. But the results are, at best, mixed. For one thing, small communities are often created and dominated by individuals. A clear example of this is *The Prime of Miss Jean Brodie* (1961). By constructing a common enemy of the administration and the rest of the school, disseminating lore concerning her romantic past, promoting secrecy among the group, and imposing uniformity, such as marching together or maintaining a certain posture, Miss Brodie creates not a community but an extension of herself. The girls become her representatives and surrogates, a process epitomized in their sitting for portraits that are really icons of herself. True, some of her efforts are defensible given economic depression, the gloomy atmosphere of the school and of Edinburgh between the wars, and the lack of adequate opportunities in the culture for young women to actualize their potentials. But the excesses of power are clearer. One encounters them in other small communities in Spark's fiction, such as the autobiographical group that Sir Quentin forms in *Loitering with Intent* (1981), the spiritualist group of *The Bachelors,* the fabricators of *Not to Disturb,* and the guests of *Symposium.*

The question of religion's role in securing personal space in contrast to social coercion in Spark's work is also not easily answered. Spiritualism in its many forms is consistently disparaged; it appears at best as only a compensation for the materialism of the culture. At worst it provides occasions for exploitation and control. The spiritualist sessions in *The Bachelors* are led by Patrick Seton, a man who has a long list of convictions for fraud and who has recently misappropriated the life savings of a widow with whom he had been intimate. In *A Far Cry from Kensington,* Hector Bartlett is associated with a black box that supposedly heals people, but the narrator is aware that this box, if it has power, has power to damage as well as to heal. Nature religion is also put under pressure. The principal example is in *The Takeover,* namely, Hubert Mallindaine's attempt to revive the cult of Diana.

This brings us, then, to the Catholic Church as a sponsor of personal integrity, but here, too, questions arise. Nancy Cowan in *The Takeover* counters the positive images of the church given by the Jesuit characters by warning that the church is involved with commercial interests that seem to compromise both its integrity and Italian society. In *The Prime of Miss Jean Brodie,* Sandy learns, when she enters the church, that there are fascists in it. And in *Memento Mori,* the priest has no interest in the old people and visits them only to perform last rites. The church seems as much affected by as it provides an alternative to modern society, and people who enter the church bring the culture with them.

However, Catholicism and the church are at times also positively viewed. For one thing, they offer a more viable religious orientation than spiritualist alternatives because the church affirms particulars and the quotidian. This is clear in *The Bachelors,* and the Irish Catholic Matthew Finch puts it well when he points out that heresies in the church have usually arisen when spiritual interests are divorced from actual particulars. The church also provides the setting for needed moral and spiritual changes in characters, although the changes are not narrated, as with Nicholas Farrington in *The Girls of Slender Means* and Sandy in *The Prime of Miss Jean Brodie.* Finally, the narrator of *Robinson* seems at home in the church because it takes an interest in tangible things and, in its attention to the Virgin, affirms femininity.

Personal space, we can conclude, is enhanced by the discipline of attention to particular things, and it is this discipline that warrants whatever authority the church, small communities, art, and exile have in Spark's fiction. Robinson, a Catholic, has strong interest in the particulars of his world. Ronald Bridges in *The Bachelors,* alienated from the culture and to a degree from the church because of his condition as an epileptic, believes that the spirituality of the church is preferable to that practiced by spiritualist groups because Catholic spirituality does not discount concrete particulars. The move of Maggie Radcliffe toward the end of *The Takeover* to a position of a pauper separates her from the world of appearance, which Hubert mistakes for reality, and yields a sense of internal rightfulness and truth. Attention to particulars forms a recurring pathway in these novels toward a sense of separation from social determinations. This is most pronounced in the interest shown by Sandy (*The Prime of Miss Jean Brodie*) in the transformation of the commonplace. This interest can become a discipline of attentiveness and a divestment of self-preoccupation. Babies at times elicit such attention, as in *The Only Problem* and *The Public Image.* Art does too, as with the poetry of Hopkins or the painting of de La Tour. Both art and religion are positively valued to the degree that they illuminate the discipline of attention to little things.

Attention to particulars also affects writing. It distinguishes the journal writing of the narrator in *Robinson* from Tom Wells's attempts in his writing to penetrate the future and to demystify life. And the narrator of *A Far Cry from Kensington,* an editor, has no use for the writing of Hector Bartlett, who is more interested in money and success than in accuracy. The recurring role in Spark's fiction of the poetry of Hopkins suggests both the combination of attention to the details of life, writing with integrity, and sacramental beliefs in the mysteries of particulars and the possibilities of personal space. It shapes the writing of Fleur Talbot in *Loitering with Intent*, a writing that contrasts with that of Sir Quentin's group, which, Fleur finds, is marked by nostalgia, paranoia, and a craving to be liked. Her own writing finds its source in affirmation and joy. This kind of writing and the disciplines upon which it depends place her in a questionable position relative to society, as though she were loitering with intent. She acts oddly, marginally, or in ways that arouse suspicion because she is not folded into the preoccupations of the society.

Personal space is clarified by exception, then, by finding and identifying with what the culture overlooks, represses, or denies. In a culture of certainty, control, comfort, and image, personal uncertainty and particularity are won at the cost of diligence and even pain. Identity is secured by reality and truthfulness. Attention to and delight in particulars or exceptions resemble ascetic disciplines that are able to lead persons to places free from the coercive forces of social space.

III

With the fiction of Muriel Spark, we engage narratives and place-relations that take into account a society increasingly determined by the mass media, representations, and duplication. These create a force too pervasive and powerful to allow characters or even narrators fully to escape from it by their attitudes or actions. Her depictions of late modernist society acquiesce to it by admitting no available spaces unaffected by it. By so doing, she describes late modernism in terms of surfaces and the power to turn everything into surface, a society endlessly self-reflective. The social space of surfaces, however, is haunted, and unseen voices play on minds grown either paranoid in it or, by virtue of its lacks, hungry enough to believe in spirits.

It is a mistake, I think, to theologize personal space and the search for it in Spark's fiction too quickly. I do not think that Spark should first of all be seen as a writer who depicts the world as she does because she comes at it with religious interests in personal space. The religious interests of characters and narrators in her work, rather than ends in themselves, are ways of granting access to personal spaces, to alternatives apart from the control of social space.

Religious quests for personal space take, as I have suggested, two forms, negative and positive. The negative form includes acts that take exception to society through dissonance, especially questioning, resisting, and suffering. The positive form is the re-creative work of transforming the commonplace, of seeing particular things differently, whimsically. Both taking exception and seeing things from the vantage point of the exception are consistent with her "nevertheless" principle. It is a principle that allows many of her characters a personal relation to their locations. It is a stance that exempts a person from the power of the Same and from the self-delusion and emptiness that submission to that power produces. The tendency of a society of surfaces to produce paranoia, the suspicion that behind the surfaces there is something more that wants to make contact or that has us under surveillance, can produce its counterpart, a suspicion of transcendent grace. The religious language of Spark's novels should be taken, then, not as an end in itself but as the language of an opposing social determination. Religious language provides her not an alternative arena but, rather, a way of articulating a human possibility.[4] In *Curriculum Vitae: Autobiography,* she says this about her preconversion beliefs: "I had no specific religion but at the same time I had a strong religious feeling. There were times when, listening to lovely music on the radio, looking at a fine picture in the Scottish National Gallery, reading or writing a poem, I was aware of a definite 'something beyond myself'" (*CV,* 115). The religious language of her fiction allows her to give substance and specificity to these possibilities.

While particular placement is secured primarily in relation to the transcendent, it cannot be dissociated from the physical and concrete. As she says: "One of the things which interested me particularly about the Church was its acceptance of matter. So much of our world rejects it. We're not happy with things. We want machines to handle them."[5] But the particular and concrete are discoveries more than recoveries, and they are brought into focus by spiritual disciplines. This is especially true of discovering the particularity of persons. She says that for her Christianity is oriented primarily to accounts of the person: "I take this attitude to Catholicism because it's really a Christian thing to me conducive to individuality, to finding one's own individual point of view."[6] That sense of the person combines vulnerability to the "beyond" and attention to concrete particulars, to "things." It is in this combination that the complexity of the person lies, and it is a complexity that religious language helps her to keep in focus. The two potentials of the person, concrete particularity and orientation to the transcendent, require and reveal one another. Seeing them in relation is consistent with the "sacramentalism" of Christian beliefs.[7] When this relation is secured, other relations follow from it. It is this emphasis that grants her work its own particularity. As one critic puts it, "She acknowledges and owes few literary debts and belongs to no school, group or movement; there is no one quite like her, and one rereads her novels in the hope of coming a little closer to their meaning."[8] Her own way of writing is similar to that of several of her characters, particularly Fleur Talbot in *Loitering with Intent.* "It is clear that although Fleur is glad of her desire and ability to write, it is life itself that is the source of her joy."[9] Important as religious language is for Spark's work, it defers to narrative discourse as the location where the convergence in human life of particulars and something more can be secured.[10]

The narrativization of personal space in her fiction, then, is primary. It locates characters who are relatively freed from the constraints and limits of society in places where the concrete particular and the beyond can be seen in their relationship. Personal places occasion this recognition. Once seen, the recognition alters everything. Personal or intimate space moves outward to the transformation of everything else. As with Forster, personal space is not a possession. It is the basis from which moral and spiritual potentials can challenge the domination and putative sufficiency of social space.

Spark's late modern social spaces are more resistant or absorbent toward personal space than are those of Forster. For Spark, late modern social space is pitted against personal and intimate space in an almost life-or-death struggle. Her brief, understated, and even elusive narratives reveal the terrifying prospect of the loss in late modern culture of the particular and the person, a loss that, she believes, would close access to the real and transcendent.

A theorist to whom later we shall turn, Maurice Blanchot, provides added weight and sharper point to Spark's discipline of personal space. He also articulates the coercions of the culture and the hazards of personal exits from it. Relying on Forster, Spark, and theorists of personal space like Bachelard and Blanchot, I shall be able, it is hoped, adequately to secure personal place-relations in their justified position within the repertoire of human spatiality.

Part Three

Toward a Narrative-Based
Theory of Place-Relations

7

The Three Kinds of Place-Relations

The task now is to gather from these narratives the contributions they can make toward an adequate theory of human spatiality and place-relations. Rather than stress, as I have been, the ways in which they differ from one another, the six writers and their fiction will be treated together as providing an incipient theory that can be extrapolated and placed in conversation with other theories about human spatiality and place-relations. The implicit theory has three components. The first is that place-relations are of three kinds.

The point that place-relations are of differing kinds is not in itself unusual. Several theorists assume or argue that this is the case. E. Relph, for example, distinguishes kinds of spaces on a continuum from direct experience to abstraction and includes six kinds, "primitive," "perceived," "existential," "architectural," "cognitive," and "abstract."[1] J. Nicolas Entrikin posits three kinds of space: subjective or local space; objective or global space; and, between them, cultural or communal space.[2] Robert Sack points out that "some places stress nature, others social relations, and still others meaning."[3] Per Raberg distinguishes kinds of spaces in this way: "The most large-scale schemata in this hierarchical structure are the geographic macro-level and the topographical landscape. An intermediate level is represented by the urban environment. At the end of the scale we find the microspace of the individual dwelling."[4] Yi-Fu Tuan locates kinds of place-relations between the contraries of "cosmos" and "hearth."[5] "Place exists," Tuan says, "at different scales. At one extreme a favorite armchair is a place, at the other extreme the whole earth. Homeland is an important type of place at the medium scale."[6] And Edward Soja, reworking the distinctions of Henri Lefebvre, posits three kinds of space: perceived space, conceived space, and lived or "thirdspace."[7] While these and other classifications have merit, I think that our narratives offer a more manageable and stable set of kinds and more fully emphasize their differential relations.

I begin, therefore, with the contention that the first component of an adequate theory of human place-relations is that they can be grouped into three kinds. While each kind contains an enormous variety of possible place-relations, each is also "sufficiently coherent to be considered as the *same* . . . as well as to be classified as places of certain *types*."[8] The three types determined by the fictional narratives are cosmic or comprehensive; social or political; and personal or intimate space. While each kind has its own defining characteristics, the three clarify one another by reason of their differences. As Henrietta Moore puts it, "To read [a space as though it were a text] is always to read in relation to other texts, [and] in relation to the codified mode of a culture's production of meaning."[9] The particular qualities of places, qualities both positive and negative, become discernible, then, for three reasons: by means of the qualities of the place with which a relation occurs, by means of comparing this kind of place with places of the same kind, and by means of comparing this place with places of the other two kinds.

The occlusion of other kinds of places seems to be more basic to a place-relation than the occlusion of places of the same kind. Indeed, a positive relation to any one kind of place may, even consciously, be enhanced by the fact that it resembles other places of that kind that also have positive characteristics. Places of differing kinds, however, even when they are positively juxtaposed, have more the impact of contrast than of similarity. The force and significance of one kind of place can noticeably be attributed to the fact that it is a place different from places of the other two kinds.

As we saw, the narratives of the six writers we studied, while all shaped by a language of place and space that is prominent if not dominant, differ from one another as to which of the three kinds of place or space is of chief significance. We should notice, however, that all of the texts draw attention to more than one kind of place-relation, even though for each writer one of the three is most important. This allows me to draw three working hypotheses. First, an adequate theory of place-relations will respect the particularity of each of the three parts that constitute the complex of human spatiality. While it appears that people differ from one another as to which of the three kinds of place-relations is most important, a theory that neglects one or more of the three kinds or transfers qualities from one kind to one of the other kinds is faulty and damages our understanding of human spatiality. Second, the value of a place-relation is a noticeable effect of its difference from place-relations of one or both of the other kinds, and the recognition of value bears an accompanying critical potential, namely, the ability granted by the differential relations of kinds of places to detect the negative characteristics of places and relations to them. Third, since the repertoire of place-relations includes three kinds, a fully developed human spatiality depends on the availability of all three kinds of place-relations. This requires the ability both to terminate and to initiate place-relations, and that ability requires mobility. This means that mobility, rather than being contrary to a full actualization of place potential, is indispensable to it.

I shall look at each kind of place-relation separately, discussing why each kind has become a problem in our own time and how that problem can be addressed so that each kind of place can more fully offer its positive potential.

Comprehensive Space and the Problem of Access

The narratives of Hardy and Greene, although different from one another in many other respects, can be yoked together as directing attention to cosmic or comprehensive space. Their narrators and characters attempt to retrieve or to search for place-relations that can be accessed outside of, prior to, between, or beyond places that are humanly constructed and controlled. Their narratives imply that modern problems of spatial disorientation and alienation can be addressed and the potentials of human place-relations actualized only if attention is first given to comprehensive place. Comprehensive space is established by these narratives as primary, and other kinds of place-relations must defer to and be corrected by relations to comprehensive space.

Since for both writers comprehensive space is sharply contrasted to spaces constructed and controlled by humans, it lacks specificity and predictability. It is a space encountered as unexpected, and this characteristic makes it both a threat and a gift. What makes comprehensive space salutary in narratives by both writers is that places of the other two kinds, especially social places, have become confining, despite their magnitude, and coercive, despite their latitude. The contrast created between comprehensive and social spaces carries an implied critique of the propensity in social space to presume the status of comprehensive space. The benefits of comprehensive place-relations arise largely from the contrast between such relations and the relations of predictability, constraint, and control that seem inevitable in social space.

Comprehensive space counters the pretentiousness of social spaces, especially large cities, in their assumptions of inclusiveness and carries a limiting and sobering effect on human excess. By clarifying the limits of human creation and control, comprehensive space also can allow human beings, even when they may in many ways differ, to feel a degree of kinship with one another and even with all living creatures. This is because cosmic or comprehensive space, unlike social space, is not perceived as structured by lines that include and exclude people.

For Hardy and Greene, modern social spaces have tended to exclude or supplant comprehensive space. Because social space has become so inclusive and powerful, accesses to cosmic or comprehensive space are located at the margins of social, political space, within interstices unincorporated by social and political structures, or at sites exposed by transitions.

A rough analogy to the interstices that provide access to comprehensive space in the fiction of Hardy and Greene is the space referred to by architects and designers as SLOIP, that is, space left over in planning.[10] Such space owes its definition to the limits of buildings and other planned areas; it lies at the edges or between planned spaces. If the analogy is extended, we can think of all social and political spaces as not comprehensive because they are constituted by particular structures of interest and coherence. What lies outside of or between those structures is SLOIP. It is noticeable at moments of transition, in gaps between structures, at the limits of institutions, and, especially in the fiction of Greene, at points of opposition between institutions. Access to comprehensive space appears when something has not been anticipated, when a human possibility or interest cannot be included, or when structures subvert their claims for totality by their dependent, contrary relations to one another. All planned, constructed, and controlled places create SLOIP between them or at their edges, and SLOIP can easily suggest a significant remainder or an access where unconstructed space becomes available.

A major question to raise about comprehensive place-relations concerns their relation to nature. While in *The Return of the Native* and *A Burnt-Out Case* we find characters in significant relations to natural places, nature cannot be assumed simply to be there. The heath and the forest, while distinguishable from social, economic, and political space, are affected by it. Nature has a culturally constructed significance and is not raw, awaiting refugees and pilgrims. While economic or political effects may be less obvious in natural space, they still are there. Natural space is not coterminous with comprehensive space, then. Only when human constructs, including cultural, economic, and political designs on nature, are bracketed can comprehensive space begin to appear.

Indeed, a significant move in the fictions of these two writers is to loosen cosmic or comprehensive space from identification with and dependence on nature. They depict nature in retreat. For Hardy, the heath is becoming more a memory to be retrieved than a contemporary reality to be encountered. But attention to the heath as it once was initiates a discipline of bracketing constructs, and this bracketing allows one to see the borders of those constructs and possible accesses to cosmic or comprehensive space, especially at points of transition and in times of "dubiousness." The spaces exposed by transitions, the narrator implies, can be discovered and hazarded not only in nature but wherever transitions, gaps, and interstices are encountered. Nor does Greene expect the denizens of modern Western culture to leave it all behind for ventures into the forests of Central Africa. But distant places can reveal, if not Western culture's limits, at least its odd and frazzled edges. There, too, the peculiarly destructive and coercive effects of modern cultural constructions can more fully be seen. Even if only by the imagination, positioning oneself at the border of Western control can bracket social space. A principal accomplishment of the fiction of Hardy and Greene, then, is not only to affirm the primacy of comprehensive place-relations but also to narrate ways by which those place-relations can be realized despite the retreat of nature. Nature is exposed at the margins of modern culture, and while not itself comprehensive space, it provides occasions for moving to a comprehensive space implied by it.

Henri Lefebvre makes clear that nature is in retreat because it has been subsumed in the modern West by social, economic space. Nature is now part of business, for example. Sun and sea, mountains and tropical islands are poster material and are incorporated by the culture of acquisition and accumulation. For Lefebvre the loss of nature poses a serious problem: "But today nature is drawing away from us. . . . It is becoming impossible to escape the notion that nature is being murdered by 'anti-nature'—by abstraction, by signs and images, by discourse, as also by labour and its products. Along with God, nature is dying."[11] He regrets the withdrawal or death of nature because nature can challenge the kind of space characteristic of modern societies, namely, mental space, space that is general, uniform, and without particular qualities. Nature in its particularities, arbitrary juxtapositions, and centrifugal effects is contrary to the prevailing tendency of social space constructed for purposes of accumulation and control. He points to the success of urban spaces to conceal their actual dependence on pieces of land and to exchange natural spaces for homogeneous volumes of vacant architectural space. Everything, as he says, conspires to inflict harm on nature, to isolate, conceal, and destroy it; "nature is now seen as merely the raw material out of which the productive forces of a variety of social systems have forged their particular spaces."[12] Against this onslaught, nature has no recourse and has largely been defeated, awaiting now its ultimate end. Rather than imposing limits to human control, nature is at best a temporary obstruction to the extension of that control.

While I agree with Lefebvre that much in modern culture conspires to extinguish nature's force and significance and its potential standing as an alternative to social, political space, I agree more with the fiction of Hardy and Greene. Nature, while it cannot be taken as synonymous with comprehensive space, continues to operate in our culture as a trope for a location that directs attention to what precedes, comprehends, and/or supports humanly constructed and controlled places. Peter Coates, for example, points out in *Nature* that the word has been used from ancient to modern times as signifying what was not humanly made and what provides the supporting, cosmic background for human life.[13] As D. W. Meinig says, "Nature is fundamental only in a simple literal sense: nature provides a stage."[14] I take him to mean by this that human spatiality requires a component that locates human constructions in relation to a space that they do not themselves provide. Human locations are dependent upon a spatiality that precedes and outstrips their constructions. Robert Sack agrees. He argues that nature, in our cultural history, has been tied closely to justice and truth because the natural connotes not only what lies beyond our control but also what relates us as persons to the most extensive context of our lives.[15]

Rather than use the term "nature" to indicate comprehensive space, Meinig prefers "landscape" as indicating an inclusive spatial category.[16] Landscape conveys the sense of spatiality that is primary, fundamental, and enduring.[17] As he puts it, "In this view landscape lies utterly beyond science, holding meanings which link us as individual souls and psyches to an ineffable and infinite world."[18] However, as Per Raberg points out, comprehensive space also has an enclosing potential. We give "our environment a visual outer boundary. This boundary very often consists of existing natural formations which we label as spatial signals."[19] Without such a sense of boundary or enclosure, comprehensive space, as Yi-Fu Tuan points out, "though liberating, can be bewildering and threatening."[20]

One can, however, err on the other side by taking nature or landscape not as a trope but as a kind of space devoid of the human. W.J.T. Mitchell warns against such abstraction, against relating large vistas to transcendence in order to occlude their ties to particular peoples and histories.[21] Comprehensive, cosmic space is also a kind of place with which, actually or potentially, we have a relation, and we cannot have relations apart from language and culture. However, while I take Mitchell's point about ignoring social, political space when considering cosmic or comprehensive space, I also counter theories of social, political space that allow such space to displace or conceal cosmic or comprehensive space. Anne Buttimer culturally establishes comprehensive place-relations by describing in detail various metaphors in Western cultural history for understanding the most inclusive context for human life, world as a "mosaic of forms," as "mechanical system," as "organic whole" (a metaphor, incidentally, that seems closest to "nature"), and as "arena of events."[22]

Amidst the qualifications and alternative tropes relevant to locating cosmic, comprehensive space, we should notice that the "natural" for us today, as for Hardy and Greene, continues to suggest what precedes human constructions and upon what our constructions depend. The fact that the word "natural" helps to sell products reveals both how thoroughly the category has been secularized by the market and how tenacious the qualities of goodness and reliability in "natural" as opposed to "artificial" are. Because of the importance of nature as a trope for access to comprehensive space, it should, as long as possible, be retained. Indeed, the moral and spiritual potentials of current environmental movements to draw attention in more tangible ways to the comprehensive context of our lives are as important as the long-term consequences they carry for the viability of the natural environment and our material survival.

Lefebvre calls for attitudes and actions that would help to retain a cultural language of natural space. One is to treat nature not as the general environment but as a variety of specific locations affected by modern societies in particular ways. A second move is to abstain from defining nature primarily in terms of its laws or design, since such notions validate the theories and planning that we so willingly impose on it.[23] We should, he urges, emphasize the complexity and even disorder of nature, its hidden, even "uterine" realities.[24] In its retreat and even in its dying, nature continues to provide access to, retrievable memories of, and tropes for comprehensive place-relations.[25]

However, as we have seen, Hardy and Greene lead us past uses of natural space toward accesses to comprehensive space provided by margins, interstices, and transitions. While nature suggests something that precedes and outstrips human constructions, margins, interstices, and transitions suggest the limits of human constructions, their incompleteness and mutual dependence. Attention to such elusive locations removes the obligation of establishing nature as some kind of prior, separate, and necessary category that is indispensable for accessing comprehensive space.

When we turn from nature to gaps, margins, or transitions as principal accesses to a spatiality that precedes and outstrips human constructions, we are aided by anthropologist Victor Turner's *The Ritual Process*.[26] Turner gives attention to in-between places within ritual processes that participants enter, places defined by being incorporated neither in the structure that precedes the ritual nor in the structure subsequent to it. His general term for such places is "liminality." Liminality provides an interim separable from the social structures that stand on either side of it, and it thereby takes on a significance and power of its own. It becomes the location from which the constructions of society arise, the potential that antedates human constructions and upon which they depend. Liminality exposes the always present but usually hidden base of all human structures and differentiations. Liminal places, of which one is reminded by the guarded thresholds of shrines, are also hazardous and threatening because they are unstructured and undesignated. Turner extends liminality and its relation to the structures of a society by identifying it not only between structures but also at their edges, with what is deemed by society to be marginal or even worthless.

I have reservations about Turner's treatment of this topic. The rhetorical force of his description is to define cosmic or comprehensive space not only by means of the differences between it and humanly constructed spaces but also by the suggestion that all unconstructed or liminal spaces are the same, indicating a shared base from which all human constructs are derived. Hardy and Greene make clear, in contrast, that relations to comprehensive space are tied to the particular kinds of accesses that people discover or receive. However, I agree with Turner's general point that all human constructions create margins, leave gaps, and cannot wholly contain transition. These points or sites form potential accesses to comprehensive place-relations because they grant persons the possibility to get out from under or stand aside from the dominance and presumed inclusiveness of space determined by human constructions.

I also disagree with Turner's assumption that one can distinguish clearly from one another constructed space and liminal, sacred space. As I shall say in my conclusion, it is not possible clearly to juxtapose nonsacred and sacred space since the binary both conceals their relation and makes access from one to the other questionable. What is needed instead is an account of human spatiality that would allow the distinctions between nonsacred and sacred to arise from the repertoire of positive human place-relations.

One component of such an adequate theory of place-relations is the language of cosmic or comprehensive space. Retrieving or reconstructing it requires at least three actions. First, it requires attention to the language both of natural space and of gaps, margins, and transitions relative to humanly constructed places. Hardy and Greene grant vitality to such language and allow it to posit sharp contrasts to social and personal spaces. They accentuate its distinctive, corrective, and forceful role. The implied critique of the language of social space provided by attention to natural and interstitial spaces is striking. The specific and vital role of this language is to grant and sustain a cultural awareness of cosmic or comprehensive space, a space that is not simple and homogeneous but variously and intermittently powerful and significant, a space that antedates, grounds, and outstrips human constructions.

Second, reconstitution of the language of cosmic or comprehensive space requires a presumption of its referential potential. Since this language does not have something specific, especially a human construct, as its signified, its referential potential is weak. It is important to affirm that when we use the language of comprehensive space, as whenever our location in its widest and most inclusive terms is being described, we take that which is indicated to exist. What is needed is an imaginary of the cosmic or comprehensive, primarily by means of bracketing the languages of social and personal spaces. This imagining can begin with but, as in Hardy and Greene, cannot be coextensive with what we mean by nature.

Finally, the reconstitution of comprehensive space requires narrative. This means accounts of why and how people hazard the risks of retrieving and searching for comprehensive place-relations. Narratives can revitalize the language of comprehensive space, and they can designate the sites of, accesses to, and relations with it. The language of comprehensive space needs to be delivered not only from the tyranny of abstractions and detachments, of what Lefebvre calls "mental space," but also from the curse of vagueness and weakness in force and meaning. The narrativization of comprehensive place-relations can help to do that.

The language of comprehensive space continues, despite its increasingly minority status, as a recurring aspect of narrative discourse. It is a responsibility of critics and theorists to enhance such narratives with analysis and commentary that will increase and refine their potential contribution to the formation of a more adequate human spatiality. Natural sites and spaces, accessed at the edges or in the gaps of our constructions, need to be retrieved and revalued in and by narratives already with us and still to come and, just as much, by our reception and treatment of them.

Social Space and the Problem of Size

Social place-relations pose a problem not of access but of totalization. Social space, especially because of its inevitable inclusion of economic and political factors, tends to conceal, swamp, or determine both comprehensive and personal or intimate spaces. As Fredric Jameson puts it, "the prodigious new expansion of multinational capital ends up penetrating and colonizing those very precapitalist enclaves Nature [which I have been discussing under "comprehensive space"] and the Unconscious [which is Jameson's substitute for personal or intimate space] which offered extraterritorial and Archimedean footholds for critical effectivity."[27] There is, in the work of all our writers, agreement that social space in modern culture threatens to take over the role of comprehensive space, has dictated the conditions of intimate space, and, by so doing, has occupied those locations from which, otherwise, checks and critiques of social space could be sponsored. Those writers who take comprehensive or intimate space as primary must establish their viability and integrity despite the size and force of modern social spaces. And Conrad and Golding, for whom social space is primary, must construct social spaces that are possible alternatives to those typical of the culture, that is, those that are self-totalizing. In other words, our writers would be unwilling to concede Jameson's point that the effort to construct or project social spaces that do not occlude comprehensive space or swamp personal space is bound to be fruitless and Quixotic.

The fictions of Conrad and Golding, then, challenge modern social spaces and imply or project alternatives. Conrad does this primarily by relating the size and power of modern social spaces to their dependence on abstract, formal relations. The tendency toward abstraction makes social spaces not only increasingly self-enclosed and divorced from and unresponsive to their physical contexts but also impersonal and lifeless. The implied corrective is to relate social spaces more fully to material conditions, especially to physical labor, to make them more responsive to changing circumstances, to consider Western social spaces as specific to their culture rather than universal, to have a higher regard for the diversity of people and interests that constitute social spaces, and to allow social spaces to be marked by uncertainty and self-criticism.

Golding's critique of social spaces in Western culture, while also emphasizing their abstract character and dominating size, emphasizes the importance of innovation and movement in social space and the role of visionaries, principally artists, for providing the impetus and direction for change. In addition, the kind of social space that appears to be advocated in his fiction is one in which differences are not absorbed by some amorphous whole but, rather, one in which differences are unified by and toward some social goal. Vision and goal, in his work, give place to, rather than repress, social contraries and tensions.

The treatment of social space in modern culture by these writers discloses how distorted social spaces become when they are all-inclusive, abstract, and rigid. It can also be said that the distortions in modern social spaces seem, as we move from an early modernist like Conrad to a late modernist like Golding, to become more severe. Conrad's depictions take the form of early detection, diagnosis, and warning. The absorption of social space by the abstractions of economic, linguistic, and bureaucratic interests and attitudes, while advanced, is not complete; the examples offered by his fiction depict, by virtue of their extremities, projected stages of a condition that will become general if advanced warnings go unheeded. But in Golding's work the situation is more severe. He employs images of disintegration and destruction to indicate that the present situation is irremediable. New social arrangements are required, and risks must be taken if a reconstitution of social space is to occur. Without a sense of direction and a creative relation to the future, the energies and skills of a society have no reason to be related to one another and are not mobilized toward purposes that advance a society. When that happens, creative potential sours and energy is used to prevent change and to keep differing kinds of people in the society from interacting with one another. Without a vision a society perishes because without a vision social structures become ends in themselves, and social resources are expended in acts either of retaining the social structure or attacking it. Mobilization, dynamism, and cooperation occur when a common enterprise, a creative, positive, forward-directing goal, is advanced by social visionaries and followed.

Golding's elevation of the social visionary may strike the reader in an age marked by the effects of tyrants and dictators as too risky to accept. But it is reasonable to argue that if charismatic figures can lead large groups and even nations to destructive ends, the solution is not necessarily to eschew the potentials of all leadership, as though it is power itself that is evil. It may mean, rather, a support of leaders who inspire people to creative, just, and edifying goals. In addition, the dangers of massive evils resulting from lemminglike allegiance to an impressive figure can be checked by an emphasis on smaller, differing groups and leaderships. It would be better, though less dramatic, to call for ways of granting real but local, temporary, and partial authority to the work of artists, visionaries, and political officeholders for the redirection, revitalization, and reintegration of particular social spaces.

One characteristic of modern social space that Conrad and Golding put clearly before us and subject to critique is its domination by rationality. The consequence of that domination is to make the placements of people and the distinctions between their positions not only formal and impersonal but fixed and ends in themselves. This characteristic of modern social spaces can hardly, in my opinion, be overestimated. The binding of social space to rational categories produces what Lefebvre calls mental space. One way of displaying how human relations become subject to formal and rational relations is to follow Conrad's cue in *The Secret Agent* and to describe modern social spaces as epitomized by bureaucracies.

In his *Economy and Society*, Max Weber distinguishes bureaucratic from traditional and charismatic forms of authority as power that justifies itself not on the basis of inheritance or personal strength but on rationality.[28] Each office in a bureaucracy holds a defined place within a rational structure, and it has that location, that "jurisdictional area," regardless of its holder. Bureaucratic hierarchy moves from particularity of function upward toward increasing generality. The rationality of bureaucracy privileges information as the material appropriately processed by it, and offices within the bureaucracy find their reality principle in their data.

Once in place, a bureaucracy cannot easily be modified. Since it is rationally structured and efficient, criticism of it will appear irrational and changes will threaten efficiency. Changes, in a word, are acceptable only if they serve to make a bureaucracy more bureaucratic. Nor are bureaucracies vulnerable to interventions from those in highest office. Those at the apex of the pyramid have and exercise their power not by their effect over the rest—the structure is a system of interlocked offices that controls its component parts—but by the more general and abstracted work they do. The system virtually runs itself. Moreover, a fully developed bureaucracy outstrips in its complexity the capacity of any one person or even group to comprehend it. The bureaucracy finally "knows" more than do its potential critics, whether they arise from without or from within.

Bureaucracy, although designed by human reason and constrained by principles of rationality and efficiency, becomes a determining, inclusive, and impersonal social environment that outstrips human potentials to limit, change, or control it. It epitomizes and warrants a powerfully determining, self-perpetuating, and proliferating social environment, and, as an expression of a rational culture, it fosters an authoritative way of organizing and deploying human energies and interests. Social spaces determined by bureaucracy are defined not by the particularity provided by physical location, by the differing kinds of people who constitute them, or by their goals but by homogeneity, a propensity toward extension, and a capacity to absorb. Social spaces, then, gradually lose the specificity that particular location, formation, and leadership would provide them.

Modern social spaces, especially because of the importance for them of bureaucracy, are closely tied in modernity to space imagined as neutral, universal, and homogeneous. Society becomes an abstract container, close in standing and primacy to notions of absolute space such as advanced by Newton. Social space becomes a mental category by which diverse spaces within a society are brought into relation to one another and subjected to an overall rational structure. The ability of this understanding of social space to accommodate the extensions created by the widening communication, transportation, and commercial relations between urban centers strengthens its authority. And when economic interests rearrange world societies into one huge and complex market, the authority of economic exchange provided by mental space is too overwhelming to resist.

Social space rationally projected becomes so normalized that it begins to represent not a particular kind of order but order itself, an order consistent with human rationality. For this reason, as Timothy Mitchell shows, European societies could assume that Western social order was not order of a particular kind but a universal that could be imposed on societies that, by lacking that kind of order, could be thought of as chaotic.[29] And William Pietz shows how by the early eighteenth century, Western societies viewed alternative social structures as irrational and needing radically to be altered if relations, especially economic relations, with and within them were to be established.[30]

Social space is so easily related to mental space also because social theorists, especially due to the influence of Auguste Comte, analyze and theorize social structures and patterns of behavior in neutral, constant, and abstract terms. Indeed, the very idea of society, as Mitchell with particular attention to Durkheim points out, rests on a notion of an encompassing, a priori container that houses the particular spaces of a society, confers on particular groups their places, and gives to all of them a shared coherence.[31]

Finally—and this is a point particularly close to the heart of Lefebvre's work—the identification of social with mental space is accomplished by the increasing ability to define society economically. Modern social systems are governed by markets that sever products from particular sites and place them together in relation not to those sources but to one another. This is made possible, among other things, by discrediting actual sources and productive capacities, particularly labor, in the name of the primacy of a general, homogenizing, and abstract space, the market as mentally conceived and projected.

The identification of social with what Lefebvre calls mental space is largely due, in all of these instances, to the fact that social spaces are primarily constructed by invisible lines of exclusion and inclusion. These lines, in a positive social space, are more enabling than restrictive. They serve to bring people together in ways they could not individually invent, and these created associations are potentially enriching both for the persons so located and for the vitality and complexity of the social whole. The problem is that in modern social spaces these lines of inclusion and exclusion are less enabling than restricting and determining for the lives of people. They separate people from one another by such categories as class, race, gender, and ethnic or religious identity, and these distinctions carry strong connotations of value and power.

Given the problems posed by present social spaces, two tasks become urgent. The first, to which attention has already been called, is to check the dominance of social spaces by designating them as only one of three kinds of equally important and powerful place-relations. The second task, to which we now turn, is to expose the fact that all social spaces are particular, relative, and dynamic.

162 | Toward a Narrative-Based Theory of Place-Relations

Social spaces are always particular human constructs that cannot be identified with human rationality and thought of as universally extendable. Lefebvre's argument that social spaces are produced counters these errors because it stresses not only the particularity of social spaces but also their relation to intention and labor. Social spaces are not self-evident or self-sustaining. They are consequences of particular human decisions and actions on particular resources.

Lefebvre questions why people allow social spaces that are their own constructions to become controlling containers. His answer is that such manipulation and control would not be possible unless sops of some kind were thrown to people in response to their demands and protestations, "replacement fulfillments" for their vital interests.[32] But it could also be said, as Bourdieu suggests, that people turn to social places to which they are assigned and develop relations with them, relations that have content, even moral content.[33] In other words, negative social spaces exist by exploiting the need that people have for positive social place-relations. A third explanation is that modernity sponsors the subjection of location to use and means. Rather than relating to locations, people use them. Consequently, social spaces are not detected as deficient when they lack real or potential significance and simply provide people, individually and in small groups, the means to prosecute their own interests and goals. The pursuit of particular interests and styles may at times indicate, as Michel de Certeau argues, improvised, temporary personal spaces, but exceptions may also be no more than ways by which social determinations are retained by thrown sops.[34] The inclusive social whole retains its authority by providing the means by which individuals and groups can pursue within limits some particular interests and styles.

The largely invisible lines by which social spaces are constructed find their counterpart in the highly visible places that constitute what Lefebvre calls monumental space, that is, space marked by buildings that represent the legitimacy and power of the lines of distinction and exclusion that grant social space its structure. Monumental space conveys the message that distinctions and separations created by the social structure are secondary to the inclusive power and significance represented by official buildings and places for commemorative displays. Monumental spaces provide the aura of concreteness, permanence, and legitimacy to arrangements that are conventional and subject to change. As he says, "Thus each monumental space becomes the metaphorical and quasi-metaphysical underpinning of a society, this by virtue of a play of substitutions in which the religious and political realms symbolically (and ceremonially) exchange attributes . . . the authority of the sacred and the sacred aspect of authority . . . mutually reinforcing one another in the process."[35]

Monumental spaces, once dominated by religious structures, are dominated in the modern period by buildings dedicated to political power and beliefs. Beginning in the nineteenth century and increasingly in the twentieth, political monuments have been displaced by monumental buildings for housing and affirming economic authority in the structuring of social space.

If social space exhibits negative qualities when it controls people, isolates them from one another, and forces them into arbitrary units, the positive potential of social place-relations is to elicit from persons their distinctive contributions to the construction of a life that is richer than could be provided by and for individual persons or small groups. Crucial to the construction of such social spaces is the belief that human activities and interactions are basic to social structure and not determined by it. Primacy in positive social place-relations, then, is held by human potentials, activities, and relationships and not by the structure that gives them order.

This means that in positive social place-relations order is enabling and flexible. Social space is fashioned in response to the abilities, interests, and activities of people rather than abstracted from or imposed on them. Some social scientists see change and flexibility as neglected aspects both of social theory and of modern societies themselves. Anthony Giddens, for example, militates against this neglect, which he sees as taking its most extreme forms in social theories formed under the aegis of structuralism. He uses the term "structuration" to introduce temporality and change into social order.[36] Theories like that of Giddens allow for a fuller consideration of what can and should be altered in our understandings of social space.

Many social theorists, however, are pessimistic about changes in modernist societies. Lefebvre's pessimism is based on social space identified with mental space, absolutism, and the ever-extending markets of advanced capitalism. His pessimism is shared by other cultural analysts, and it even becomes cynicism. A good example is the work of the French sociologist Jean Baudrillard. The rhetoric of his argument is determined by what could be called the logical force of the synecdoche. What Baudrillard often does is to take a particular aspect of the social space characteristic of late modernity and to see that particular as epitomizing the whole. For example, in his *America* he takes freeways, even more particularly interchanges on freeways, as representative of the whole.[37] Drivers are directed not by their sense of left and right or east and west, say, but by signs. Signs take the place of physical orientation. Without minimizing the importance of his many insights into late modernist societies, I would also say that the presumptive totality of social space is reinforced by Baudrillard's work, since he has little appreciation of other kinds of place-relations as critical alternatives by which the domination of human spatiality by social space, especially by its means of transportation and communication, could be countered. One finds a similar form of argumentation with similar results in the work of Fredric Jameson.

While I minimize neither the present homogenizing and totalizing of social space nor the force of ideologies designed to maintain them, I think that the logic of cultural analyses such as these and the cynicism from which they arise and that they support must be questioned. As David Harvey points out, they concede to social space so conceived what it most wants, its own logic, universality, and irreversibility.[38] These discourses focus on transportation, commerce, and communication as so determining social space as to force particular places to lose their distinctiveness and to be incorporated by an abstract world network of economy and means. Furthermore, by being quantifiable and universal, information and its communication become reality, a kind of actual absolute.

What is called for to open up alternatives to the present direction and perception of social space, in addition to recognizing the primacy of human activities and relationships and identifying the means and goals of social change, is to relativize social spaces. This means taking large social spaces not first of all in their totality but in their diverse particularities, seeing them as aggregates of many social spaces formed into federations. A "society" is actually constituted by many social spaces, and the most inclusive, although it often is so taken, should not be understood as primary despite the fact that all people, however much they identify themselves with smaller social units within it, are also part of the larger whole. Social spaces are formed by distinctions and relations that penetrate one another.[39] This means that social spaces should not be analyzed and interpreted as single texts, since they are composed of many texts.[40]

Gillian Rose has criticized the entire project in social, especially urban, geography for its privileging whole and homogeneous at the expense of particular and differing social spaces. She argues that one of the features of Marxist social analysis that, by all means, should be retained is its recognition of differentiations between locations.[41] She argues that social geography persists in favoring the all-inclusive in the face of a growing number of scholars who, for differing reasons, are able and willing to see "that cities are divided along increasing numbers of social axes, and that this results in a growing diversity of spaces." Rose singles out feminist geographers as those who "are understanding the contemporary city not as the increasing fragmentation of a still-coherent whole, but rather in terms of a challenge to that omniscient vision [of hegemonic geography] and its exclusions."[42]

These characteristics of positive social spaces, namely, their responsiveness to human activities and interests, their dynamic character, and their particularity, can be identified and articulated in narrative discourse. Narrative discourse can relate social spaces to the complex of human potentials, to other kinds of human place-relations, and to norms as to what in social space harms and what helps human relations and cooperative human activities. The narrativization of social space counters the authority of mental space, that is, space as unconstructed, unalterable, homogeneous, and universal. Narratives can give attention to the particularity of social places. The narrativization of social spaces formed by people who are not fully integrated into the larger society—formed, for example, by ethnic behavior and values, by opposition or nonconformity, or by festivals and play—can be subversive of the present habits of construing modern social space as uniform, totalizing, and unalterable.

Social spaces must be understood as particular material or physical locations. But social spaces are also projections of hope and desire, and they have an effect on the human spirit. Social spaces have not only their own force but also their own real or possible significance for human potential. When the complexity and particularity of social spaces become recognized, narratives can begin to take a more positive, mimetic stance toward social space. For now, narrative discourses must largely continue to expose the threats that modern social spaces pose for human well-being and recall or project possible countersites to them.

Another way of saying this is that narratives should have the kind of importance for our understanding and depicting social space that is now held by maps. The mapping of social spaces, especially of cities, privileges abstraction and the total grid. We need to augment maps with stories. Maps can affect social place-relations in ways similar to the effect on human temporality posed by standard time and clocks. While we need not—indeed cannot—get on without maps and clocks, their partial and abstract roles ought always to be kept in mind. Narrative space and narrative time are powerful and meaningful counters to the effects of abstraction created by clocks and maps.

Intimate Space and the Problem of the Personal

The narratives of Forster and Spark, with all of the differences between them, clarify place-relations that foster personal identity and intimate relations. For both writers, personal place-relations are crucial to the actualization of human potential and integrity, and their absorption or displacement by social spaces in the modern West, especially social spaces that are impersonal and homogeneous, is an alarming prospect. The principal difficulty for both writers is designating the personal. They do not, for example, define it in terms of ownership or privacy. In *Howards End*, houses are owned by the

Wilcox family, but ownership primarily reveals how fully people are identi-fied with spaces as socially and economically defined and defining. While people do construct their identities by means of property, these identities lack integrity. And in *The Only Problem,* Harvey's ownership of the house in the northeast of France is preliminary to the work of securing his own particularity and integrity in a society that is bent on dissolving them into categories. While it is important to have what Virginia Woolf called a room of one's own, possession can be more a deferral to the power of social space than an exception to it.

In addition, personal space is not defined by these writers only as contrary to social space. Rather than only negative, the force and significance of personal places are positive and distinctive. They are places that enhance the potentials of persons and of personal relationships that have content of their own. Indeed, personal space would be unable to take its place in an adequate theory of place-relations if it had no characteristics of its own. But this requirement presents a difficulty because personal or intimate places must to a large degree elude categorization. The particularity of personal integrity and relationships is threatened when they are generally described. While this is true, as well, of each of the other two kinds of place-relations, relations that are comprehensive and social are shared and suggest inclusiveness. But personal or intimate places are largely hidden. This means that they are recognizable, more than is the case with the other kinds of place-relations, analogously, that is, by similarities and contrasts between what is described and kinds of relations that the reader also has experienced.

Third, personal and intimate places, while needing to be clarified prima-rily by positive potentials that distinguish them from the other kinds, also have negative potentials. As comprehensive space can have the negative ef-fect of placing a person in so vast an arena that orientation is lost, and as the structure of social space can grant a person a stronger sense of exclusion than inclusion, so personal space has a negative potential. All three kinds carry negative possibilities. As Alan Thomas puts it, "Places may be vari-ously valued: thus, spaciousness may elate or terrify; small enclosures may be sought-after refuges, wombs where the spirit may be reborn, or they may be prisons, the place of despair and death; a forest may be a sheltering grove or a dark wood to get lost in, a place of freedom or of horror; and a garden may harbor earth's delights or earth's poisons."[43] However, the negative potentials of personal places are particularly complex. They carry, for ex-ample, direct relations to gender politics. Personal and intimate places have become, especially since the beginning of the nineteenth century, locations to which an increasingly male-dominated social space has assigned women. They have become, therefore, sites for confinement, implicit prisons. However, it is also the case that personal space for this very reason has been undervalued. Because it is associated with women, "the domestic is not addressed as the Other of public space—it is ignored," as Gillian Rose points out. Spatial theory is conflicted in regard to personal places because they are both "sites of oppression," as Rose puts it, and underappreciated locations because women tend to occupy or preside over them.[44] Spatial theories, especially theories of social space, that discount the importance of personal places cannot be taken as free from gender bias. What needs to be done is both to theorize the importance of personal or intimate places for all human beings and to identify those features of personal spaces that may contribute to their becoming enabling and liberating instead of repressive and confining.

Finally, the problem of personal place is aggravated by the standing of individuality in modern culture. Individuality, while a staple of the culture, is largely illusory or ideological. A theory of personal places must distinguish the person from the individual, and it does so by clarifying that personhood is not a given but is a consequence of relationships, including relations with places. The personal is actualized in relations both with other persons and with places.

The difficulties of defining personal places are, then, no less daunting than those associated with comprehensive and social places. But these difficulties should not dismiss those who address them as nostalgic, naively humanistic, or bourgeois. Forster and Spark, instead, point the way toward affirming that personal places can still be found, places that nurture identity, and that personal identity and relationships require places for their discipline and development. The need for and the benefits of personal places may be greater than we realize.

Gaston Bachelard in *The Poetics of Space* provides a theory of particular places for personal nurture. His theory helps to elaborate the kind of place-relations that are central to the fiction of Spark and, even more, of Forster.

Bachelard's basic point, one particularly relevant to *Howards End*, is that memories, with all of the import that they carry for a sense of continuity, identity, and worth in personal life, have a spatial more than a temporal quality. While we also remember things as having occurred at certain times, we remember more clearly where they occurred. In fact, early memories are "housed"; they are distinguished from and related to one another more by space than by time. This housing of memories, while not identical to the houses in which we grew up, derives much from them.[45] Among the qualities of the house that Bachelard finds most important is the contrast between up and down. The house's verticality is central, and the values of locations are affected by the range from basement to roof. We go down to the basement and up to the attic, and the two extremes have contrasting qualities. The solid geometry of carpentry and the sense of security and simplicity it imparts grant the attic its significance, while the grounding of the house and the darkness of the subterranean basement give a sense of foundation.[46] Bachelard supports his description of the housing of memories not with a theory of psychic structure but with an emphasis on the various contributions that differing parts of a house can make to the sense people have of places as distinctive in value and force.

While he privileges the past by his discussion of the relation of place to the formation of memories, Bachelard also relates personal or intimate space to the future. Houses frame the sense of personal possibility. We tend to think of personal possibilities as related to some kind of place or housing. Often we think of the future in terms of a dream house. The fact that we can imagine our house of the future variously, that we can project many desirable locations, reveals that we can imagine several, sometimes conflicting futures for ourselves.[47] This desire for housing of a new and better kind is not merely ambition or a desire for accumulation or self-expansion. It is a desire for a location that will allow latent potentials of the person or between persons to be actualized.

Bachelard clarifies the human need and capacity for personal attachments to place most fully in his discussion of the role of particular places within the house. He suggests a set of concentric forms of human relations to personal places, and the centermost form can be located in the relation children develop with very particular, often hidden places in the house. Such special, perhaps secret locations are retreats or places where personal treasures are kept. Sometimes these are locked places, and Bachelard relates the child's fascination with locks and keys to this desire and need for a personal place rather than to an incipient interest in sexuality.[48] The force of these places can be calculated not by the public worth of what is stored there but, instead, by the relation of such valued places to the child's sense of personal worth. A specific and secure location anchors or validates a child's growing sense of personal worth. This need and potential for a relation to personal places continues with us. A culture that militates against the attachment of people to places of particular, personal worth either threatens their identity and self-worth or else forces the value of personal life to become entirely internal and unsubstantiated.

Bachelard implicitly deploys his theory of the indispensable role of personal place against Bergson and the early Heidegger. It is obviously Heidegger that he has in mind when he contends that we are not cast into the world but placed in it, put into a place that was prepared for us by parents.[49] This means that our primordial experiences are more related to place than to time, and for early experience place has a positive meaning. Life begins in relations, including relations to a significant, protected, and integrated location. Implied as well is a move to counter Bergson, for whom personal experience is temporally defined and for whom spatialization has depersonalizing consequences. Bachelard secures positive place-relations as both primordial and personal.

However illuminating it may be, Bachelard's theory also raises questions. For example, he assumes a cavalier attitude toward social and economic differences and inequalities regarding the places where children grow up. Only a minority of the world's children live in houses that have attics, basements, and particular places for self-investment. A way must be found to argue for the importance of personal attachment to places that will not warrant wealth by attaching it to personal identity and psychological health. Bachelard's theory of personal place-relations is also deficient because it fails to take into account the negative potential of intimate places, particularly that they can be confining. This failing is tied to the fact that he does not see personal places in relation to the other kinds of place-relations, social and comprehensive.

It is not only children who, for economic reasons, lack felicitous personal places. As Virginia Woolf makes clear in *A Room of One's Own*, economic factors have prevented women from having places of their own. Personal places, while not identical with ownership, are often dependent on it. Personal space and financial dependence are to a great degree contraries. But she goes on to say that women have not had the benefit of personal space also because their work was thought to be insignificant and therefore interruptible. Men have had personal places where they would not be interrupted because their work was deemed to be important enough. She ties personal space, then, not only to economic factors but to the cultural evaluation of persons and their particular interests.[50] Woolf, in ways similar to Forster and Spark, identifies personal place-relations not only with self-worth and human relationships but also with creativity. She marvels, given the lacks women have suffered in personal place-relations, that there have been any women writers at all. And the existence of any women writers at all is even more surprising when one takes into account the fact that people of genius, rather than less sensitive to negative criticism and acts of devaluation, are more sensitive than others to them. We should see Woolf's argument regarding the relation between personal space and personal worth as fundamental. She makes it clear that women have not had the benefit of personal space because they have been undervalued and that women deprived of personal space will find it difficult to develop or maintain a sense of personal worth. Indeed, the implication is equally clear: Women have been deprived of places so that they will not develop a sense of personal worth.[51]

The qualities of personal place, finally, can be related not only to personal identity and worth but also to morality and spirituality. This potential in personal space accounts for the religious language that Forster and Spark use in their narrativization of personal place-relations. Personal space is the site from which moral critiques of society can take shape and where new forms of moral identity and human relations can be created. Forster makes clear that personal place-relations potentially counter social space because they can foster, primarily by physical residence and relations, new, morally charged possibilities for personal life. In Muriel Spark's fiction, the spiritual qualities of personal identity and relations require intimate places that counter the designs of modern social space. Not only are people who engage in disciplines that cultivate personal place-relations perceived by society as odd or dangerous, as is Harvey Gotham; the personal, by being mysterious and hidden, is a threat to society, especially a society that tends toward totality and control.

This identification of personal places as not only a refuge from social space but also as a site of morally and spiritually grounded resistance is offered by bell hooks in her graphic and moving autobiographical essay, "homeplace: a site of resistance."[52] She describes the walk that, as a little girl, she took through white neighborhoods to reach the home of her grandmother. Arrival was a homecoming, a restored sense of worth and assurance. More than that, for a life lived under "the brutal reality of racial apartheid, domination, one's homeplace was the one site where one could freely confront the issue of humanization, where one could resist," where people could become "subjects" instead of "objects."[53] Such spaces allowed black people to affirm one another and by so doing heal many of the wounds inflicted by racism. Personal space was a "site of resistance and liberation."[54] She identifies the racism of modernity with the widespread construction of domiciles that no longer provide what she calls "the subversive value of homeplace," and she believes that oppressed people have not recognized the value of personal places of which they have been increasingly deprived and are depriving themselves.[55]

While hooks writes out of and to the experience of black people in a racist society, I think that the integrity of her work is not diminished if her point is extended. For morally and spiritually sensitive people, for people with personal integrity, there always will be at least some tension between social space and "homeplace." While vastly differing in degrees and kind, the nurturing of "subjects" as an alternative to "objects" will always require particular places, at times places of resistance and subversion. Identity, integrity, self-worth, and the actualization of personal potential are relational, and those relations are not only with other persons but also with the places that provide for, sustain, and protect them.

This contrary relation between the search for personal place, with its moral and spiritual implications, and social space, with its implicit drive to contain and explain, is also clarified by Maurice Blanchot. The search for a place not assigned and controlled by the surrounding culture is one that constitutes for him a moral and spiritual discipline. And, as bell hooks can be read as deepening and extending Forster's principal interest in personal space as a form of moral resistance and correction to social space, Blanchot can be read as deepening and extending Spark's interest in personal space as a location for cultural divestment and exit.

Blanchot characterizes modern society as governed by a thirst for answers. This suppression of questions and uncertainty conceals the fact that answers are secondary and partial and that questions are finally primary and unyielding. He says, in *The Infinite Conversation,* that "the answer is the question's misfortune, its adversity."[56] Answers are so highly valued in modern society because they resemble commodities and appeal to the culture's desire to possess and control. Answers are abstracted from the questions that give rise to them as commodities are abstracted from the conditions that produce them. Even when modernity addresses unspeakably painful matters, such as disasters, it does so with a language of social control.[57] Blanchot diagnoses the modern desire to control as concealing a penchant for violence. The notion that we must get the answer, must get something or someone to yield up a secret and to conform to the general scheme of things, is consistent with the potential for torture.[58]

Blanchot accounts, thereby, for the intrinsic impatience in modern society with and suspicion of personal places, of the secrets and particularity that they sponsor and house. Blanchot implies that the Holocaust can be seen as an exaggerated and intensified expression of modern social impatience and suspicion directed toward particular peoples, their distinctive practices, and the homes that provide arenas separable from the coercions and conformities of modern social space. The questions posed by such personal places require an answer, a "final solution." The concentration camp is the ultimate, inevitable modern response to the question created for society by dissonant personal places.

The discipline of personal place that Blanchot implies is one by which, like Harvey Gotham, a person becomes an enigma to other people. Personal identity appears in the process by which a person sheds the identity that the society constructs for the person. The result is something like anonymity. Blanchot points out that anonymity is a suitable response to modern society, a society of violent answers. In a concentration camp, for example, the last thing one should do is to become noticed, to have one's name known.[59]

One of the striking aspects of Blanchot's theory of particularization and its relation to place is that he often illustrates it with biblical examples. Particularly important are departures from familiar social locations and events that occur at night. He cites stories of the patriarchs, particularly of Abraham, who leaves his hometown to journey to an unknown place. Jacob wrestles throughout the night with the guardian or messenger at the border of the Jabbok brook. Night is also the setting of the perilous escape of the people from Egypt. Such references help us to relate the discipline of personal integrity to the fiction of Muriel Spark, especially its attention to textual patterns of social divestment, of moral and spiritual formation, and personal identity and worth.

Personal place, as narrated by Forster and Spark, is the location of identity, moral integrity, and mystery. Personal place-relations, when not subordinated to social space, reveal their own real and potential value. Cultivating relations to personal spaces requires moral sensitivities that are separable from social acceptability and a personal resistance that allows persons not only, as Spark puts it, to *take* exception but to *be* exceptions. We need meanwhile also to keep in mind that while supporting fuller actualizations of human potentials for relations to personal places we must be ever more attentive than even these writers and theorists have been to their negative possibilities. As David Sibley reminds us, "While the home can have these positive symbolic qualities [for example, as providing a haven], it also provides the context for violence, child abuse, depression and other forms of mental illness."[60]

It puts no unrealistic burdens on a narrative discourse to anticipate that it will and can convey all three kinds of place-relations. Indeed, as we saw, modern fictions can do just that. The crucial role of narrative and its languages of place and space is not only to reveal the particular problems and potentials in each of the three kinds but also to reveal the full repertoire of human place-relations and the possibilities of moving between them. This does not mean that all three will be for any one person of equal importance or that they can be equally important at any one time. It only means that optimal place-relations always are both of a particular kind and hold within them the counter claims and possibilities of the other two.

8

The Two Sides of Place-Relations

Now that I have clarified the first component of an adequate theory of human place-relations, namely, that there are three kinds, that they are related differentially, and that one of the three will dominate the other two, we can turn to the second required component. This component is revealed by the contrast drawn in the study between earlier and later modernists.

The earlier modernists, it was argued, responded archeologically to the growing costs for spatial orientation exacted by a history of cultural change. That is, they looked backward to retrieve kinds of place-relations characteristic of an earlier period but still viable, and they diagnosed the problem as the loss of tangible, physical aspects in place-relations. In contrast, later modernists, due to the disillusionment caused primarily by the traumas of war, turned not to the past, which they treated as largely inadequate to and even deceptive regarding the actual conditions of human life, but to the future. They responded teleologically. That is, they stressed the spiritual and future-directed aspects of place-relations. While the earlier modernists were not indifferent to the spiritual aspects of place-relations and the later modernists were not indifferent to the physical aspects, the earlier stress the physical and the later the spiritual side of place-relations.

It can be inferred from these narratives, then, that all three kinds of human place-relations are two-sided, that both sides need to be present, and that one side can be more important than the other in any positive place-relation. The potential for the dominance of one side can occasion the occlusion of the other. When that occurs, place-relations can become deficient, even distorted. An adequate theory of place-relations should not emphasize one side at the expense of the other. As Michael Keith and Steve Pile point out, space has been too often treated as either opaque and inert or as transparent and dematerialized. They call for a spatial theory that retains the ties between the real and the symbolic, the literal and the metaphoric.[1] And Edward Soja and Barbara Hooper put the matter in the strongest possible terms: "It is easy to say (as most geographers do) that both [real and imagined aspects of space] are important and should be combined in good geographical analysis, but too often in the history of geographic thought, subjectivism and objectivism, imagined and real geographies, have been placed in rigid opposition, especially when couched in extreme or essentialist forms of idealism and materialism."[2] I shall look at the physical and then at the spiritual side of place-relations and conclude by advocating a theory of human place-relations that holds both of them together.

The Physical Side of Place-Relations

Physicality is required in place-relations because they ground and steady human life and support modes of relationship between people, bodily identities, and the physical contexts of people's lives. We saw this potential in place-relations in our studies of Hardy, Conrad, and Forster.

For Hardy, the physical aspect of space is associated with the cosmic context of human life shorn of cultural attempts to conceal or blunt its force. Social, political, and religious constructions fall short in their ability to house or account for the physical space that forcefully comprehends human life. Human beings must choose, therefore, between a partial and fragile world of human constructions, a world that tempts them by its apparent security and predictability, and a world comprehended by a physical space that, while difficult, grants human life the gravity and truth of the "real."

For Conrad, the physical aspect of social place-relations is provided by human labor. Human labor, while it carries unavoidable ties to economic and political causes and consequences, is primarily directed toward the threats and potentials of the physical world. Labor becomes distorted when it is defined and controlled primarily by the economic and social ties it carries. The absorption and abstraction of human labor by economic and social structures is the last stage in this falsification. Behind Conrad's many depictions of distorted social space stands, it was argued, the norm of social place-relations that are primarily physical and that do not conceal their basis in physical labor.

The physicality of space for E. M. Forster is provided by the human body, its accommodation by locations that also support relations, especially, but not necessarily, sexual, to other bodies. Distortion of personal space in his fiction occurs when personal places are determined by economic forces and social control. The social context in which his characters find themselves is increasingly shaped by places constructed in that distorted way. Personal integrity and intimacy require and establish their own place-relations. The validity and significance of those relations are based on the reliability or trustworthiness of the sexually intimate body, and places created by it have the potential, if heeded, to alter and revitalize social space.

Kant, in his early writings on space, makes clear that human place-relations and spatial orientation are grounded in physicality. While Kant privileges absolute space, imputing to it a primacy independent of the existence of all matter and a ground for the existence of anything material, he recognizes that human judgments about space are radically affected by physicality. The two sides of the human body, for example, grant us knowledge of the positions of places relative to one another. Since we cannot perceive universal space, what we do perceive are differences between bodies and the relations imputed to them by our own physicality.[3] Our understanding of how things stand in spatial relation to one another, then, is first of all based on our own physicality, on distinctions between left and right, front and rear, above and below. Although I do not agree that externality forms an adequate account of the relations of beings to one another, it certainly is a basic factor, one, moreover, that helps to establish the physical side of place-relations.

In addition, it is basic for Kant that a person cannot conceive of something unless it is taken as being in a space distinguishable from the space in which the person stands. This relation is basic to the understanding that things are distinguishable from one another because they occupy differing places. Perception, then, presupposes and does not construct spatiality, and that presupposition is bodily grounded.[4] As Reingard Nethersole points out, the physicality of space for Kant is very much grounded in the body because the crucial distinction the body allows us to make is between near and far: "Motility means the distinction which is made between those things a person is himself close enough to interact with and those things that he could interact with only if he (or they) moved."[5] When perceptions of and orientations to places are extended beyond reference to bodily location, they have their standing by analogy with bodily location.

Lest we get too physical with Kant, we should note that he subordinates spatiality to temporality precisely because spatial relations are more physical. Time is more universal, for Kant, than space, for time embraces everything, including space.[6] I do not agree that time should be taken as always more important than place in a human world, but it is impressive that Kant, given his priorities, directs so much attention to spatiality in its physicality and in its focus on the body.

Edward Casey extends the bodily orientations of Kant's theory of space toward a fuller comprehension of human physicality. He argues that not only the distinctions, along with their qualities, that Kant makes between right and left or above and below but also sexual distinctions are important in a theory of place: "Much as Kant had demonstrated that the mere difference between the right and left hands has everything to do with our insertion into surrounding cosmic regions, so the body in its equally binary sexual differentiations leads into whole interpersonal and extrapersonal worlds."[7] As sexuality makes clear that human life is fundamentally relational, so it indicates that people are related not only to one another but also to places. As he says: "Just as there are no places without bodies that sustain and vivify them, so there are no lived bodies without the places they inhabit and traverse. . . . Bodies and places are connatural terms. They interanimate each other."[8] Gillian Rose reinforces this stress on sexuality and gender in space theory by contending that their neglect, along with a neglect of the physicality of spaces, is a mark of masculine habits of mind.[9]

We expect theorists who are materialist rather than idealist in their assumptions to stress spatiality in its physicality, particularly in relation to the human body. An example is the work of Henri Lefebvre, to which, in this study, I have on several occasions already turned. *The Production of Space,* a culminating work by this major theorist, develops his theory that "the material conditions of individual and collective activity" antedate the coherence by which people are related to locations, that the language of space derives from and is secondary to labor, and that the body and other forms of physical location and activity are basic to the construction of space (*PS,* 71).[10] Lefebvre argues from the conviction that the significance of space and place-relations arises from and defers to the body, labor, and material conditions.

Lefebvre attacks the abstraction of space and the construction of what he calls "mental space." The abstraction of space represses the reality of human labor and the body and the dependence of space on them. Abstract space opposes human interests; "its *modus operandi* is devastation, destruction" (*PS,* 289). Its violence has been concealed, however, and abstract or mental space has become "the stuff of 'common sense' and 'culture'" (*PS,* 297).

Even more disturbing for Lefebvre is the conflation of absolute or mental space with social, political, and economic order. Such conflation allows a particular system of order to look as though it flowed "directly from the Logos—that is, from a 'consensual' embrace of the rational" (*PS,* 317). When this occurs, a historically contingent order is made absolute, and particular places are subordinated to it. Such subordination conceals the fact that all social spaces are shaped by particular political, social, and economic interests and are derived from and dependent upon conditions that the human body and human labor provide.

Lefebvre does not see abstraction as in itself unnatural or sinister. He recognizes that a society will theorize a sense of the whole within which diverse human initiatives and actions can be seen as related to one another (*PS*, 94). But when such constructed wholes become primary and absolute, they take on a power of their own, controlling particular places. Absolute space becomes a surrogate reality, an agent that particular political and economic interests can employ in order to validate and advance themselves.

Lefebvre provides a historical narrative of the growing prestige of abstract space in Western cultures. Until the twelfth century, Christendom's towns were centered by tombs to which pilgrimages were made. But when increasingly important roles in commercial trade made towns more powerful, market places were brought from outside the town to its center. As commercial centers, towns soon became involved in economic networks in which some towns dominated. This development was paralleled by Christianity, which transposed its center from crypt to monument. Cathedrals signified the stature of a town and represented emancipation from cryptic physical space (*PS*, 262ff.). Economic order placed a high value on the rational arrangements of increasingly complex systems of commercial and communicational interrelations. Rationality became closely aligned with economic power and its bureaucratic structures. The relation of rational order to economic and political power produced the modern period and culminated in the present use of absolute mental space as a metaphor for social and economic order.

Lefebvre counters with the primacy of the body and human labor for the spaces they produce. He sees the subjugation of particular places and what produces them to general space as a means of control, and he opposes the denigration by such moves of what he considers to be human reality, particularly the labor of human bodies. The homogenized spaces of modernity, in which everything looks like or is interchangeable with everything else, are not real spaces but ideas of space imposed on or concealing the real spaces that human labor produces.

Lefebvre also opposes the hegemony of abstract space by siding with those who are excluded from and by the determinations of modern space. He believes that resistance and conflict can reveal spatial distinctions and diversity (*PS*, 55). Differing, particular spaces, unlike "mental" or abstract space, are real and already there and need only to be recognized and released.

We should notice that Lefebvre relegates language and culture to a secondary position when he argues that labor forms the physical basis for social space. He posits the laboring body as "base and foundation, *beyond philosophy*, beyond discourse, and beyond the theory of discourse" (*PS*, 407). His use of "beyond" rather than "prior to" is rhetorical; the physical or material body and the reality of labor provide a physicality to which the language of space ought to defer (*PS*, 30). While the laboring, space-generating body is not without "non-formal knowledge," it is posited as antecedent to such knowledge and prediscursive. Narrative discourse and its language of space for Lefebvre, then, derive from and should refer to working bodies and the places they produce.

An important addendum to Lefebvre is provided by the work of Michel de Certeau. *The Practice of Everyday Life* gives attention to the ways by which people in their daily activities counter and subvert the otherwise complete control over them of designed and imposed social space. Particularly by what he calls "style" or a "way of operating," which includes the full range of human practices, he focuses on individuals and groups as they counter uniformity and predictability by their distinguishable ways of operating. This addendum extends the category of "labor" in a very helpful way. The daily activities of people and the results of those activities, and not simply what usually counts as "labor," augment attention to the physical aspects of social space. However, it is important to see a limitation in de Certeau's contribution to the physical aspect of social space.[11] While it is important not to minimize the tensions between particular styles and the determinants of social patterns, a particular "way of operating" need not be construed only as oppositional. While some social spaces may resolutely resist alterations proffered by the initiatives of persons and groups, they need not, and surely ought not, do so. In addition, it could be true that particular styles are allowed by social spaces in order to perpetuate themselves by concealing how determining they actually are. And we know that personal styles are vulnerable to social invasion and absorption. Moreover, de Certeau is so fully focused on social space that he does not relate particular styles to personal places. Some distinction, it seems to me, ought to be made between gestures and styles that are personal in ways supported by personal space and particular ways of doing things that are socially affected or directed.

We can extend de Certau's addendum to Lefebvre further by returning to Kant and recalling that place-relations have a physical aspect not only because of such bodily activities as laboring and walking, but also by the body's simply being there. We need not, with this thought, follow Heidegger in undercutting social with individual or historical with ontological categories. We can simply posit a physical base beyond labor and even beyond de Certeau's everyday activities, a physical ground, so to speak, in the polyphony of human spatiality provided by the constant of bodily presence.

While any viable theory of human place-relations must take the work of

Lefebvre into account, I also have two reservations about it. The first is that Lefebvre discounts the complexity of human spatiality. His attention is almost exclusively on social space, especially social space in its economically and politically constructed forms. There is nothing wrong with a theory that focuses on one rather than on all three kinds of human place-relations, but it becomes a problem when the other kinds are assigned to the margins and discounted. We saw that Lefebvre does this in regard to comprehensive space both because he thinks that "nature" can no longer serve as an access to comprehensive space and because he thinks of social space, especially in its economic form, as comprehensive. Personal space has little place in his theory. In contrast, I think that to check the power of social space it is important to include all three forms of human place-relations and to insist on the potential, if not actual, value of place-relations of the other two kinds. Indeed, one of the symptoms of a diseased social space is its occlusion or swamping of place-relations of the other two kinds.

Second, Lefebvre treats the nonphysical or spiritual side of place-relations primarily under the category of "mental" space. Given the power and prestige of rationality in the modern period and its alliances with economic and social order, his attack on "mental" space is valid and valuable. However, this attention to "mental" space allows Lefebvre, in my opinion, to neglect what, for lack of a better word, I refer to as the spiritual side of human place-relations. The question Lefebvre lays before anyone who attempts to do justice to the spiritual in place-relations is whether that can be done without slipping into the well-worn ruts of modern rationality in general and popular idealism in particular.

The Spiritual Side of Space-Relations

As we saw, Greene, Golding, and Spark extend the language of space not in a backward and downward direction toward the past and the physical but in a forward and upward direction, toward the future and the spiritual. While positive human place-relations in the earlier modernists have to be largely recovered, for the later modernists they need primarily to be envisioned and discovered.

Comprehensive space in Greene's work, a space that his characters desire and seek, is located at the edges of constructed spaces and in the interstices between competing human institutions. However extreme in location and partial or fleeting in actualization, comprehensive place-relations in their spiritual quality are positive alternatives to the controlling, conflicted, and inadequate constructions particularly of politically and religiously defined spaces.

Golding's fiction identifies vision as crucial to vital and renewed social spaces. Without vision, social space hardens and fragments, and people perish. Social space must be oriented upwardly and toward the future by goals and aspirations. Predictability and certainty at least partially defer to the inviting and edifying possibilities of a social space structured by vision. The results of new social reconfigurations cannot be wholly predicted or assured, and positive consequences of the fulfillment of vision are also received as gift, as innovation.

Finally, Muriel Spark's fiction discovers personal place-relations distinguishable not only from materially constructed space but also from the virtual, nonmaterial space projected by the image making of modern media. In a culture of media and image, almost nothing personal can be defined, and the culture of images so mimics the aura of spirituality that it is difficult to define personal space in an upward and forward direction without being usurped by it. Personal space spiritually defined is furtively located at exits from the culture. The accent on possibility emphasizes the dependence of personal space on the future and on space not so much constructed as discovered or received.

The spiritual side of positive place-relations is secured, among other things, by the fact that places are significant. As E. Relph says, "places can only be known in their meanings."[12] We have relations with places not only, as we saw in the last section, because of our bodily locations but also because places have real or potential significance. We are drawn to places because of what they mean to us. Places have qualities. As Alan G. Thomas says, "All places . . . serve figurative ends and thereby sacrifice part of their concreteness as they cater to some human desire or craving beyond present reality." He notes further, "Even for modern realists there is sometimes a curious removal from the physicality of place to the realm of spirit."[13]

A literary theorist well known for his interest in the spiritual qualities of spatial orientation is Joseph Frank. He attempts "to outline the spiritual attitudes that have led to the predominance of spatial form" in his influential essay "Spatial Form in Modern Literature."[14] This essay has spawned a school of criticism very likely because it depends on idealist philosophical beliefs consistent with long-standing modern views of literature, art, and high culture. Such views, which come into English literary and cultural theory from Kant and Hegel by way primarily of Coleridge and Arnold, posit art as standing above the contingencies of history either by being itself transcendent to them or by granting access to a noncontingent and stable moral and spiritual world beyond temporality and physicality.

Although Frank begins by explicating Lessing's genre distinctions, he takes from Lessing not so much a theory of genres as of aesthetic form.

Frank applauds Lessing's break with eighteenth-century theories in which form was something objective into which, so to speak, particular works were poured. For Lessing (and for Frank), form is a relation, a moment of coincidence between the "art medium" and the "conditions of human perception." It "issue[s]d spontaneously from the organization of the art work as it present[s]ed itself to perception" (*SF*, 8).

By being a distinct instant of interrelationship, "form" is distinguishable from time and becomes spatial. Frank uses Lessing's ontology of aesthetic form to define modern literature as work that should be apprehended in a nontemporal, spatial way. The reading of modernist work not only should be a conjunction between the work and the reader's perception of it but also a reconstitution of Lessing's attempt "to rise above history, to define the unalterable laws of aesthetic perception" (*SF*, 4). Frank subsumes his theory of spatial form under this idealist agenda.

Frank reads the poetry of Pound and Eliot spatially, that is, as producing moments of pure relation between poem and reader. Their poetry does this by avoiding both sequential relations between parts of a poem and the poem's referential thrust (*SF*, 13). If sequence and reference are suspended and if the perception of the poem is deferred until the whole of the poem is read, its sundry parts can combine and occasion a spontaneous, self-referential, and momentary unity with its reader.

When Frank turns to modern fiction, he gives some attention to the narrative language of space and place, by, for example, stressing Flaubert's comment that all three levels of the county fair scene in *Madame Bovary* should be viewed, so to speak, simultaneously. But as he moves from Flaubert to Joyce, his attention shifts from spatial language in narratives to the moment of reception. Frank argues that the reader of *Ulysses* cannot apprehend the work until all of it has been read and "viewed as a whole" (*SF*, 16). And when he discusses Proust, whose work seems most compatible with Frank's philosophical agenda, he points out Proust's orientation toward momentary experiences that, by means of spiritual techniques, transcend time. Frank represents his own interests well when he remarks how Proust "believed that these transcendent, extra temporal moments contained a clue to the ultimate nature of reality; and he wished to translate these moments to the level of aesthetic form" (*SF*, 20). Frank's analysis of modernist literature in terms of "spatial form" closely resembles Proust's attempts to rise above time and to unite past and present simultaneously and nontemporally in a moment that Proust called "pure time" and that Frank calls "form," a moment, as he goes on to say, that "is not time at all" but space (*SF*, 24).

We reach the clearest declaration of Frank's aim when he discusses Wilhelm Worringer's *Abstraction and Empathy* (1908) and its theory of relations between art and history. Following Worringer, Frank argues that sequential and referential styles are typical of cultures in which people have a positive relation to their historical environment, while non-naturalist styles, which for him define literary modernism, arise when such rapport is lacking. For Frank, modern literary culture holds a negative relation to social, historical circumstances, and spatial form is the principal locus or effect of that negative relation. Frank then goes beyond Worringer to endorse the philosophical implications to which his argument leads. He affirms the latent idealism in several of the writers he has considered, especially Proust, and turns, in his last paragraph, to the religious idealism of Mircea Eliade and his "timeless world of myth" (*SF*, 60). Modern literature, Frank concludes, by transmuting time into timelessness, is not specific to a particular historical period but transcends history and reveals what art always is and can provide. Literature today plays the kind of role that myths played in earlier culture. It can grant access to moments that, by transcending history and being self-referential, are not only spatial but also ideal and absolute.

What is most powerful and enticing about this essay is not so much its comments on modernist writers, which are often apt and insightful, but its implied narrative, an understanding of literature's gradual and now complete divorce from and elevation above history and the access to transcendence that reading it provides. Frank ties moments of transcendence in modernist writing to one another, to his own distrust of history, and, finally, to the ideal, spiritual, or transcendent defined as a spatial reality. While not all the critics associated with the spatial form school follow him along this entire route, a potential idealism lurks behind any attempt to posit human space as constituted apart from physicality and in relation to the spiritual taken as in some way stable and already there.

Before leaving Frank and an exclusive focus on the spiritual side of spatial theory, a postscript should be added about cyberspace because it seems to offer a spatiality without physicality. Largely, this technology is a continuation of other technologies and not a departure. It is a means of communication, and, as with photography, it makes places available by means of images and simulation. In addition, the storehouses of information that cyberspace provides resemble libraries that undercut chronology by surrounding a person simultaneously with texts from many ages. But, as Timothy Luke makes clear, cyberspace also departs from earlier forms of technology and their consequences. Cyberspace can become a kind of social space: "Cyberspaces are both fascinating and problematic social sites." He says that they are neither utopian nor "atopian" but "'ectopian,' or outside of ordinary space, and open to multiple contradictory appropriations by those who create and then traverse their spatial properties." Furthermore, like other spaces, cyberspaces have "a material origin" or "location," and like other spaces, "they generate value."[15] The suggestive power and spiritual qualities of cyberspace appeal to theorists of religion and spirituality, and Lily Kong reviews much of the literature that is developing along these lines. She points out that there are close ties being constructed between theories of cyberspace and human spirituality.[16] However important studies of this kind of spatiality, especially its relation to spirituality, may be, they should be shadowed by an insistence on the importance of the physical side of place-relations. Virtual space, while destined to affect more and more of our spatial orientations and understandings, must always be seen, it seems to me, as a metaphor for something more basic, namely, the relations of people to actual places, relations that have a physical as well as a spiritual side.

Lefebvre's materialism and Frank's idealism, when taken together, reveal the archeological (Lefebvre) and the teleological (Frank) sides of places and our relations to them. Their work also reveals how one side of place-relations can exclude the other side, especially when pursued by someone in strong reaction to the threats of dominance from the other side. While I prefer the work of Lefebvre to that of Frank because, among other reasons, Lefebvre analyzes so well how philosophical notions of nonphysical space have become welded to social, economic, and political interests in the modern West, I disagree with both him and Frank in their one-sidedness. This fault in their work is enlarged by the fact that each, in ways contrary to the other, posits something that is taken to be prior to or beyond language, a material or a spiritual reality. They subject the language of space to one or the other of these prediscursive realities. What is needed, rather, is a stress on the language of space as holding these two poles, the archeological and the teleological, together.[17]

I posit instead the primacy of narrative discourse and the attention narrative discourse can give to both the physical and the spiritual aspects of place-relations. The language of space is a necessary part of narrative discourse, and it can convey both the physicality of location and its real or potential relation to the moral and spiritual well-being of persons. Narratives and human spaces are inseparable from one another. What needs to be restored is the importance of places in our narrative worlds, how they come to recognition, what they mean to us, how they affect us, who constructed and inhabits them, and what changes should be made in them.

The narrativization of space is not only an act of recounting how places have come to be as they are in our worlds; it is also an act, sponsored by protest, need, and desire, of projection, of articulating what place-relations can and should be like. The narrativization of space extends the language of place and space toward both the past and toward the future, both the actual and the possible, and both the physical and the spiritual.

Reuniting the Two Sides of Place-Relations

In order for a theory of place-relations to approach adequacy, there should be an understanding of place and space that neglects neither its physical nor its spiritual side. A theorist who deals with location as crucial to cultural theory and criticism, who is also oriented toward narrative and narrative theory, and who combines the physical and the spiritual in his understanding of human spatiality is Raymond Williams. His work not only affirms both the physical and the spiritual sides of place-relations but also traces the historical, social process by which these two sides fell into separation from and opposition to one another.

Williams pinpoints the closing decades of the eighteenth century as a time when aspects of society normally in complex, mutual relations to one another fell out as contraries. This process continued for the subsequent two centuries. The precipitating occasions were the three revolutions that occurred during this period of history: the democratic, the industrial, and the communications revolutions.[18] While all three were changes in means rather than goals, they were sufficiently far-reaching to alter the culture's sense of the world and of the relation of humans to it and to one another.

The principal consequence of these changes was the separation that grew between the material or physical and spiritual sides of human life. "Against mechanism, the amassing of fortunes and the proposition of utility as the source of value, [cultivation or culture] offered a different and a superior social idea" (CS, 63). Despite the efforts of people like Carlyle, Arnold, Ruskin, T. S. Eliot, and F. R. Leavis to see culture as "a whole way of living," the two directions of interest became contraries. This was due primarily to the tendency of literary theorists and cultural advocates to take a recognizably idealist view of the "whole way of living," and that idealist tendency, which easily accompanies any attempt to configure the "whole," found its inevitable contrary in naturalism and materialism (CS, 39). Theories, even when they attempted to accommodate a "whole way of living," privileged one side or the other, and they continue to do so.

Williams poses, in contrast to the separation of material and spiritual, an inclusive theory. He puts the options clearly: "Either the arts are passively dependent on social reality, a proposition which I take to be that of mechanical materialism or a vulgar misinterpretation of Marx. Or the arts, as the creation of consciousness, determine social reality, the proposition which the Romantic poets sometimes advanced. Or finally, the arts, while ultimately dependent, with everything else, on the real economic structure, operate in part to reflect this structure and its consequent reality, and in part, by affecting attitudes toward reality, to help *or hinder* the constant business of changing it" (CS, 274). Williams identifies with the third of his options.

It should be noted that, while not Marxist in any blunt or simple way, Williams favors the material side. He does not do this because he is committed to viewing the primacy of economic factors in the constitution of society. Indeed, he says that he finds the question of whether the economic element is dominant in the configuration of a "whole way of life" "unanswerable" (CS, 280–81). Even if it were determining, it is not the economic element but the "whole way of life" to which literature is or should be related. Rather, Williams sides with the material side because he believes that it is among workers that one finds an alternative to the corrosive threat toward the "whole way of life" posed by individualism (CS, 326). The almost sacred datum of his theory is "common loyalty," and it is primarily found among workers. The loyalty that marks a society of workers creates a social base he sharply distinguishes from both bourgeois individualism and state primacy. His emphasis is on social space created by the loyalty of workers and its resulting culture.[19]

Williams's theory of social space is based more on internal than on external relationships, on mutuality more than competition, and on inclusion more than exclusion. The relation he poses between the physical and spiritual sides of social space is philosophically grounded, therefore, in a sense of human life itself as basically relational rather than oppositional. As he says: "Politics and art, together with science, religion, family life and the other categories we speak of as absolutes, belong in a whole world of active and interacting relationships, which is our common associative life. . . . Yet we begin, normally, from categories themselves, and this has led again and again to a very damaging suppression of relationships" (LR, 39). These relationships include the relation of people to one another, the relation of people to locations, and the relation of "man's ideal development" to "his 'animal nature' or the satisfaction of material 'needs'" (LR, 43).

Although he accounts for the loss of the primacy of relationships historically and socially, Williams also suggests a philosophical basis for that loss, namely, Cartesianism, which he opposes. This modern habit of mind posits a fundamental separation between human consciousness and objective reality, particularly the physical world. This separation has created, he argues, a "contrast between art and reality" that should be seen as false (LR, 19). Theories of art and culture come to be based on the assumption of this separation. Williams proposes that we think, instead, "of human experience as both objective and subjective, in one inseparable process" (LR, 20). He concludes: "The antithesis of nature to the mind, 'as object to subject,' we now know to be false, yet so much of our thinking is based on it that to grasp the substantial unity, the sense of a whole process, is to begin a long and difficult revolution in the mind. Yet it is certain that theories of art which begin from the separated categories of 'artist' and 'reality' are, from now on, irrelevant" (*LR, 23*). He defines cultural theory, then, "as the study of relationships between elements in a whole way of life" (*LR, 46*). His emphasis is unmistakable: "Yet I am saying that cultural theory is at its most significant when it is concerned precisely with the *relations* between the many and diverse human activities which have been historically and theoretically grouped in these ways [that is, 'literary' and 'social'] and especially when it explores these relations as at once dynamic and specific within describably whole historical situations which are also, as practice, changing and, in the present, changeable" (*PM, 164*). By emphasizing "*relations*" and "a *common* element of the culture," cultural theory criticizes the "divided and fragmented culture we actually have" (*RH, 35*).

Spatial theory continues to suffer from the bifurcations against which Williams militates. Edward Soja, for example, recognizes that Lefebvre, while still largely Marxist and materialist in his spatial theory, was trying to overcome the "dualism that had developed between Marx's historical materialism and Hegel's philosophical idealism."[20] But Soja, rather than, like Williams, pursuing that corrective project, appears to oppose it by positing "first" and "second" space, that is, perceived and conceived space, as contraries and as primary while making "third" or lived space subsequent to them. I think that Williams would respond by affirming what Soja calls lived or "third" space as primary. Work or livelihood is the way, for Williams, by which our relations to and within our world are defined and secured. Perceptions and conceptions of place and space, if they are not, when so separated, to repeat the Cartesian, subject/object split, should be drawn from and recognized as dependent on the primarily relational character of human spatiality.

Another form of such bifurcation is offered by J. J. van Baak, who distinguishes between conceptual and cultural space, a distinction that sounds quite a bit like Soja's distinction between conceived and perceived spaces. This is how van Baak puts it: "In nearly all studies of literary space . . . somehow a difference is made between theoretical conceptions of homogeneous, mathematically unlimited, continuous and empty space, and, on the other hand, the socio-dramatic . . . cultural space which is the essential space of literature. This space is presented not as homogeneous, but as subject to limitations, hiatuses and discontinuities, filled with obstacles, privileged points and directions . . . , with colours, sounds, smells, and tactile properties."[21] Such distinctions between what I have been calling the two "sides" of place relations—the physical or material and the spiritual or mental—can easily draw us back to the split. This does not mean that we should avoid distinguishing the two sides from one another, but it should be remembered that these two sides, while distinguishable, should not be taken as separate, even less as oppositional, in human place-relations.

A relational theory of space such as Williams suggests will also emphasize, as he does, the role of language as integrative, constitutive, and inclusive. He rejects both the reification or abstraction of language in idealism and the dependent or secondary role given to language by naturalists, materialists, or social realists.[22] The relations between what in modern theories have become separated components are not imposed by language but are intrinsic to it (*ML*, 98). "Language, then, is not a medium; it is a constitutive element of material social practice" (*ML*, 165).

It should be clear that I largely agree with Williams, especially in regard to the fundamental, relational model that underlies his spatial theory. However, I have two reservations. The first concerns the privileged place that Williams gives to social space. I realize that this is due to what he considers an overemphasis on the individual and its contrary, the state. I also realize that he tries at times to make room both for particular persons and for what lies beyond and outstrips social space. But he gives to comprehensive and intimate kinds of human places and place-relations a marginal and secondary role. They are the dissidents that indicate a society's failure to be wholly adequate. It is because "*no dominant culture ever in reality includes or exhausts all human practice, human energy and human intention*" that such alternatives to it are constructed. He identifies these alternatives "as the personal or private, or as the natural or even the metaphysical" (*ML*, 75, 61). But the identity and role he gives to comprehensive and personal spaces allow them no real and constant significance. His own "alignments," to use his euphemism for beliefs, keep his otherwise capacious cultural theory focused on what he takes to be primary, namely, social space.

My second reservation is that, despite his inclusive, balanced, and relational theory, Williams still favors the materialist side. When he says, for example, that "social being determines consciousness," he does not—no matter how he objects to "the mechanical materialist reversal of the idealist dualism" that posits "*first* material social life and *then*, at some temporal or spatial distance, 'consciousness' and 'its' products"—finally avoid that position (*ML*, 75, 61). This is because his account of culture includes an account of how high culture has been so constructed as to devalue the locations of workers. Consequently, his relational theory carries traces of resentment that continue to affect it. But I believe it is important to press beyond such resentments and to affirm a fully relational theory. This means, first of all, making the spiritual side of place-relations as important as their physical side. His theory would be more adequate if he were to stress spiritual needs and potentials as he emphasizes those that are physical and economic. Place-relations have a spiritual as much as a physical side. This means that power and material conditions may as easily be subordinate to culture as culture may be to them. Indeed, a number of cultural theorists have, without slipping into idealism, made this point. Culture not only is basic; it also can mobilize and direct material conditions and power. Social tensions and conflicts are based not only on establishing and distributing power but also on establishing and disseminating meaning.[23]

A theory of place that attempts to account for both the physical and the spiritual aspects of place-relations but that comes, in contrast to Williams's, from the more idealist side suggested by phenomenology is offered by Edward Casey. Drawing on the work of M. Merleau-Ponty, Casey argues that places are "meaningful" as well as "sensuous."[24] He argues this point by contending that the dependence of bodies on physical places yields to the fact that both places and bodies are bearers of culture. "Bodies and places are connatural terms. They interanimate each other," he says.[25] More exactly, "Perceiving bodies are *knowing bodies,* and inseparable from what they know is culture as it imbues and shapes particular places. It is by bodies that places become cultural in character."[26] Casey is not implying that people and places are predetermined by culture; he also insists that his emphasis on perception excludes neither the particularity, expressivity, and ever-changing character of language nor the particularity and alterity of places, what he calls their "autochthonous being."[27] Nor does he, by granting potentials to place-relations that outstrip or antedate language, think of these relations as standing to any degree outside of culture. To safeguard his position, he deploys a view of culture as particular as well as inclusive and as changing as well as stable.

Williams and Casey are closer to one another than are Lefebvre and Joseph Frank, and by joining Williams, who moves from a materialist side, and Casey, who moves from a more idealist side, I think that we begin to have a balanced and sufficiently resonant account of place-relations as both physical and spiritual. Even more, we find in their theories a strong emphasis on the role of narrative discourse for articulating place-relations. As Casey puts it, "places happen," and "it is because they happen that they lend themselves so well to narration."[28] I would add that they lend themselves to narration also because narrative discourses always contain a language of place and space and because narratives arise from and return, either to confirm or to challenge, to the relation of physical entities, including places, to moral and spiritual beliefs.

The narrativization of space, then, represents a project of uncovering the interrelations between places and their human significance before those relations are broken apart and the spiritual and physical sides of place-relations are projected as basically separated from and contrary to one another. Human place-relations are marked by both material and spiritual components. If we understand that narrative discourses are not secondary or derivative but primary and originating, we can also understand why they are crucial to our experiences and evaluations of human place-relations.

The physical and spiritual sides of positive place-relations, while inseparable from language, cannot wholly be captured by it, even by the language of place and space in narrative discourses. There are complexities, resonances, and particularities in positive place-relations to which language can lead but not duplicate. The inadequacy of a narrative fully to account for and to validate place-relations means that narrative discourses are partial in both senses of that word. Place-relations, in their physicality and spirituality, outstrip the archeological and teleological directions of language, including narrative. However, those directions of language are also indispensable to place-relations. Narratives make us aware of the specificity and the significance of places. They are not only responses to those relations but guides and guardians of them. Place-relations cannot occur without the placements that language, particularly narrative discourse, provides.

9

The Single Norm of Place-Relations

Emphasis on the three kinds and the two sides of place-relations reveals the complexity and instability of human spatiality. When we turn to evaluating place-relations, we also face instability. To a large degree the quality of a place-relation is judged by comparisons with other possibilities or experiences, either associated with the other kinds or with the other side of place-relations.

However, we should see that evaluation, while calling attention to variety and instability, is also steadied by a single norm. This norm runs between places of differing kinds and between place-relations that are dominated either by their physical or spiritual side. Consequently, it supplies a continuity to spatial theory that counters variety and instability. Having said this, however, I must add that this norm, though constant across the kinds and sides of place-relations, is intricate. A simple norm will fall short of adequacy. For example, Robert Sack's norm, namely, that positive places are those that allow us to see the "real" and to see the real as complex, seems to relate more to one than to all three kinds and more to one than to both sides of place-relations.[1] In our search for a single norm we should not compromise variety and instability. Nor should we favor one kind of place-relation or one side of place-relations.[2]

I

It will be helpful for approaching the norm of positive place-relations to look first at examples of deficient or questionable kinds of place-relations. One such kind includes place-relations marked by exclusion and/or detachment from place. Exclusion is imposed, and detachment is chosen. Both of these kinds of nonrelations can be housed under the category of "place-lessness."

Placelessness is *imposed* for a variety of reasons. The most general reason is that exclusion is a primary consequence of social space. Social spaces are marked by boundaries most of which are set to designate areas of inclusion and exclusion. This runs, for example, from parking zones to men's and women's restrooms to work places that admit only employees. Some exclusions involve everyone; some are for the convenience of the majority; some are for the benefit of a few. We take exclusion as a normal part of daily life, although at times we are offended and even injured by it.

Placelessness is imposed, furthermore, when places admit people but discourage or even prevent attachment. Places designed for efficiency keep relations between people and place at a superficial level. Relph mentions commercial strips as one kind of space designed to be purely functional. By being duplicated in many locations, commercial strips promote recognizability, easy accessibility, and utility rather than attachment. Relph suggests that commercial interests in the construction of space create a sense of nonrelation so that people will enter such places easily and, it is hoped, often.[3]

To move from ordinary to graver placelessness, we saw that one consequence of modern history has been a pervasive sense of dislocation and disorientation. Wars, urbanization, suburban migrations, changes wrought by social movements, and new forms of technology and communication, especially the computer age: such aspects of modern culture have loosened the ties of people to places.

Placelessness is imposed on us, then, by the boundaries and exclusions basic to social space; by the construction of kinds of places that, by being efficient and functional, promote easy access and repetition rather than attachment; and by a history of social changes and reconfigurations. However, we also *choose* placelessness. We often create and maintain stances of detachment from places because we do not want the responsibilities and limitations resulting from identification with them. Mobility is related to freedom; it allows us to move on to the next, more satisfying interest or location. J. Nicolas Entrikin points out that people consciously construct a sense of detachment from places in order to hold open accessibility to other kinds of relations. Although some benefits are lost when people minimize their attachments to places, other benefits are gained.[4] Erazim Kohak argues that wayfaring is not necessarily unfortunate and questionable but is a characteristic of human behavior: "The problem is not just that we are alienated dwellers, but that we are irreducibly both dwellers and wayfarers."[5] The cultural emphasis in recent decades on liberation from restrictions of many kinds, restrictions not only of race and gender, for example, but also restrictions imposed when particular places determine behavior, should not be suppressed by an overemphasis on rootedness at the expense of mobility. Cell phones, for example, give people the freedom to call and receive calls almost anywhere. Jean Baudrillard, along with cataloging the negative effects of placelessness, argues as well that those effects are offset by what he calls "the ecstasy of communication."[6] Placelessness is a result, then, not only of imposed social boundaries, of the architecture of convenience, and of accumulated social and cultural changes; it is also the result of our own decisions, decisions often made out of a desire for the mobility, freedom, and variety that detachment offers.

Placelessness, while widely recognized as an aspect of late modern culture, is evaluated by theorists in contrasting ways. Simone Weil, for example, views it as wholly negative. She sees it as arising from the fact that modern people have bonds of attachment not with places or with other people but with abstractions, particularly money and the state.[7] While she admits that uprootedness is also a consequence of education, she implies that something is wrong with education when it uproots people.[8] Weil's advocacy of roots finds its contrary in the work of Gilles Deleuze and Felix Guattari, who see rootedness as submission to political order. Indeed, Weil is vulnerable to their judgment. She *advocates* hierarchy and submission, although qualifying the latter with consent. She calls order the first need of all, and she identifies obedience as "a vital need of the human soul."[9] Deleuze and Guattari call, on the contrary, for rootlessness: "We're tired of trees. We should stop believing in trees, roots, and radicals. They've made us suffer too much."[10] Their alternative metaphor, the rhizome, stresses movement, variation, and unpredictability. Their anthropology posits, against Freud, an unconscious that is both positive and disordered. They are suspicious of order, even the order implied by language. They tie order to political order and, ultimately, to death.[11]

While not all theorists, in their evaluation of rootedness, can be so sharply contrasted with one another as can Weil and Deleuze and Guattari, the topic can hardly be broached without some evaluation of the options. Entrikin, for example, sees uprootedness or destabilization as a consequence of modern life that should, at least in part, be consciously resisted. People should cultivate places for themselves in an otherwise dislocating world. Consciously constructed places can, at least in part, compensate for the loss of "natural" places.[12] David Sopher takes a position contrary to Entrikin's when he points out that fewer and fewer people in our society live, as they once did, surrounded by family and lifelong friends. And people take this state of uprootedness, this nomadic style, as natural: "If we must use botanical metaphors, shouldn't we rather think of rhizomelike connections on the surface of the land forming a dense mat of human interchanges?"[13] E. Relph leans more toward Weil's side and the need for rootedness: "To have roots in a place is to have a secure point from which to look out on the world, a firm grasp of one's own position in the order of things and a significant spiritual and psychological attachment to somewhere in particular."[14] Madan Sarup would counter, "It is nearly always assumed that to have deep roots is good."[15] She argues that while "exile can be an affliction . . . it can also be a transfiguration—it can be a resource."[16] I could go on. The contrasting evaluations of a rooted or of a nomadic life seem clearly to divide many spatial and cultural theorists.

While it may be difficult to secure a norm for place-relations that is not finally a victim of this root and rhizome conflict, we can begin by recognizing positive elements on each side of the divide. As we already have seen, mobility is crucial to positive place-relations. And, as Yi-Fu Tuan points out, nomads are not only mobile; they also "establish camp at roughly the same places," and "the paths they follow also show little change."[17] Indeed, having no relations to places at all seems not only exceptional but also difficult, while lack of mobility may easily become imprisoning. Mobility and place relations should not, therefore, be seen as contradictory but as complementary.

Edward Casey deploys a single term to contain both mobility and rootedness, "habitation," a kind of commitment to place that is "capacious enough to include nomadic life as well as settled dwelling."[18] This seems, however, to collapse the contraries and to underestimate the tensions between them. But I would agree that the two emphases must be retained in spatial theory, and one need not decide in advance why and when the positive and the negative aspects of either rooted or nomadic states appear or what distribution or weighting between the two is optimal. It seems that, like preference for one of the three kinds and for one of the two sides of place relations, some people seem inclined by nurture and disposition more toward mobility and others more toward settledness.

The second kind of questionable relation to places, one that, we shall see, stands as a contrary to some forms of "placelessness," is ownership. Ownership should be seen as a contrary to imposed placelessness. Virginia Woolf makes this very clear in "A Room of One's Own." As a person who, by virtue of gender, had placelessness imposed on her by a society that considered (and often continues to consider) women's work as readily interruptible, Woolf counters by calling for the financial power to construct and maintain private space. Owned space counters the power of imposed placelessness. It answers force in kind. Ownership counters exclusion not only by the inclusion that ownership secures but also by the power it grants to exclude others.

It is not only to imposed placelessness or exclusion that owned space offers an alternative. It is also an alternative to chosen placelessness or detachment. Ownership grants a sense of specific location that counters mobility. The responsibilities and opportunities created by ownership can be a welcomed alternative to the kind of detachment that often marks other place-relations. Ownership allows a person to have things the way he or she wants them, and people are willing to expend the care and cost that makes them so. Simone Weil is sufficiently dedicated to rootedness that she advocates ownership strongly: "Private property is a vital need of the soul. The soul feels isolated, lost, if it is not surrounded by objects which seem to it like an extension of the bodily members."[19] And when J. Douglas Porteous divides places into two categories, "home and non-home," he means by "home" a place one owns: "Home is that place where we are most secure, where we can drop personas and become ourselves."[20] Ownership is a contrary to both imposed and elected placelessness; it becomes clear that these contraries intensify the force and significance of one another.

Indeed, ownership becomes an almost necessary alternative to placelessness, the sense we often have of being outsiders especially as we traverse social spaces. Not only are there many places that are not open to us; we also have no or very little effect on the social spaces that we encounter daily. By owning places we counter some of the determinations and limitations of our relations to social spaces.

While placelessness is elected as well as imposed, so ownership is not only chosen but is also required. We are socially positioned by private space, a place of residence, for example, that we own or rent. Indeed, ownership of property is part of our identity in a largely economically defined society. Having an address has been naturalized as a criterion for full or normal social identity.

While exclusion and detachment are not entirely negative, ownership of place is not entirely positive. Relations to places based on ownership are questionable because of the control that ownership provides. While there are likely to be inherent resistances in any place that keep its owner from exercising complete domination over it, ownership is inclined to reduce and even to eliminate reciprocity between person and place. The two, ownership and placelessness, stand, then, as mutually clarifying, contrary attitudes toward places, attitudes that, while not without positive characteristics, are noticeably deficient. They constitute as well, it is important to add, the most common forms of place-relations in our own culture. Imposed placelessness and private ownership, while having positive aspects, become problematic in our culture because, first, they largely determine our relations to places and because, second, they act as contraries, their negative aspects, which are largely attached to power, securing and aggravating one another. We are excluded from some places, and we own and control others and exclude people from them. It is a temptation to bewail the fact that our relations to places are so often defined by these two mutually aggravating contraries. Clearly, each kind of relation has deficiencies, and they are readily detectable by the critical eye. But we should also keep in mind that they also are not only mutually exacerbating but also potentially complimentary kinds of place-relations that help to sustain a very complex human world. They allow people both to move about and to have locations in society. Despite the real and potential negative factors in each—the distortion to place-relations produced by their domination of our relations to places and the fact that their often oppositional relations intensify their negative potentials—I discredit neither functional spaces and the nonrelations that they foster nor ownership and the sense of control over place that ownership provides. What needs to be done instead is to reduce the dominating, even defining, roles of placelessness and ownership in our spatial repertoire so that more complex and resonant relations to places can emerge.

II

If placelessness and ownership are bracketed, a center range of place-relations emerges, relations defined neither by placelessness nor by ownership. A term often used, especially by sociologists, to describe this middle, elusive range of relations is "attachment."[21]

A very important part of current spatial theory is the attention being given to the need for and experience of place-attachments, of meaningful relations with places, relations that include feelings, memories, and beliefs.[22] The general point is that place relations need not be defined exclusively either as functional, thereby deflecting attachments, or as commodities, thereby allowing full control. Places are also repositories of significance. As the editors of a collection of essays on place-attachment say, "the notion of valued environments emphasizes the benefits that are to be derived from association with, attachment to, and love of, certain places and landscapes: a perspective that has helped to balance the 'bias in favour of mobility' . . . in much contemporary social science theory."[23]

Two points become clear when studies of place-attachment are surveyed. The first point is that any of the kinds of human places that we earlier discussed—comprehensive, social, and intimate—can be the repository or locus of significance and the object of attachment. D. W. Meinig argues, for example, that landscape grants the sense of inclusion within something that antedates human constructions. An important correlate of landscape is nature, which means primarily, he suggests, what lies beyond human control, the ultimate backdrop or stage of human activities.[24] Porteous agrees: "We need a feeling of at-homeness, of course, not only with regard to our house, neighborhood, or country but also, according to philosophers of the environment, with the earth as a whole."[25] Sociologists, however, locate place-attachments primarily in social space. Places are repositories of meaning because they are sites of social relationships. Typical questions are these: Do place-attachments become less important or less possible in a more highly mobile society? Are place-attachments secondary effects of social attachments or do places have qualities of their own that serve to foster attachments? And can place-attachments be reestablished when once they have been disrupted?[26] More humanistic theorists associate place-attachment with intimate places, as in the essays edited by Leroy Rouner in *The Longing for Home*. Personal tastes, memories, and interests are stamped on intimate places, and they become associated with the person(s) that inhabit them.[27]

Several theorists recognize that place-attachments, because they are of many kinds, are differential. Yi-Fu Tuan counterpoises hearth and cosmos as contrary but also complimentary kinds of spaces with which people have meaningful relations.[28] Rather than discrete kinds of place-relations, Tuan posits hearth and cosmos as poles between which a range of place-attachments can be located: "If lovers of the hearth need the cosmos, so do lovers of the cosmos need the hearth."[29] J. Nicholas Entrikin projects a sense of attachment that includes meaningful relations with places of three kinds—objective or global space, places understood by means of cultural or communal symbols, and subjective or personal space.[30] Kinds of place-attachments need not be placed in exclusive relation to one another but can also be understood as having, at least on some occasions, a kind of nested relation. As J. E. Malpas puts it, "places are juxtaposed and intersect with one another; places also contain places so that one can move inwards to find other places nested within a place as well as move outwards to a more encompassing locale."[31] And Per Raberg argues not only for a three-tiered understanding of human place-attachments—the geographic macrolevel, the intermediate level of urban environment, and the microspace of the individual dwelling—but also for interactions "between the spatial layers," interactions that describe a complex but meaningful pattern or "existential totality."[32]

The second point about attachments to places of all three kinds is that their meanings can shift, sometimes suddenly and without detectable cause, between positive and negative effects. Comprehensive space can be exhilarating and expanding, but it can also become disorienting and intimidating. Social space can grant inclusion and direction, but it can also exclude and control. And intimate space can be a haven and a realm of freedom, but it can also become a prison and a place of lonely exile. J. Douglas Porteous says, for example: "Home is not wholly positive, however. It can, in its security, its routine, its well-knownness, become a prison."[33] And since, as David Sopher points out, "home" "can refer with equal ease to house, land, village, city, district, country, or, indeed, the world," the negative potentials of any kind of place-relation must be taken into account.[34]

The negative potential in each kind of place relation is, as I have already suggested, not entirely or necessarily bad. If the whole of the spatial system is intact, negative effects in relation to any kind of place can become a stimulus for finding alternative or complementary attachments with a place of that or of another kind. The optimal condition is that the negative potential of each kind of place-relation, even before it makes itself felt, defers to the positive potentials of another kind. However, it seems to be the case that people often lack positive attachments to places that complement and correct one another in this kind of ready way. This may be because the negative effect of one kind of place is so great that it reduces the ability to have a positive relation with a place of another kind. When giving critical attention to such negative states as these, we should keep in mind the possibility as well that people may have negative relations to places not only because of the nature of those places but also because of the inability of people to relate positively to them. Mobility, for example, may stop being an enabling potential that allows persons to move from one location to another and become a deeply engrained disposition that prevents any kind of relation to place at all. Conversely, ownership may create in people a habit of mind that allows them to treat all places with a desire to control them and with a consequent lack of restraint or respect when they cannot.

Place-attachment, however, is largely positive, and it is viewed as a normal, desirable aspect of persons' lives. Malpas, for example, believes that subjectivity is deformed without place-attachments: "place is not founded *on* subjectivity, but is rather that *on which* subjectivity is founded."[35] In addition, "the social does not exist prior to place . . . and so it cannot be that out of which, or solely by means of which, place is 'constructed.' It is within the structure of place that the very possibility of the social arises."[36] And speaking of what I have called comprehensive place, he says, "What enables our detachment from particular subjective spaces, then, is just the idea of objective space as that which is independent of any particular experience, and yet which provides a framework within which particular agents can be located and within which the particularities of experience can be explained."[37] Lack of place-attachment of any of the three kinds, then, is taken to have disabling consequences for human development, interrelations, and identity.

What commends the category of "place-attachment" as a description or norm for positive place-relations is that it recognizes both the differing kinds of place-relations and their two-sidedness, their physical and spiritual sides. It represents an attempt, especially by sociologists, to do justice to the combination within places of their physical specificity and the meanings places accumulate for people especially by the fact that they have done important things in or to them.

My dissatisfaction with the term "attachment" as a norm, however, is that it rests largely on notions of projection and deposit, acts of attaching oneself to a place, often consciously. It carries very much the sense that places are passive, locations where meanings are stored. People, such as Jonathan Z. Smith, who adopt this way of viewing place even analyze what are for people sacred places as places that are sacred because of the actions of people and their projections of meaning onto place. He says, for example, "Ritual is not an expression of or a response to 'the Sacred'; rather, something or someone is made sacred by ritual."[38] Since I do not believe that action or projection is always primary, I would want to look for another way of designating this single norm.

A contrary option is "home." It is not an uncommon designation for the positive relation that persons can have with places, and I have cited several theorists who use the term. As we saw, it is not a designation that is limited to intimate or personal space, although when applied to social and comprehensive spaces the term becomes recognizably metaphoric, an extension of one kind of place-relation or feeling to another. While the effect of the metaphor is powerful, it neglects the claims of the other kinds of space that their positive potential be recognized as relatively distinct from the privileged position that intimate space is given when "home" operates as a norm for all three kinds of place-relations.

I am also uneasy with "home" as a norm for place-relations because it stresses too heavily arrival and completion. There is too much a sense of finality about being "home." Perhaps it is because of the force and significance in my mind of "home" in baseball that the term has for me a strong sense of finality. The designation "home" neglects the negative potential in place-relations, and it discounts mobility as a factor that can enhance place-relations by allowing movement between kinds of places.

There is, now, a steady stream of studies of human spatiality that counter the sense of placelessness and ownership as well as mobility in modern culture with an emphasis on "home." Many of these studies, while not neglecting the physicality of places, emphasize their spirituality.[39] Such studies are constructive responses to the commercialization of places. They also counter the emphasis of the preceding decades on liberation, which, as Yi-Fu Tuan points out, always carries spatial implications, namely, liberation "from bondage to a fixed condition—to place."[40]

While there is much that is thoughtful and sensitive in these studies, I am also dissatisfied with "home" as a norm for positive place-relations. This is not only because it privileges personal space, suggests completion or finality, and ignores the important role of mobility for optimal place relations but also because those who use "home" as a norm tend to give too much authority in place-relations to the place itself. Belden Lane says, for example, "Indeed, it appears that, from one point of view, place creates people."[41] While I want to retain the force and significance that places can generate or hold, I think that this way of formulating place-relations tips the balance too much toward the place. While "place-attachment," by emphasizing places as passive to deposits of meaning, makes place too secondary, "home," by suggestions of places that are meaningful prior to the relations of persons to them, makes place too primary. While positive place relations can largely be described in these two ways, I think that, for reasons given, we cannot rest with either of them as our norm.

III

The designation I prefer for positive place-relations is "accommodating," and I place it *between* its nearest relatives, "place-attachment" and "home." There are several connotations of the term "accommodating" that serve it well as a normative designation and make it more useful and inclusive than Edward Casey's "habitation."

"Accommodating" suggests, first of all, that there is a fittingness and adaptability of persons and places to one another, an adjustment by both so that they are mutually suitable and appropriate. There are several things that I like about this way of designating the norm in place-relations. First, the cause of a positive place-relation is not located on only one side. There is an adjusted compatibility or reciprocity between person and place. The place draws something from and adds something to the person, and the person draws something from and adds something to the place. As Robert Sack puts it, "mutual dependency and causality are exactly what I mean by relational."[42] Relations to places are richly positive when places are both depositories of meaning and themselves evocative and significant. As places evoke something from persons and persons evoke something from the places, both are altered. There is a potential in both persons and places that is actualized by their relation to one another. Casey puts it this way: "A place, we might even say, has its own 'operative intentionality' that elicits and responds to the corporeal intentionality of the perceiving subject. Thus place integrates with body as much as body with place." It is clear, I should go on to say, that what Casey means by "body" is not only its physical but also its cultural make-up.[43] There is in optimal place-relations, then, first of all a reciprocal accommodation of place and person to one another.

The second thing that commends "accommodating" as a designation for the positive potential in place-relations is that it suggests capaciousness. Places and persons are mutually accommodating because both are complex. Places and persons not only accommodate both the physical and the spiritual but also grant the realization that the physical and spiritual are not separate but united or interpenetrating. Places and persons also accommodate both past and future, both memories and aspirations. They grant, furthermore, both restfulness and exhilaration. Optimal place-relations are accommodating, then, because they are multidimensional and inclusive, capacious enough to evoke and sustain a range of factors and dimensions, some in tension with one another, in a complex unity.

Third, "accommodating" is a helpful designation for the norm in place-relations because it suggests something temporary. This sense of impermanence sets off my norm from the finality suggested by "home," "dwelling," or even "habitation." It preserves, in place-relations, the fact that there are negative potentials in every place-relation, including home, and that there are no permanent placements. This is not to neglect the welcoming force and meaning of "accommodating." There is a fully positive sense of being accommodated by a place. In addition, awareness is preserved that one can be accommodated by all three kinds of places and by many instances of each kind. This also means that connotations of one kind of place-relation, such as personal or intimate place, are not applied to another kind, expecting, as seems to be the case with "home," "dwelling," and "habitation," that all positive place-relations are of one kind. Optimal place-relations, then, are firm but not final, locating but also liberating.

Finally, "accommodating" suggests an element of the unexpected in positive place-relation, of relation to place as gift. Positive place-relations cannot wholly be accounted for in terms of expectation and planning. There is something gratuitous and surprising in positive place-relations. As Yi-Fu Tuan puts it, "One can no more deliberately design such places than one can plan, with any guarantee of success, the occasions of genuine human exchange."[44] One is unexpectedly reassured or exhilarated by the sense of or relation to comprehensive place. One is incorporated, valued, and enriched by a relation to or participation in social space. And one is restored, particularized, and deepened by relation to personal or intimate space. These positive relations delight because, among other things, they carry the implication not only of something unexpected but also of something undeserved. Accommodation, therefore, suggests not only reciprocity, comprehension, and impermanence but also surprise. Positive place-relations hold gifts that we do not know we need and desire so much until we receive them.

The positive place-relations narrated by the texts to which we gave primary attention in this study have these characteristics. It may be helpful briefly to catalogue them as a way of substantiating the designation of "accommodating" as a norm for positive place-relations. I think that it is possible to recognize the aspects included within this norm, that is, mutually adjusting, inclusive of the past and future and the physical and spiritual, secure but impermanent, and giftlike, in each instance.

Clym Yeobright, in *The Return of the Native,* returns to the heath with expectations and plans that are unrealistic. His exposure to the heath's harshness requires accommodations by him, and those changes are a measure of his increasing wisdom. The heath, in turn, becomes a fitting arena in which Clym can carry on his pedagogical program, since it is, along with him, a teacher of wisdom. Clym's relation to the heath as comprehensive space is one of mutuality between his expectations and the realities of life's conditions.

In addition, the heath is commodious. It grants a sense of continuity between past and present, physical and spiritual. The sense of continuity with the distant past is expressed in the ancient monuments and the rituals still enacted on the heath. The future is adumbrated in the kind of teaching ministry that Clym will pursue. And the relation of physical and spiritual to one another on the heath is secured not only in and by the rituals but also in the moral integrity and charitable qualities that are recognizable in people who, like Venn, live close to the heath.

The temporary quality of place-relation is detectable in Clym's sobered attitude toward his environment. He has been made aware of its negative potentials, and there is little chance that he will feel entirely rooted to the heath. However expanding and revealing it may be, the heath is too difficult and unpredictable a place to allow return to become complete and final.

Last, the giftlike quality of relation to the heath is clear in that the heath not only is anything but humanly constructed but also that it is thereby also a welcomed relief. Relation to such a place is exactly what Clym needs, given the superficiality and self-deception associated with the constructed social space of Parisian life. The gifts bestowed by relation to the heath, especially by its magnitude and vicissitudes, are a sense of reality and an identity free from illusion.

In *The Secret Agent,* we are dealing with a wholly negative depiction of social space. We have to infer from its negative characteristics what a positive social space and relation to it would be like. So, for example, mutual adjustment is exactly what is lacking in the relation of Verloc to his social context. He and the political bureaucracy stand in no mutuality at all.

The social space is also confining rather than commodious. It does not allow Verloc to relate his past to his present or future. Winnie also experiences no connections between her past attempts to provide security for her family and the future thrust upon her by what Verloc does to Stevie. The social space, although total, is confining, even imprisoning. Efforts toward greater freedom only create more restrictions. The futures projected by the anarchists offer no connections with the present and are highly improbable.

What further contributes to the negative coloration of relations to social space in *The Secret Agent* is that there are no alternative spaces to which one can move, spaces either of a comprehensive or of an intimate kind. No relief can be found. There is no chance of significant mobility, social, cultural, or geographical. The social space is permanent and total.

Finally, there is nothing giftlike about the environment. All surprises are bad ones. The revelations to Verloc about his prospects and the truth about Verloc's relation to Stevie are all bad news. Social space reveals itself not as a gift but a bane, a prison, a den of horrors. It has a contrary relation to human aspirations and abilities.

Mutual adjustment is very much a part of the situation of Margaret and Helen at the close of *Howards End.* The house can accommodate change, suggested by Helen's pregnancy, as it can also accommodate the Schlegel furniture. The ability of the women, especially Margaret, to adjust to the house and its legacy is also clear.

The close of the narrative also makes clear the commodious character of personal space, its ability to hold past and future as well as physical and spiritual together. Margaret, by taking Helen and her child in, betokens a future that will mark departures from the past. In addition, the spiritual inheritance of Mrs. Wilcox is a part of the house's legacy, but the turn of Helen toward the realities of economic and social class and injustice indicate a strong injection of material and historical factors.

The house, while it grants security in a time of transition, is also not confining. Helen and her child, particularly, may not remain in the house, and it is for them especially a temporary lodgment. It offers security but not finality.

Last, the house is very much a gift, a bequest from Mrs. Wilcox, and Helen's inclusion in the house is a gift to her from her sister. The gift-quality of the place and of the sisters' relation to it is clear in contrast to considerations of property and propriety, the economic interests of the Wilcox family houses, and the attempted exclusion of Helen from Howards End because of the social embarrassment caused by her pregnancy.

Querry and the heart of Africa evoke something from one another by the end of *A Burnt-Out Case*. The location has a positive, quickening effect on Querry, although the place, due to European imperialism, is ambiguous. But he is able to take up, howbeit in modest form, his own work, and Querry, by his work, is able to contribute something to the place.

The relation of past and future and of physical and spiritual aspects in Querry's relation to the place can also be seen. His past architectural training can be retrieved from its cultural determinations, and the designs he offers hold open a direction for the future that will be less marked by the disdain and conflicts of the past. His attention to the physical realities of the location, especially the forest and the bodies of the ill, are tied very closely for Querry to matters of spiritual integrity, charity, and a lack of anxiety toward his own dying.

There are enough ambiguities and uncertainties in Querry's African location, however, to keep it from becoming final and complete. Indeed, Querry repeatedly realizes that he wants and needs to go further. While Querry becomes increasingly a part of the life of the colony and of some of the indigenous people, especially Deo Gratias, these ties are tentative. The heart of Africa forms for him no permanent abode.

Finally, the location is giftlike, and the comprehensive space to which it grants Querry access is a gift as well. He did not go to Africa as part of a plan, and he has no objectives for his stay there. He simply allows the place to affect him, and his attitude toward his own death puts him in relation to a reality that he does not control. By his acceptance of death he has access to a way of being in the world that prevents him from absorption into the comforts of institutions and their ideologies. The asylum Africa grants from constructions imposed on him by the culture he left behind and the sense of mystery that the location provides are gifts.

The mutual adjustment, in *The Spire*, between Jocelyn and the cathedral, while not by any means without its painful and injurious sides, is evident in the fact that the cathedral evokes from him the aspiration to build the spire, and the spire is completed largely because it draws so much from him. Social space is changed by the contributions of persons, and their potentials are actualized by the roles provided to them by the construction.

The capaciousness of the social space binds together past and future and the physical and spiritual. The life of the cathedral, although temporarily disrupted by construction of the spire, is embodied in the various offices and the vocations it includes and requires. But the future is very much a part of the reconfiguration of social space consequent to the construction of the spire. No less are physical and spiritual factors revealed as mutually dependent and clarifying in this social space. The question of foundations, for example, is crucial to the construction, and the weight and strength of the structure are indispensable to its overall effect, which is an edifying, upwardly directed one. The narrative in many ways makes clear the important role that a social place and relations to it can play in confirming the interdependence of past and future and of the physical and spiritual.

The negative aspects of building the spire, especially the pain and even deaths it causes for others, are due to the confinement of Jocelyn to the project. Jocelyn has access to no alternative places, neither comprehensive nor personal, and the dedication of his whole life and of everything under his jurisdiction to the project is obsessive, confining, and coercive. His deficient relations to personal and comprehensive places make him more a prisoner of his project than he could or should have been. So strong is this meaning-effect in the novel that the language of obsession and confinement threatens the language of exhilaration, joy, and creative fulfillment. While it is very likely that if it were not for his lack of self-criticism and his pride, the spire would not have been built, it also seems clear that his attitudes are excessive and objectionable and that Jocelyn, by a more inclusive repertoire of place-relations, could have accomplished the task without so heavy a cost.

Finally, the spire and the social space that it creates are a gift, a surprise. Despite the storm, it stands. While planning, resources, and skills go into its construction, it is also unprecedented, improvised, and gratuitous. Its effects, such as reconfiguring the town, are also a surprise. Golding weaves a language of grace and a language of judgment together in the narrative to convey the very ambiguous nature of human creativity, its costly and its edifying sides.

In *The Only Problem,* Harvey, at the end, seems to have discovered a personal place at least partially outside of and free from the determinations of social categories and identity constructions. It is a place that allows him to pursue his own interests, and its effects on him are registered by the caring roles he assumes at the end.

The past that Harvey takes to the discovery of personal space is his long-standing interest in the particular suffering of Job, an interest focused by the de La Tour painting. The future that the place opens to him is one of caring for others, particularly the young. Such caring points outward, toward growth and change. And it is a place where physical location and moral and spiritual clarification are interrelated. The place and the actualization of personal integrity are inseparable.

Harvey's newly achieved personal place is bound to be temporary, if for no other reason than because it is oriented toward the nurture of children. It seems clear, too, that personal space, given the force and pervasiveness of the social environment, cannot be permanent but must be won over and over again.

Finally, personal space at the end of *The Only Problem* is not only the result of disciplined withdrawal but also is a gift. Harvey, while pursuing the possibility of taking or being an exception, did not know beforehand how personal place would appear or become accessible. Indeed, almost by definition, personal space cannot be scripted. If it were it would become part of the culture of duplication and categorization. Instances of taking or being an exception can be scripted, but what that would be like in particular cases must be clarified anew each time.

The four connotations of "accommodating"—namely, mutually adjusting; inclusive, especially of past and future and of physical and spiritual factors; tentative or releasing; and giftlike—serve to give content to the norm for positive place-relations that runs throughout kinds. These narratives directly or indirectly advocate *accommodating* as the norm for optimal place-relations of all three kinds and of place-relations regardless of which of their two sides is the dominant.

IV

The characteristics of positive place-relations that I have gathered under the single norm "accommodating" bear, as the quotations from Tuan and Sack included above indicate, similarities to the relations that we have with other people. Indeed, one could turn not only to those characteristics but to all the attitudes toward place that we have considered and see analogies to the relations people have with others. Relph says as much: "A deep relationship with places is as necessary, and perhaps as unavoidable, as close relationships with people." And, as in our relations with people, "there is not merely a fusion between person and place, but also a tension between them." He adds, "Our experience of place . . . is a dialectical one—balancing a need to stay with a desire to escape."[45] Gillian Rose's spatial theory is grounded in her belief "that identity is relational," a belief that she finds nurtured by feminist theory, and the relational character of identity pertains to places as well as people.[46] Robert Sack concludes, "People and places are then mutually constitutive."[47] Our relations to places and our relations to persons have much to do with one another. If we think of our relations to people as contrary, antagonistic, or competitive, it is difficult to imagine how we will be able to increase the positive qualities, as I have tried to secure them, in our relations to places. However, if spatial theory charts the way toward a revitalization and enrichment of our relations to places, it will also carry a subtext about the role of personal relations in human identity. While it is not clear to me that, in securing the relational character of human identity, one kind of place-relation should be emphasized, it does appear that social space, especially given the fact that social spaces in modern culture carry particularly grave problems, deserves special attention.

Michael R. Curry, in his discussion of the ethics of places and place-relations, says that places deserve ethical consideration because all human activities take place somewhere. However, social places are not only contexts for human activities; they can also influence behaviors: "'That's how we do things here'"[48] While Curry stresses, in his discussion of ethics and place, that social places have ethical importance because human actions occur in places, he does not simply make place a passive context for human activities so that the ethical standing of place is derived passively from the human activities that occur there. Places affect human activities, attitudes, and behaviors, and their effects can be beneficial or harmful. Spatial theory, then, because it cannot be separated either from personal identity or from the relations of persons to one another and because it can give directions for improving the qualities of place-relations, has obvious moral and spiritual content.

The moral and spiritual status of social spaces would benefit from the kind of concern that recently has begun to enhance our relations to what I have been referring to as comprehensive space, especially in regard to the natural environment. Environmental ethics and the attitudes of responsibility and care that mark the ecological movement offer a ready and rich resource for cultivating a sense of the ethics of comprehensive place-relations. More incipient but also available are the ethical considerations that go into theories and policies regarding personal or intimate spaces, policies concerning adequate and fair housing, for example. But when we come to social spaces, we find ourselves in a less promising position. We have largely given over our sense of social space, especially in the form of large urban spaces, to what we take to be the inevitable effects of "public" life, that is, impersonal, functional, and commercial effects. A deficiency in positive attitudes toward social space, especially urban space, poses a serious problem. I shall take up this question more fully in the conclusion by asking, to sharpen the point: Can urban spaces be freed from the negative, even evil, status assigned to them, including those projected by some of the texts treated in this study? Can urban space be freed from its roles of epitomizing meaningless or negative space and of standing to the sacred as its contrary? If urban spaces are freed from confinement to the cultural construction of "profane space," can they become social spaces that, along the lines of the norm of "accommodating," are more aligned with and helpful in defining what could be culturally understood as "sacred space"?

Conclusion

Freeing the City from the Factual Profane

A fracture separates two contrary sites for articulating and defining modernity. I have emphasized one of them, particularly in the introduction. That site is the modern in its massive and external form, the complex that finds its center or epitome in vast urbanization. I charted briefly the history of this site's formation, and in the chapters on social space I took the measure of some of the problems that urban spaces pose for human place-relations. Their size, for example, tends to occlude comprehensive space and to swamp personal spaces. With the help of several theorists, particularly Lefebvre, I described, especially in response to Conrad's London, the tendency of large urban spaces, because of their hidden, determining structures, toward abstraction, rigidity, and depersonalization.

The second site for articulating and defining modernity has only, in all of this, been suggested. It is a site that, from the Romantics to the present day, stands as a contrary to the massive modern, namely, the self, subjectivity, and the personal. This preoccupation is part of the entire modern agenda, beginning with Descartes and continuing in Locke, primarily in the question of personal identity. It becomes an urgent preoccupation in the Romantic period in direct response to the emerging modern in its massive forms. Toward the end of the nineteenth century, this culture of personal identity and subjectivity takes a more radical turn through the growing attention to, even fascination for, what William James called the subconscious continuation of the conscious life. Indeed, internality became not only an alternative to, or retreat from, the massive modern but also a spiritual resource to evaluate and oppose it. For James, the subconscious is the locus of revelation, for "whatever it may be on its *farther* side, the 'more' with which in religious experience we feel ourselves connected is on its hither side the subconscious continuation of our conscious life."[1] If our lives, for James, are invaded by a spiritual reality, this invasion takes place through the subliminal door.[2] By the end of the nineteenth century the religious importance of internality—which is manifest in such occult explorations as theosophy and the Hermetic Order of the Golden Dawn—pits the internal self against the massive, external modern as the sacred is pitted against the profane.[3] And that opposition, however attenuated or complicated, continues to have determining cultural effects today.

Modernity, indeed, is most accurately articulated and defined neither by the site of the massively urban nor by the self as site of the sacred but by the distance or contrary relation between the two. While this split marks the entire modern period, it takes on a new profundity in the period of time covered by this study. The two sites of the modern define and deepen one another. Peter Calthorpe describes the dynamic this way: "As our private world grows in breadth, our public world becomes more remote and impersonal. As a result, our public space lacks identity and is largely anonymous, while our private space strains toward a narcissistic autonomy."[4] On the one side is the construction of that matrix of power concentrated in the urban. On the other side are internally oriented and spiritually resourceful selves, standing apart from—often in critical postures against—the city.

It should be clear that the six writers I have examined, including those who emphasize social space, militate against this defining and mutually exacerbating split. Their underlying theory of human spatiality posits social place-*relations* instead of this split. The writers, in their differing but complementary ways, understand and depict human spatiality as relational. However, when confronting the massively urban in the figure, say, of London, the attitude is one of warning and fright.

The task before us, however daunting, cannot be dodged. If massive urbanization is not simply a phenomenon of the nineteenth and twentieth centuries but will continue during the new century and even increase in pace, a viable theory of human spatiality as relational needs to deal with this sign of the modern as *split*. We can see even more reason for urgency perhaps than they do when Edward Soja and Barbara Hooper remark, "the whole focus comes upon the importance—no, the *necessity*—to re-cover 'urbanness.'"[5]

I think that the task of addressing the split should begin with the modern cultural construction of massive urban space rather than with its contrary, the spiritually resourceful self. I suggest this for two reasons. First, the modern as massive externality is what we as moderns more fully share. We tend far more to agree on the nature and moral standing of the urban than we do on the spiritual resources of the self. Indeed, we take the urban as shared fact while we take the personal as the arena of freedom and variability. Second, I think that because personal identity cannot be formed without regard to place-relations and given the importance of massive urban spaces for defining place, it follows that personal identity and subjectivity, along with whatever else contributes to them, are affected by the urban. I find it requisite, therefore, to raise the question of the urban in order to enhance the possibilities of the personal and to counter the invalidation of a relational theory of social spatiality posed by urban space as the factual profane.

I

As striking as the massive size of urban centers is the negative view that we tend to have of them. As Sol Linowitz says regarding cities, "Despair from within and indifference from without have taken the place of vision."[6] The negative thrust of our sense of the city is not wholly unwarranted. It has two causes. One is material: Cities have been exploited by people who neither reside in them nor have their nurture in mind. Much urban space has been constructed, as Linowitz says, by "land speculators and builders [who] wanted to make money" and had no interests in cities apart from exploiting their economic potentials.[7] The result is a city shaped by commercial interests, skyscrapers, freeways, and single-function sites "which systematically sought to remove the content of everyday culture."[8] Cities are also put at a disadvantage materially by the fact that they receive large numbers of people who emigrate to them from rural locations or small towns and from other countries, bringing with them little in terms of skills and wealth to cope with their new, vast, and complex environments. As a consequence, populations often grow more rapidly in cities than the facilities and opportunities to accommodate them, and a lag appears between the needs and potentials of people and the capacity of cities to respond to them. This produces large groups of people who are not only impoverished but also frustrated and even desperate, and such conditions can be expected to breed crime. Crime, while having its impact on the larger urban setting, most directly worsens the lives of people living under the conditions that breed it, people whose lives are already difficult. Finally, a city, while we refer to it in the singular, is far from unified. It is a complex aggregate of differing power groups and competitive financial interests. This means that generating resources, developing policies, and constructively addressing the problems of the city fall victim if not to particular interests than to the difficulty of finding a public will between them.

Along with these material causes for the negative positioning of the city, there is also a powerful cultural cause. The deeply damaging colonization of urban spaces and the problems that cities create by virtue of size, complexity, and scarcity of material resources for public use are intensified and even justified by a cultural construction of the city as profane space. Theories that often are shaped by positive moral intentions can be seen as actually abusing cities by identifying them as concentrations of all that is wrong with modernity. Cities and city-parts are displayed as epitomes of what is worst in the society. David Harvey, a social, economic geographer, recently exposed Baltimore and its most neglected and abused parts to demonstrate the negative consequences of the history and practices of capitalism. While it is not his purpose to support the abuse of cities by regimes of economic exploitation and indifference, his depictions of the city warrant a degree of hopelessness concerning them, an attitude of indifference of which Linowitz speaks. This attitude serves to accept the colonial role of cities and the majority of their populations until such time in the vague future when as yet unrealized economic and political replacements can be initiated, "spaces of hope," as Harvey refers to them.[9] The tendency in all of this, although not part of Harvey's intention, is to locate the problem in the victim and not in the cultural attitudes that construct the city itself, at least in part, as the cause of the problem. Edward Soja and Mike Davis do similar things to Los Angeles. Davis, for example, calls it the first among the "fortress cities"; "Los Angeles, in its usual prefigurative mode, offers an especially disquieting catalogue of the emergent liaisons between architecture and the American police state."[10] Cultural evaluations of urban spaces as epitomes of what is wrong, even evil, in modernity support the colonization of cities and locate the possibilities of their rectification outside the history of which cities are viewed as epitomes. Modernity constructs urban space as the profane, as the agreed upon, indisputable negative upon which tentative forms of internal, utopian, or sacred spaces are projected as contraries.

Such cultural constructions of the city as profane carry consequences. As Roy Eyerman points out, physical realities are not necessarily all-determining in the formation of places and of relations to and attitudes toward them. Culture, what he calls "symbolic frameworks of meaning," mobilize and direct "realities" as much as realities and power determine culture. Extending his observations, we can say that what too often happens in regard to cities is that cultural evaluations of them have sponsored "realities" that have allowed cities to be victimized by powers with little interest in their general well-being.[11] On this view of things, "cities are often criticized because they represent the basest instincts of human society," and they have come, whole or in part, to be associated with evil.[12]

If, as Richard Rorty points out, "fact" is an honorific we apply to what we agree on, the profane character of the city has become a fact.[13] The city as factual profane establishes the secure base upon which various, more personal constructions of "sacred" spaces are erected. As a result, a moral resignation regarding urban spaces is commonplace in modernity. The separation of moral and spiritual hopes and needs from the historical realities of urban spaces causes and confirms the role of cities as actualizations of the factual profane.

This construction of the city as the factual profane is the result of a long history. I suggested this history when, in the introduction, I gave some of the causes for the gradual exchange of historical for spatial categories in the self-description of some early modernists. I pointed out that, while historical categories dominated from the eighteenth century on (I cited Vico as a crucial theorist for this shift), modernism, beginning already in the nineteenth century, became increasingly defined by more spatial than temporal terms, a process that comes to completion in late modernity or postmodernity and helps to define it. The violence, dislocation, and alienation that mark twentieth-century cultural history provide mounting evidence for a narrative of loss and degeneration in social, particularly urban, spaces.

Raymond Williams, to whom I already have turned, is well known among historians and theorists of English literary culture for his analysis of this history and its consequences. One of his main points is that culture, because of this history of rapid and often traumatic change, increasingly was defined, from the beginning of the nineteenth century on, as an ensemble of understandings and values standing above and apart from history. Literary culture became a kind of steadying constellation to guide generations otherwise at sea on the swells and troughs of frequent and radical spatial changes. This separation between a history of change and a sacred culture of stable values and significance is well established by the close of the century. The project continues through the middle of the twentieth. When Wyndham Lewis mounted his campaign in 1927 against philosophers of time, especially Bergson, his aim, despite all his appeal to external reality, is to argue for "Space" as a refuge from a history of disruption and disorientation. For him the great appeal of "Space" is that it "keeps still, not (ideally) occupied in incessantly slipping away, melting into the next thing, and repudiating its integrity."[14] Lewis was so influential not by strength of his philosophical argument but by positing "Space" as apart from change and above time and history. The bifurcation between a history of physical disruption, altered identities, and spatial dislocation and a realm of stable value sponsored by moral and aesthetic genius, personal character and virtue, and the spiritual resources of the self grows from the end of the eighteenth century well into the twentieth, and its consequences are with us still. Among the many outcomes of this history is the identification of modern urban centers with a history of violence and alienation and the exclusion of cities from the values located in a realm of cultural significance apart from or above material history, a realm sponsored by and relevant to creative, moral, and spiritual subjectivity.

When cities are seen as the principal products of material history, cities are not only bereft of culture but posited as its contrary, as the profane. The classic statement of this development is by Marx and Engels: "all that is sacred is profane." As Marshall Berman says, Marx and Engels mean by this clause that the "aura of holiness is suddenly missing" and that we are "all in it together, at once subjects and objects of the pervasive process that melts everything into air."[15] That clause in the "Manifesto" yields to what follows it, namely, that "man is at last compelled to face with sober senses his real conditions of life and his relations with his kind."[16] "Reality," exposed by the loss of the sacred, is harsh. Engels describes the city as revealing the truth of the relations of human beings to one another. In the city "the war of each against all, is here openly declared . . . , people regard each other only as useful objects; each exploits the other, and the end of it all is, that the stronger treads the weaker under foot, and that the powerful few, the capitalists, seize everything for themselves, while to the weak many, the poor, scarcely a bare existence remains."[17] This reality and what, as Berman puts it, we all have in common come together as the construction of the factual profane. In the profane, the real and what we have in common have been revealed. It is the yield of history, the truth we all can be expected to accept. It is the city as factual profane, and "spaces of hope," culture, and the sacred, if entertained at all, must be projected as its personally sponsored contraries.

There is a remarkably tenacious and pervasive agreement in our culture that modern history is deficient in meaning, is determined solely by power and struggle, and is wicked, and that this history finds its principal consequence or product in urban space. A remarkable confluence of agreement on this point spans distinctions between people with religious and with nonreligious interests and between people whose orientations are political and those whose orientations are aesthetic. Whatever sense of agreement we may have as a culture arises not primarily from beliefs about positive values in our common life but from a shared belief about the negative effects of modern history and their principal concentration in the city. Modernity is unified primarily by the certainty of the city as increasingly and inevitably profane and evil and as the negative warrant for the moral and spiritual resources located in the self.

This shared belief about modern history and the city as profane provides a solid, shared basis upon which various less certain forms of sacred places can be affirmed, projected, or imagined. The only continuity that exists between beliefs in and projections of sacred spaces is that they are all based on the certainty of the factual profane. The sacred becomes some version of dissociated place, a social utopia, the realm of spiritual internality, a religious community or tradition, a canon of texts viewed synchronically, and so on. However much sponsors of alternatives to the profane in other ways differ from one another—Marxists and post-Marxists; cultural critics who call for a return to a shelf of texts that teach virtue; spokespersons of the church and theologians; those interested in myth, whether for Jungian or literary reasons; and those attracted to premodern societies—all can be seen as standing together not only in their judgment of modern history and the city as profane but also in their attempts to establish, on the basis of the putative factuality of the profane, a place or space free from and contrary to that profane, a sacred place or space offering a more moral, fully human, and meaningful alternative.

A scholar who shares much with all of the above, who clearly depends on the factual profane for theorizing sacred space, and who is the still influential is Mircea Eliade. He comes to his advocacy of sacred space by way of a condemnation of modern history, a condemnation that he shares with many cultural and religious theorists emerging from the First and Second World Wars. A displaced Romanian, Eliade inherited and cultivated a deep distrust for modern history, and he militated against progressive theories of history and historicism. Under the banner of what he called the "terror of history," he advocated a reinstatement of sacred space as an antidote to the consequences of dislocation, alienation, meaninglessness, and trauma caused by modern history in general and the history of war and Western European political domination in particular.[18]

The need to establish sacred space is created, for Eliade, by the experience and threat of the profane. As he says, "The first possible definition of the *sacred* is that it is *the opposite of the profane*."[19] The disorienting effect of the profane compels people to construct or intuit a space defined as center and as open to the transcendent. The sacred is present to modern awareness in recognizable vestiges, an awareness quickened by it negative contrary, the profane: "Man becomes aware of the sacred because it manifests itself, shows itself, as something wholly different from the profane."[20] Awareness of the profane triggers recognition of the sacred, a recognition moderns, however jaded, continue to carry as a potential in their subjectivity.

It would be easy to dismiss Eliade's theory of sacred space because of the idealism upon which it is built and the ontological claims that it carries. But we should notice that his construction of sacred space gains credibility from the agreement it holds with many diverse theorists who also read modern Western history as profane, disorientating, meaningless, and alienating. What needs to be questioned, then, is not the idealism, which is, I think, of secondary standing in his argument, but the move that he makes, along with so many others, from the putatively secure, agreed upon ground of modern history as the factual profane to the desirability and authority of a sacred space recalled from or modeled on *homo religiosis*. What points can be raised against this formidable construction of the profane as a fact supportive of theories of the sacred?

The first is to question positing the profane as primary, as preceding and warranting the sacred. Why is it the case that the profane, the negative, has a primary and causal position that grounds the sacred, the positive? Why can a theory of sacred space not be based on and derived from positive place-relations?

The second reason to question this construction and use of the profane is that the profane, even if only as its contrary, will determine the force and significance of the sacred. If a person turns from the profane in order to pursue the sacred, the person will do so from motives and needs derived from the rejected negative. Should the nature and role of sacred space be determined by the threats and lacks posed by the profane? Is it not possible that the sacred answers questions, so to speak, that it itself poses and fulfills needs that it itself clarifies? Why cannot positive place-relations in their incompleteness or impermanence point beyond themselves to sacred space as something that exceeds them?

Finally, if the profane is so closely tied, as it is in these constructions, to history, the sacred is projected as a space at least partly separate from history and change. Indeed, a recent collection of essays on sacred places as pilgrimage sites attacks, precisely on this point, such notions of the sacred as we have in Eliade. The sacred places to which people make pilgrimage are not uncomplicated, separated from the history of change and struggle, and whole. Rather, they are complex, contested, and subject to change. As the editors say, "it is necessary to develop a view of pilgrimage as a field of social relations but also as a *realm of competing discourses.*"[21] The essays and the editors' introduction draw on an array of anthropological testimonies that sacred places are the goals of pilgrimage not because they are constant, unified, and simple but because they are complex. The editors conclude, "This, in the final analysis, is what confers upon a major shrine its essential, universalistic character: its capacity to absorb and reflect a multiplicity of religious discourses, to be able to offer a variety of clients what each of them desires."[22] Such places mean many things and possess various potentials for disparate people. People go to sacred places for differing reasons and with various results. Sacred places generate many kinds of significance. Indeed, the management of pilgrimage sites often involves ordering the differing interests that give rise to the presence of the pilgrims and that the sacred place is called on to address.

A recent version of an Eliade-like use of the factual profane to secure projections of the sacred is Graham Ward's *Cities of God*. The visibility of this study is extended by the fact that it represents a widely noticed movement in current theological studies called "radical orthodoxy." This means, among other things, that it is representative of a group of theologian who would consider themselves as in every important way distant from such work as Eliade's represents. It may be helpful to point out, then, that there is large agreement not only between them and Eliade but also between them and, as I have said, many other witnesses, nonreligious as well as religious, political as well as aesthetic.

What is striking about Ward's book is that its author can call on many, various scholars to support him, so that however specific his theological interests may be, they look, given that support, not of parochial but of public standing. His thesis that the modern city is a concentration, an inevitable outcome, of all that is wrong with modern culture and modern history is amplified by its wide support. He names some of its members: "We are heading in this direction if the Haraways and Posters, the Sassens and Castellses, the Featherstones and Harveys, the Baudrillards and Lyotards, the Vattimos and Baumans, the Nancys and Zizeks, the Urilios and Giddenses are to be believed."[23] Although he could have named more, he draws on a large repertoire of studies that assume, along with him, this role of the modern city as profane space and the principal product of modern history.

Ward's diagnosis of urban space as profane is based primarily on his assumption that the city is constructed as a fulfillment of every conceivable human desire. In what may be his most provocative move, Ward shifts from the city as synecdoche of modernity to the pornographic shop as synecdoche of the city. The pornographic shop distils the essence of the city, enticing people with promises of fulfillment and luring them with images more vivid than reality.[24] The veritable sinkhole or heart and soul of modernity can be found in the city's pornographic shops.

Ward's construction or projection of spaced space is, therefore, a conventional move. The fact that his sacred space is parochial does not matter; variety and particular interests in projections of the sacred are tolerable since all find their shared and sure base in the factual, univocal profane. Since Ward sees the fountainhead of profane history in Protestantism generally and in Calvinism particularly, he can pose his personal, sacred contrary as a form of Catholic hierarchical sacramentalism. It is the church as "a community [Note the built-in contrary relation of "community" to urban space.]²⁵ that produces and occupies a space transcending place, walls and boundaries, a liturgical, doxological space opening in the world onto the world."²⁶ In other words, it is not an actual but a potential space. What Ward and others who pursue this line want to do is to restore the public offices of the medieval church despite the fact that the church, in the modern city, holds nothing like the position relative to public life that it held in the medieval state.²⁷

Eliade and Ward jointly tap into a cultural agreement about modern history and its principal consequence, urban space, namely, that they are profane, even evil. Their theories reveal a belief that many people, despite widely differing interests and beliefs, share. Indeed, it is difficult to be certain about what will unify modern culture if it is disabused of this "fact," this shared belief. The profane has, for a long time now, provided the common ground that holds us together, despite radical differences. But however useful the belief may be in unifying the culture, it has run its course because it has done so much damage. It has, among other things, culturally warranted the material exploitation and colonial oppression of cities and their populations.

II

The question to ask, then, is whether or not the city can be freed from its cultural captivity as the epitome of profane history. The answer is affirmative, and it is not based simply on wishful thinking.

While there were earlier, more positive assessments of the city and its prospects,²⁸ it has been since the publication in 1961 of Jane Jacobs's paradigm-altering book, *The Death and Life of Great American Cities,* that the negative cultural attitude toward the city has begun to change. As David Byrne says, "the city is 'being seen anew' by those who write about it. There is a clear cultural turn in the nature of accounts of the urban and urban change."²⁹ This change is caused by at least three factors.

The first factor is a new appreciation for ethnic and racial particularity and diversity in cities. Identity is increasingly related to ethnicity, and differing but interacting racial groups are most clearly to be found in cities. To the degree that we value ethnicity, racial diversity, and the importance of differing people living side by side, even creating a common life without jeopardizing their particularities, the more we begin to see the city not as an obstacle to our future but as a guide.

The second reason is that during the last few decades, culture, especially as creativity and performance, has been released from its ties to high or elite culture. It is not only that a serious interest is now taken in popular culture but also that categories distinguishing kinds of creativity and performance have become more permeable. Culture and its effects extend beyond the boundaries of former cloisters. The result, again, is not a melting pot, a loss of particularity. The extension and diversification of performance and creativity and the juxtaposition and interaction of differing cultures do not jeopardize multiplicity, particularity, and difference.

The third factor is that culture itself, even in terms of the beliefs, values, and hopes that constitute it, is, as I have already suggested, increasingly seen not as secondary to and derivative from material conditions but as standing with the material as primary and powerful. This change of attitude toward culture has much to do with the social changes wrought during the period in racial and gender issues. Cities have been places where nonwhite people and women have sought and found greater freedom of movement, economic opportunity, and places to actualize their identities and integrity. As Elizabeth Wilson argues, men have viewed cities as threats because cities have been places "of liberation for women."[30] She calls for "a new vision, a new ideal of life in the city—and a new 'feminine' voice in praise of cities."[31] This also is true for gay and lesbian people. As Wilson points out, "'gay identity' appears to be a creation of the urban scene."[32] While cities have granted marginalized peoples a place from which to generate material strength, it has, at the same time, given them opportunities for developing a culture of their own or of altering dominant cultural constructions of them. To the degree that people of color, women, and homosexuals have places to flourish, their cultural as well as material standing is enhanced. And the contrary is true: cultural condemnation of cities inevitably carries the connotation that the identities and cultures of oppressed peoples have no value or power. I think that Doreen Massey should be taken seriously when she says that negative appraisals of cities are often deeply gendered and that they arise not only from the feminization of space but also from the city as lacking order and producing vertigo in the male observer. She points out that Fredric Jameson and other male theorists refer to urban spaces as producing "vertiginous terror."[33] Since cities are the sites of greater material and cultural opportunities for women and other oppressed peoples, negative appraisals of the city cannot avoid an implied negative appraisal of these recently actualized spaces of freedom.[34]

It is not surprising, then, that, beginning with Jane Jacobs's book, many of the geographers and urbanists who call for changes in our cultural attitudes toward urban spaces have been women. Sharon Zukin, in *The Cultures of Cities*, brings all of this together and adds a great deal more. She points out that in cities the culture of identity and the culture of civility—

these are Terry Eagleton's terms, not hers[35]—do not oppose one anther but mutually thrive. Zukin also takes seriously the significance of the links cities have, by virtue of their various cultures, with peoples and locations distant from them and that this has an enriching and not only a distracting effect. She also views the city's markets as places not only for consumption but also as places where differing people acknowledge one another, where people can be mobilized to address shared problems, and where people can receive information about their common life. She also points out that the common critique of consumption, especially of shopping, cannot be divorced from a male perspective, since shopping is a performance that women practice more fully than men.[36]

In her book *Feminism and Geography,* Gillian Rose argues that it is primarily the male perspective dominant in geography that views the city from above and as primarily an abstract totality. She calls for a recognition that cities are constituted by particular social locations and axes and that they should be viewed not as single texts but intertextually.[37] One could say, drawing on her position, that cities are federations of differing institutions, neighborhoods, and cultural interests and expressions. In addition to the work of Zukin and Rose, we have the challenges to entrenched negative urban images offered in the essays of feminist critics and theorists recently collected by Ruth Fincher and Jane M. Jacobs in *Cities of Difference.*[38]

Rather than being constructed in contrast to characterizations of modern history and the city as profane, a theory of the sacred, if it is to have plausibility, should emerge from attitudes and practices of positive social place-relations. If one moves toward a theory of sacred space, it should be from an understanding and appreciation of experiences of positive place-relations and an adequate theory of human spatiality. This means that sacred space need not be posited as a contrary to urban space. If there are positive potentials and consequences in the relations of persons to urban spaces, why not see them as contributing to a theory of sacred space? Earlier on, while considering comprehensive space, I noted some positive consequences in the new cultural awareness of the natural environment. Why not extend or duplicate this awareness to and for the urban landscape? As Richard Rogers says, "Ecologists' description of our relationship with nature—we are not its owners but its trustees, and have responsibilities toward future generations—applies just as well to the public life of cities."[39] Why not look for positive moments in urban place-relations and move from them toward a theory of optimal social spaces? Do our cities, especially since the destruction of the World Trade Center, require from us anything less than that? As Gianni Vattimo says, "A secularized culture is not one that has simply left the religious elements of its tradition behind, but one that continues to live them as traces, as hidden and distorted models that are nonetheless profoundly present."[40] Or, as Jeremy Carrette says, "As Foucault's work demonstrates, a culture cannot understand itself without first understanding its implicit connection and development within the constructs of religious belief and practice. Contemporary culture is born out of religious traditions and the conditions of our knowledge are therefore embedded in religious discourse."[41]

Not only will a change in cultural attitudes affect our sense of the relation of urban and sacred spaces; it will also affect the deployment of material resources. As David Byrne points out: "the city is 'being seen anew' by those who write about it. There is a clear cultural turn in the nature of accounts of the urban and urban change."[42] By the mid-seventies, "a critique had emerged that the planning and design of the modern city was a blueprint for placelessness, for anonymous, impersonal spaces, massive structures, and automobile throughways." David Ley argues that the modern "reduction of culture has provoked an important counter-current in the past 20 years." He sees new attitudes arising from and affecting urban spaces, a movement that "attempts to create smaller units, seeks to break down a corporate society to urban villages, and maintain historical association through renovation and recycling."[43] Richard Sennett comments: "And I suppose because I am an urbanist, I want to believe physical places such as cities could play a role in creating that social sense of place. A city might ideally provide . . . a site that offers relief from the burdens of subjective life."[44] Indeed, city planners have shifted their interests, as Peter Hall points out, from land use in the 1960s and traffic patterns in the 1970s to the needs and desires of community groups in an "attempt to organize against hostile forces in the world outside."[45] Paul Davidoff warns us that these community groups not only may have differing agendas but may also be in conflict with one another, with the welfare of the city as a whole, and with poorer and less organized groups within the city. Despite these obstacles and handicaps, he calls city planners to a dedicated will to make urban life "more beautiful, exciting, and creative, and more just."[46] And adding substance to this call, Stephen Wheeler points out that there is widespread agreement as to what ingredients in planning make cities more livable and sustainable.[47]

An application of postcolonial theory to this reconsideration of urban spaces is sharply stated by Homi Bhabha. Primarily under the figure of "hybridity," Bhabha argues that the space of culture is not simple, static, and coherent but is complex, changing, and conflicted. The location of culture so described is for Bhabha the city: "It is the city which provides the space in which emergent identifications and new social movements of people are played out."[48] Although Bhabha is far from sanguine about the prospects for urban cultural hybridity, he recognizes the vitality and richness of urbanized human resources. Indeed, while he eschews attempts to cast a unifying metaphor around the many cultural borders that mark urban cultures, the struggle for cultural survival, however improvised on the margins and within the interstices of the dominant culture, creates an unpredictable solidarity and sense of moral purpose.

Sharon Zukin provides an even more detailed program for revising our attitudes toward and relations to urban spaces. She criticizes the erection of desired, utopian, or sacred spaces as contraries to actual urban space, alternatives like Disney World that profit from the widespread cultural pessimism concerning cities. Disney Worlds absorb and exploit our potential for constructing more positive social place-relations.

It may be possible to redress the injustice done to cities because we have come to view "culture" not as something unified, stable, and transcendent but as multiform and changing. Indeed, "culture" becomes a way of establishing a niche in the larger society. The multicultural and ethnically diverse character of urban life does not threaten culture but liberates it. The consequences of interaction in cities between differing peoples is not a loss of identities but their intensification. It produces not conflict but civility. Cities stimulate a process by which the cultures of identity and of civility emerge mutually rather than antagonistically.

Zukin, Homi Bhabha, and the many others who take a more positive view of the city are not blind to the problems of the city and to what causes them. But they are convinced that vision, a sense of positive prospects for cities, has power and can occasion incentives for change.[49] Elizabeth Wilson puts the issue clearly when she says: "Those who believe that spiritual values can develop only in an atmosphere of calm and orderliness will always dislike and fear the city. For others it will represent the possibility of the highest level of spirituality in its excesses and extremes: the city as the ultimate sublime."[50] The point is that urban spaces will not diminish in their size, number, and influence but will increase. And the question is whether we will let the future of expanding urban space be determined by those whose interests, material and cultural, are not in its well-being.[51]

III

Among those who have much to lose from the waning cultural force of the urban as profane space are, as we saw already, religiously positioned cultural theorists or critics and theologians. They have depended heavily on this cultural agreement to secure a place in academic culture provided for them not by their religious interests and constructions but by their confirmation of the factual profane. But once weaned from this dependence on the cultural construction of the city as the factual profane, genuine challenges for understanding sacred space begin to appear.

Whether construed as religious, cultural, or political, "sacred" spaces should be posited as contraries neither to the city nor to the dynamics of complexity, contestation, and change. This means that the language of sacred space should not be deployed in opposition to history, and it should not be detached from the complex repertoire of positive human place-relations. If there are spaces that could be called sacred, they are places in which the kinds of place-relations that we have examined are found not in states of mutual exclusion but interrelationships. Indeed, I think that a theory of sacred space can be warranted by places where the three kinds of place-relations are experienced as "nested" and where the negative potential of each kind is absorbed by the other kinds. Pilgrimage sites, for example, would be recognized, then, as sites that people seek for access, at the very least, to the more than human that comprehends them, for incorporation within a gathering of diverse peoples, and for the fulfillment of personal potentials, needs, and hopes. If we appreciate what places are and can be for people in the everyday, we can begin to move from the positive characteristics of those places to their fullest actualization in places that deserve to be called, correspondingly, sacred.

Indeed, an adequate theory of positive place-relations should include sacred space because positive place-relations, like all relations, outstrip language and point beyond themselves to further possibilities. As Leonard Talmy puts it, "those spatial characterizations that are expressed overtly . . . ultimately rest on certain unexpressed spatial understandings."[52] This is because place-relations, in what I have called their physicality and spirituality, include the two directions of language, the archeological as well as teleological.[53] That is, positive place-relations not only relate the physical and spiritual to one another but also confirm possibilities that outstrip language as ground and goal, that should not be divorced from one another, and that are not available apart from language. The language that can appropriately arise from or lead to sacred places is a language that can include not only potential references to all three kinds of place-relations but also to their differing sides, physical and spiritual, past and future, archeological and teleological.

I ask that we take seriously and support the relation between urban and sacred spaces suggested by Philip Sheldrake in his recent book, *Spaces for the Sacred*. He calls for a more positive assessment of the relation of urban to sacred space. He encourages an appreciation for "the civilizing possibilities of the city and the opportunity it may offer for community, or social, humanization and cultural meaning."[54] Is this a call we can answer? Is it possible to posit sacred space without relying on the modernist construction of the city as the factual profane?

What needs to be done, it seems to me, is the following. First, we should bracket as extreme the negative images of the city and the effects and warrants of those images that increasingly dominated the culture from the 1920s to the 1960s. Second, we should ferret out and affirm what, in our place-relations, is or can be positively viewed and advocated. Third, we should affirm and extend countersites, places that, by actualizing or adumbrating positive social place-relations, begin to isolate, marginalize, and defuse the negative. Rather than construct the city as the factual profane against which the sacred is posited as contrary, we should recognize the city as a place where suggestions of what the sacred might be like can be discovered, places where identity and civility are mutually nurtured, where oppressed peoples find sites to articulate and cultivate their identities and cultures, where people can be contributors to a larger human enterprise, and where people can experience the fact that human life is not only individual but also relational and corporate. These all, it seems to me, are powerfully important messages, and the sacred places that churches hope to and can provide have, I would add, much to learn from them. The most important gift churches and other religiously based institutions can give to cities, as is the most important gift that anyone can give to a victim, is a willingness to take them seriously, to listen to and to receive from them. As Peter Sedgwick puts it: "Urban theology needs to be small-scale and particular. It should listen to the stories of where people are, how the destructiveness can be turned around, and what a new way of life would be."[55] Meanwhile, we should also become, as David Harvey wants us to be, "insurgent architects," but I would amend Harvey by saying that this means not only projecting something detached from what cities now are but taking what are life-giving aspects of them and finding adequate sites for their expansion and fulfillment.

Sacred space can take its place in an adequate theory of human spatiality because the norm of "accommodating"—mutually adjusting, inclusive, releasing, and giftlike—could be more fully recognizable in such a theory. The four aspects of this norm could be explicated more largely because the language of the sacred can deal effectively with such human longings and experiences. The sacred stands to the quotidian and general as the concentrated to the diffuse, as, that is, an epitome or synecdoche.

Imagination has least two roles in this effort. It, first of all, exposes and affirms what, in our daily place-relations, is potentially or actually positive. Second, it projects and makes available countersites, places that, by extending and normalizing locations and relations that are positive, marginalize and bracket the negative. We should as much as possible become what David Harvey calls us to be, people who imply a spatial sense as they go about daily activities and who already have one foot in an alternative space, a space that portends more potential for being what I call "accommodating."[56] The urban imaginary, while political and economic, is not only so; it is also religious. As Robert Orsi puts it, "Religious imaginings have taken up the life of the city—its spaces, pains, and dangers as well as its hopes, excitements, and possibilities—and have made life in the daunting and exciting conditions of industrial and post-industrial cities not simply possible but enjoyable and meaningful."[57] And James Dougherty, having drawn on thinkers and writers from Augustine to Auden, concludes, concerning the religions imagination and the future of the urban, "'Building the city' is not Babylonian arrogance, but a process of devotion and charity. . . ." The political and religious imaginations can support one another in the task of renewing the communal bonds between human beings."[58]

Countersites, imaginary, insurgent constructions, can be articulated most fully in narrative discourse. Spatial theorists have increasingly come to recognize this mutual relation between narrative and human place-relations. Denis Cosgrove and Mona Domosh, for example, call for narratives that, by virtue of internal consistency, have positive moral and political potentials regarding our spatial relations, especially regarding social spaces.[59] The editors of a set of essays in humanist geography point out the importance for themselves as well as for many of their essayists of narrative and storytelling.[60] I hope that this study provides additional ground for the recognition that narrative discourses are sites of our experiences of and search for positive place-relations, that by means of narrative discourses a more adequate theory of human place-relations can be secured, that the potential for more positive place-relations can be more fully realized, and that a more viable understanding of sacred places can emerge.

Notes

Introduction: Narrating Place-Relations

1. Crang and Thrift, eds., *Thinking Space,* 1.

2. Kant, "Dissertation on the Form and Principles of the Sensible and Intelligible World," 19–29.

3. See Foucault, "Questions on Geography" and "The Eye of Power," in *Power/ Knowledge: Selected Interviews and Other Writings, 1972–1977,* 63–77, 146–65.

4. Kort, *"Take, Read,"* 41–58.

5. Jameson, "Postmodernism and the Cultural Logic of Late Capitalism," 64.

6. Foucault, "Of Other Spaces," 22.

7. Soja, *Thirdspace,* 2.

8. Bradbury and McFarlane, eds., *Modernism,* 182.

9. Tindall, *Countries of the Mind,* 119. Tindall points out that other countries developed more positive evaluations of large cities—Paris, Vienna, Florence, and so on. In England, human values were associated more with rural and small town than with urban life, and this general tendency in English culture exacerbates the negative depiction of London.

10. Golding, *The Hot Gates,* 100.

11. Vattimo, *The Transparent Society,* 3.

12. Bradbury and McFarlane, *Modernism,* 51.

13. Crang and Thrift, *Thinking Space,* 1.

14. See Venturi et al., *Learning from Las Vegas*; Harvey, *The Condition of Postmodernity*; and Lyotard, *The Postmodern Condition.*

15. See Giddens, *The Constitution of Society*; Bourdieu, *Distinction: A Social Critique of the Judgement of Taste*; and Gadamer, *Truth and Method.*

16. See Foucault, *The Order of Things*; Weedon, *Feminist Practice and Post-structuralist Theory*; Hutcheon, *The Poetics of Postmodernism*; and, especially, Macdonell, *Theories of Discourse.*

17. Laclau and Mouffe, *Hegemony and Socialist Strategy.*

18. I have in mind such work as Berman's *All That Is Solid Melts into Air*; Baudrillard's *America*; and Jameson's *The Geopolitical Aesthetic.*

19. Said, *The World, the Text, and the Critic,* 242. On the exchange between Said and Walzer over the political consequences of cultural constructions of place and space, see William Hart, *Edward Said and the Religious Effects of Culture.*

20. I agree that "the use of spatial metaphors is, ironically, encouraged by the very fact that spatial discourse has been so underdeveloped" (Smith and Katz, "Grounding Metaphor," 74).

21. Derrida, "Architecture oue il desiderio puo abitare," 17–24.

22. Soja, *Postmodern Geographies,* 81, 15.

23. Soja, *Thirdspace,* 182–83.

24. Casey, "How to Get from Space to Place in a Fairly Short Stretch of Time," 14.

25. Lefebvre, *The Production of Space,* 296–97.

26. Lefebvre is thoroughgoing in his evaluation of the effects of abstraction on our conceptions of social space. See, for example, *The Production of Space,* 298–99.

27. Pratt, "Scratches on the Face of the Country," 138–63.

28. Timothy Mitchell, *Colonising Egypt,* esp. 34–62.

29. Pietz, "The Problem of the Fetish."

30. Lefebvre, *The Production of Space,* 373.

31. See Hutcheon, *A Poetics of Postmodernism,* 28–29.

32. Kermode, *The Sense of an Ending*; and Kermode, "A Reply to Joseph Frank."

33. Genette, *Figures of Literary Discourse,* 133.

34. Ibid.

35. Ibid., 136.

36. Ibid., 141.

37. Ibid., 142.

38. See Ricoeur, *Time and Narrative.*

39. Chatman, *Story and Discourse.* See also Culler, "*Fabula* and *Sjuzhet* in the Analysis of Narrative."

40. van Baak, *The Place of Space in Narration,* 21.

41. Lutwack, *The Role of Place in Literature,* 17; Malmgren, *Fictional Space in the Modernist and Postmodernist American Novel,* 26.

42. See especially Said, "Narrative and Social Space," in his *Culture and Imperialism,* 62–80.

43. Smitten, introduction to *Spatial Form in Narrative,* ed. Smitten and Daghistany, 42.

44. Kestner, *The Spatiality of the Novel,* 70.

45. Ibid., 94, 110.

46. Spencer, *Space, Time, and Structure in the Modern Novel.*

47. Wallace Martin, *Recent Theories of Narrative,* 116.

48. Entrikin, *The Betweenness of Place,* 128.

49. Malpas, *Place and Experience,* 186.

50. Soja, *Postmodern Geographies,* 42.

51. Lemon, "The Hostile Universe."

52. See Ricoeur, *The Conflict of Interpretations,* 21, 117, 120, 171, 175, 325, 333. These designations in Ricoeur distinguish kinds of hermeneutical practices. Archaeological hermeneutics brings the interpreter to the border between language and life, and teleological hermeneutics brings the interpreter to the border between language and spirit.

Chapter 1. Thomas Hardy: Facing the Physicality of Comprehensive Space

1. See Lemon, "The Hostile Universe."

2. "[*The Return of the Native*] is often recognized as a model of modern fiction's advances in the technique of spatialization" (Springer, *Hardy's Use of Allusion,* 98).

3. Raymond Williams, *Country and City in the Modern Novel,* 10.

4. Florence Emily Hardy, *The Early Life of Thomas Hardy,* 43.

5. For a concise description of these effects, see Scott, "Thomas Hardy and the Victorian Malaise," in his *Craters of the Spirit,* 45–69.

6. Schwartz, "Beginnings and Endings in Hardy's Major Fiction," 19.

7. For an excellent study of the role of human labor and kinds of work in Hardy's fiction, see Merryn Williams, *Thomas Hardy and Rural England,* esp. 122–99.

8. See Miller, *Thomas Hardy: Distance and Desire,* 80; and T. R. Wright, *Hardy and the Erotic.*

9. Morton, *The Vital Science,* 196.

10. Webster, *On a Darkling Plain,* 127.

11. Quotations from Thomas Hardy's works are cited in the text with the abbreviations listed below.

DR *Desperate Remedies* (New York and London: Harper and Brothers, 1905).

FMC *Far from the Madding Crowd* (New York and London: Harper and Brothers, 1905).

JO *Jude the Obscure* (New York: Harper and Brothers, 1896).

MC *The Mayor of Casterbridge: A Story of a Man of Character* (New York: Rinehart, 1948).

RN *The Return of the Native* (New York and London: Harper and Brothers, 1905). Citations refer to volume and page numbers.

TD *Tess of the D'Urbervilles: A Pure Woman* (New York and London: Harper and Brothers, 1920).

12. J. B. Bullen suggests that Hardy derived his evaluation of northern over southern cultures from Ruskin's descriptions of Northern European Gothic in *The Stones of Venice.* See his *The Expressive Eye,* 259.

13. Alcorn, *The Nature Novel from Hardy to Lawrence,* 67.

14. For comments on the positive assessments of the conditions of life and of

registering those conditions in human awareness in Hardy's fiction, see Beer, "Finding a Scale for the Human."

15. "[I]t is his ability to make concrete the relationship between character and environment in a way that is both sensuously particular and symbolically suggestive that makes him such a powerful and original novelist, in my opinion, rather than his skill in story-telling, his insight into human motivation or his philosophic wisdom" (Lodge, "Thomas Hardy As a Cinematic Novelist," 81).

16. Springer, *Hardy's Use of Allusion*, 100.

17. "Being an innkeeper is in itself a somewhat suspect vocation, for Hardy's novels contain ample illustrations of the danger of drink. . . . Wildeve's profession, in fact, is almost as destructive as his emotions" (Merryn Williams, *Thomas Hardy and Rural England*, 140).

18. Raymond Williams, *The English Novel*, 98–99.

19. I do not agree with J. Hillis Miller that Hardy's narrators move inwardly toward a location in their own consciousness. I believe his narrators direct attention outwardly toward a difficult spatial reality (see Miller's *Thomas Hardy: Distance and Desire*, esp. 39).

20. See Miller, *Thomas Hardy*, 83–85.

21. "The business of the poet and novelist is to show the sorriness underlying the grandest things, and the grandeur underlying the sorriest things" (Florence Emily Hardy, *The Early Life of Thomas Hardy*, 223).

22. Tristram, *Living Space in Fact and Fiction*, 119.

23. It is important to keep in mind that Hardy retained a complex and fairly constant contact with the church. In addition to the many "between" positions that he took up, Hardy also stood between secularism and Christianity and between identification with and rejection of the church. His fascination with church architecture and music never flagged, and he had close friends in the clergy. In the summer before his death, he told John Middleton Murry that he at times regretted not following through on his youthful goal of entering the clergy. For more on Hardy's complex relation to the church, see, for example, Jedrzekewski, *Thomas Hardy and the Church*.

24. I add this comment concerning Hardy's use of biblical texts to the general point about his biblical references often made by commentators. For example, "Biblical echoes are almost legion in Hardy's fiction, and where they refer to well-known events and figures . . . they still have a universalizing effect" (Pinian, "The Ranging Vision," 5).

25. For an excellent discussion of various framing techniques in Hardy's fiction, see Berger, *Thomas Hardy and Visual Structures*.

26. In a fascinating study of the relation of Hardy's fiction to Marxist analysis, John Goode points out how close Hardy seems to come to Marxism only to turn away: "We have seen Hardy move close to a picture that accords with Marxist perspectives. We also see him move sharply away, into a kind of cosmic wisdom that leaves him in pain and leaves the world he portrays still full of injustice" (Goode, "Hardy and Marxism," 37). Goode does not castigate Hardy for this turn, but he does see it as a deficiency. The problem with Goode's analysis of Hardy is that Goode

wants Hardy to share his own belief in the primacy of social place or place-relations. The difference between Goode and Hardy is not in their estimation of social evil or in their belief about the primacy of the material conditions of social life. The difference is this: for Goode, as we shall see for Conrad, the rectification of place-relations pertains primarily to social space. For Hardy, that rectification can occur only when people have a truthful relation to a space that precedes, outstrips, and comprehends social space. Hardy believed, I think, that a primary relation to the physical conditions of comprehensive space would ameliorate social problems because it would make social spaces secondary and create a sense of commonality among people. While this expectation on Hardy's part may seem a bit easy, it serves to stress, given his obvious awareness of social and economic distress especially for the working class, what kind of value Hardy placed on the relation of people to the physical conditions of their lives.

27. Lefebvre, *The Production of Space*, 220–26 and passim.

28. "To the very end, Hardy's novels are stories of entrapment. Yet Hardy is at pains to let his reader know that this power is fabricated in large part by man's own folly" (Alcorn, *The Nature Novel from Hardy to Lawrence*, 73). Ian Gregor agrees (see Gregor, *The Great Web*).

29. Many critics have cited Hardy's interest in and use of Arthur Schopenhauer's *The World As Will and Idea* (1818) to develop his sense of the ultimate cause of events (see, for example, Collins, *Thomas Hardy and His God*, 60–65).

30. Stock, "Reading, Community, and a Sense of Place," 317.

Chapter 2. Joseph Conrad: Labor and the Physicality of Social Space

1. See Hewitt, *Conrad: A Reassessment*, for example. He argues that external situations actually are reflections or extensions of the internal conflicts of characters (13).

2. See, for example, Erdinast-Vulcan, "'Sudden Holes in Space and Time,'" 207–21.

3. See, for example, Walter F. Wright, *Romance and Tragedy in Joseph Conrad*.

4. Curle, *Joseph Conrad: A Study*, 66.

5. Ibid., 76.

6. Parry, *Conrad and Imperialism*, 4.

7. Raymond Williams, *Country and City in the Modern Novel*, 11.

8. Purdy, *Joseph Conrad's Bible*, 99.

9. "There is isolation on every level—among colleagues, among friends, among families, even between husband and wife." "Linked to the group of words suggesting unreality and illusion are all those relating to masks. Mist and fog mask the sun; darkness veils day" (Claire Rosenfield, *Paradise of Snakes*, 116, 117). Characters conceal their feelings and thoughts from one another.

10. Hawthorn, *Joseph Conrad's Language and Fictional Self-Consciousness*, 74, 78. Hawthorn ties the use of people as go-betweens to the rise of capitalist social relations.

11. Piper, *Cartographic Fictions*, 33. However, while I disagree with Piper con-

cerning the relation of the Verloc home to the social space of London as Conrad depicts it, her placement of the novel in the context of the women's movement is very interesting. She inquires as to why Conrad should write the novel, which gives so much attention to anarchists and revolutionaries, without taking into account the suffragette movement that, with the founding of the Women's Social and Political Union in 1903 by Christabel Pankhurst, gave the movement a decidedly revolutionary or anarchist direction and reputation.

12. Fogel, "The Fragmentation of Sympathy in *The Secret Agent*," 190.

13. Ibid., 169.

14. Quotations from Joseph Conrad's works are cited in the text with the abbreviations listed below.

C   *Chance* (New York: Norton, 1968).

HD   *Heart of Darkness,* ed. Robert Kimbrough (New York: Norton, 1963).

LJ   *Lord Jim: A Romance* (Harmondsworth, England: Penguin, 1949).

N   *Nostromo: A Tale of the Seaboard* (London: J. M. Dent and Sons, 1947).

NN   "The Nigger of the 'Narcissus.'" In *Typhoon and Other* Stories (New York: Knopf, 1991).

SA   *The Secret Agent: A Simple Tale,* with an introduction by Frederick R. Karl (New York: Penguin, 1983).

SL   *The Shadow-Line: A Confession* (London: John Grant, 1925).

T   *Typhoon and Other Stories,* with an introduction by Martin Seymour-Smith (New York: Knopf, 1991).

UWE   *Under Western Eyes,* with an introduction by Boris Ford (New York: Penguin, 1985).

V   *Victory* (Garden City, N.Y.: Doubleday Anchor, 1957).

15. Religious language in Conrad's fiction, which will be taken up later in this chapter, plays in this novel largely one of two roles: it either is ironic—as is the attribution to Providence of Verloc's appearance into Winnie's life—or indicative of excess, as here. As we can see with the professor, extreme or excessive behaviors can quite directly be traced from extreme and excessive religious orientations, but also preoccupation and obsession are now and again described by Conrad in religious terms. This should be taken to mean that Conrad, while he promotes shifting religious language from its confines in particular institutional and theological contexts to illuminate the importance of various broader life situations, also uses such language implicitly and negatively to judge forms of behavior and attitudes that are distorted or excessive.

16. See Hay, *The Political Novels of Joseph Conrad,* 245.

17. The professor's notion of work, namely, perfecting a detonator, stresses *means* and destruction. His work is in both respects antisocial.

18. Jacques Berthoud identifies "indolence" as a key ingredient of Verloc's character. It "shows him to be as parasitic on the labour of others as the most socially exalted *rentier*" (Berthoud, *Joseph Conrad: The Major Phase,* 147).

19. For an excellent study of the revolutionary character of the program envisaged by the Goulds, see Hay, "*Nostromo*," esp. 90–92.

20. "'Ah! You are all alike, you fine men of intelligence. All you are fit for is to betray men of the people into undertaking deadly risks for objects that you are not even sure about. If it comes off you get the benefit. If not, then it does not matter'" (*N*, 459).

21. Reading Conrad's depiction of Russia as ambiguous counters somewhat readings that emphasize Conrad's resentment and disdain toward Russian political and religious life. As Jeffrey Meyers puts it, Conrad had an intense dislike for "the hypocrisy and mindless destruction; the compulsion to betray, to repent and to debase themselves as a way of recovering lost honor; the Dostoyevskian combination of instinctive cowardice and anguished longing for spiritual absolution." "Conrad's attitude toward Russia was consistently negative," he concludes (Meyers, *Joseph Conrad: A Biography*, 253, 329). However, it should be remembered that Russia is viewed in the novel both in contrast to the West generally and Geneva particularly and by a narrator who suffers from the effects of cultural abstraction. Russian society, while diseased, seems more vital and interesting than Genevan.

22. For a provocative analysis of the attitude of Conrad toward imperialism in *Heart of Darkness*, see Brantlinger, *Rule of Darkness*. Brantlinger argues that Conrad associates Africa with evil and African customs with bestiality, death, and darkness, associations drawn from the repertoire of Victorian imperialism and racism (262). Interpretation depends on one's understanding of Marlow, whose position as observer, mediator, and purveyor abstracts him from the economic, political, and personal matters he narrates. If, as I think, the destructive results of the culture of abstraction are exposed and criticized by Conrad's fiction and if Marlow shares in this culture, then the role and attitudes of Marlow subvert the authority of his descriptions of Africa and African cultures.

23. We should keep in mind, as we look at the sea stories, that they are reconstructions. "The farther Conrad's sea years receded into the past, the more he idealized not only [sailing] ships but seamen" (Najder, *Joseph Conrad: A Chronicle*, 162).

24. "[T]he vision of a community bound together by common duties and a common ideal—these are visions of a moral order, not reflections of reality" (Najder, *Joseph Conrad: A Chronicle*, 163).

25. One should keep in mind that Conrad's use of sea, ships, and crews to reveal the human possibility for constructing positive and morally resonant social spaces does not mean that he stakes his identity as a writer on that kind of material. As Jeffrey Meyers points out, Conrad "hated the reputation he had acquired as a novelist of the sea" (Meyers, *Joseph Conrad: A Biography*, 173; see also 130).

26. Taussig, "The Beach (A Fantasy)."

27. See Ricardo, *The Principles of Political Economy and Taxation*, 5–32.

28. Parry, *Conrad and Imperialism*, 4.

29. For a critical comment that locates work on the conservative side of Conrad's political influences, see Knowles, "Conrad's Life," 6.

30. Benson, "*Heart of Darkness*: The Grounds of Civilization in an Alien Universe," 213.

31. See Raymond Williams's section on Conrad in his *The English Novel*, esp. 141–42.

32. Krajka, *Isolation and Ethos*, 123, 145.

33. See Lothe, "Conradian Narrative," 162. I disagree with Lothe, who concludes that Conrad, in such pivotal narratives as *The Nigger of the 'Narcissus,'* reveals an "undertone of nostalgia and collective loss—of a *Gemeinschaft* that can now only be found aboard a ship and that is threatened even there" (164). Conrad's evaluation of physical labor as the basis for social space subverts the contrary relation of *Gesellschaft* (society) and *Gemeinschaft* (community). The result, indeed, has qualities of both. For comments on the sharp popular contrast between the two as a distortion of Ferdinand Tonnies's original distinction, see Isenberg, *Between Redemption and Doom*, 11–17.

34. These effects of Conrad's narrators and implied authors are a common target for objection in analyses of his work. One finds this reaction summarized by Daphna Erdinast-Vulcan in her "'Sudden Holes in Space and Time': Conrad's Anarchist Aesthetics in *The Secret Agent*." She points out that many readers have been perplexed by the failure of Conrad to supply, particularly in and by his narrators, some "superior structure of meaning which can be related to the authorial-authoritative origin of the text." This "refusal" she attributes to a kind of moral exhaustion in Conrad, the plight of the political conservative "with nothing to conserve" (209). I would argue that to provide readers with what such critics want would be to place the value in ideas divorced from their physical base. I think that Conrad's narrative techniques imply that also the work of writing is not exempt from the negative effects of a social space that has become diseased and destructive. To bring the narratee into a privileged position above or apart from the social space created by the novel would be flattering to the narratee but distorting as well.

35. Foucault, "Of Other Spaces," 27.

36. As John Lester points out, Conrad employs religious language most fully and least ironically when referring to the life of sailing crews at sea. I agree with Lester that much of the religious language in Conrad's fiction and correspondence serves to enhance the importance of vocation and that Conrad seemed to relate the positive model of work inherent in his depictions of sailing crews at sea to the vocation and labor of writing (see Lester, *Conrad and Religion*).

37. See his "Author's Note" of 1920 in the 1984 Penguin edition of *The Secret Agent: A Simple Tale*.

Chapter 3. E. M. Forster: The Body and the Physicality of Intimate Space

1. As Francis King points out, Forster's father received architectural training from the same man who trained Thomas Hardy. Indeed, Forster kept his father's architectural sketches as "treasured relics" (see King's *E. M. Forster and His World*, 9). This relation of Forster to his father delivers his interest in houses and intimate spaces from the exclusively maternal and female associations with intimate spaces secured in the dominance of Rooksnest by Forster's women.

2. Stone, *The Cave and the Mountain*, 16.

3. Forster, "What I Believe," in *Two Cheers for Democracy*, 68.

4. See Bourdieu, *Distinction*.

5. "Between 1880 and 1910 England gradually changed from the leading industrial power in Europe into the leading financial power, and along with this change went an ethical shift from what might be called Victorian work values to Edwardian money values" (Stone, *The Cave and the Mountain*, 250).

6. Quotations from E. M. Forster's works are cited in the text with the abbreviations listed below.

HE	*Howards End* (New York and London: G. P Putnam's Sons, 1911).
LJ	*The Longest Journey* (Norfolk, Conn.: New Directions, 1922).
M	*Maurice* (New York: Norton, 1971).
MT	*Marianne Thornton: A Domestic Biography* (New York: Harcourt, Brace, 1956).
PI	*A Passage to India* (New York: Harcourt, Brace, 1924).
RV	*A Room with a View* (Norfolk, Conn.: New Directions, 1922).
WA	*Where Angels Fear to Tread* (London: Edward Arnold, 1924).

7. Forster does not deny the actuality of force in social life. What he does deny is the idea that force is the exclusive or even dominant factor in human relations: "I realize that all society rests upon force. But all the great creative actions, all the decent human relations, occur during the intervals when force has not managed to come to the front. Those interests are what matter. I want them to be as frequent and as lengthy as possible, and I call them 'civilization'" ("What I Believe," in *Two Cheers for Democracy*, 68).

8. "Paradoxically, those individuals like Margaret and Ruth who are sensitive to the unseen most clearly see the concrete entities of their daily lives for what they are, neither ignoring them as the idealistic Helen would nor putting too much weight upon them as the materialistic Wilcoxes would" (McDowell, *E. M. Forster*, 78).

9. We are told that "Tibby's attention wandered when 'personal relations' came under discussion" (*HE*, 310).

10. "[T]he inner life is nothing less than the sole emblem of divinity: to affirm its primacy would seem the novel's major interest" (Barbara Rosecrance, *Forster's Narrative Visions*, 117).

11. Stone, *The Cave and the Mountain*, 227.

12. "Forster is so concerned for his message—. . . that Sawston and all it stands for is evil and that Monteriano, with all its selfishness and brutalities, is good—that he is prepared to break right out of the comic mode and address us directly in the most solemn language known to him, which is at bottom, that of the religion in which it is clear that he does not believe" (Hewitt, *English Fiction of the Early Modern Period*, 70).

13. Wilfred Stone, who tends toward a psychoanalytic interpretation of Forster's fiction, says: "The desire to hide in dells is the desire to hide in the mother. Such a desire is a normal expression of infantile sexuality, but in the grown boy or man it is

felt as shameful, for his fantasy-return symbolically violates the strictest of our ta-
boos, that against incest" (Stone, *The Cave and the Mountain,* 197). I think it is a
mistake to dissolve the physicality of intimate spaces into something psychological or
symbolic. They are spaces that present alternatives to social space, but this does not
make them in some way suspect or unreal. Without denying the psychological needs
that intimate spaces may satisfy, it is necessary, with Forster, to recognize intimate
spaces as in some way more physical and stable than social spaces. One's world
moves outward from them, as Margaret orients herself spatially by beginning with
Howards End and moving out toward the whole of England.

14. "Krishna appeals to Forster as a sage, a visionary, and a rounded individual
whose engaging humanity, manifest in his love of fun and occasional stupidity,
propagates the value of life over abstraction, renunciation and otherworldliness"
(Advani, *E. M. Forster As Critic,* 85).

15. Stone, "E. M. Forster's Subversive Individualism," 33.

16. Tolley, *Domestic Biography,* 18.

17. Ibid., 38.

18. See Colmer, *E. M. Forster: The Personal Voice,* 2–4.

19. Francis King writes, for example, "He was obliged to find a whole series of
metaphors for his real sexual preoccupations and it is in these metaphors that so
much of the power of his writing resides" (King, *E. M. Forster and His World,*
113).

20. Robert K. Martin and George Piggford, eds., *Queer Forster,* 4, 13.

21. Advani, *E. M. Forster As Critic,* 79.

22. Ibid., 78.

23. Forster "values social-political order only to the extent that this enables a
world made up of free individuals to develop their unique personalities"; "[H]e is
centrally concerned with arguing that no contemporary social order is viable unless
it integrates within its structure liberal . . . values of creative individualism and
cultural tradition" (Advani, *E.M. Forster As Critic,* 3, 12).

Chapter 4. Graham Greene: Mystery and the Space Between

1. For example, Michael Shelden attributes the negative attitudes of Greene toward the recent past to Greene's hatred for his father and his upbringing and to his
botched attempts at suicide (see Shelden, *Graham Greene: The Enemy Within,* 52,
100).

2. Whenever Greene lists a small number of contemporary writers whom he
highly regards, Eliot is among them (see, for example, Adam, "A Pantheon of Contemporary Writers," 137; and Parini, "Getting to Know Graham Greene," 444).

3. I view the work of Woolf and Lawrence to be dominated more by temporality
than by the language of place and space, however important spatial matters are for
them (see my *Modern Fiction and Human Time*).

4. Winter, *Sites of Memory, Sites of Mourning.*

5. "Some critics have referred to a strange violent 'seedy' region of the mind (why

did I ever popularize that last adjective?) which they call Greeneland, and I have sometimes wondered whether they go round the world blinkered. 'This is Indochina' I want to exclaim, 'this is Mexico, this is Sierra Leone carefully and accurately described'" (Greene, *Ways of Escape*, 80).

6. I do not know of any specific comments by Greene about similarities between his own spatial orientation and Hardy's, but he often refers to Hardy the poet, along with Yeats, and to Hardy the writer of fiction, along with James. He also could recite much of Hardy's poetry from memory (see Cassis, ed., *Graham Greene: Man of Paradox*, 266, 313).

7. "I suppose you could say that, just as landscape painting was behind Sir Walter Scott, film is behind or before me" (Adam, "A Pantheon of Contemporary Writers," 318). Gene D. Phillips comments, "Graham Greene is one of the first major literary talents of our time to have shown serious interest in the motion picture medium" (Cassis, *Graham Greene: Man of Paradox*, 203). And Greene tells Maria Couto: "I belong to the age of cinema. I have tried to make my descriptions with a moving, hand-held camera" (ibid., 423).

8. Porteous, *Landscapes of the Mind*, 142.

9. Quotations from Graham Green's work are cited in the text with the abbreviations listed below.

BOC *A Burnt-Out Case* (London: Heinemann, 1961).
C *The Comedians* (New York: Viking, 1966).
DF *Doctor Fischer of Geneva or the Bomb Party* (New York: Simon and Schuster, 1980).
HC *The Honorary Consul* (New York: Simon and Schuster, 1973).
HF *The Human Factor* (New York: Simon and Schuster, 1978).
LC *The Lost Childhood and Other Essays* (New York: Viking Press, 1951).
MQ *Monsignor Quixote* (New York: Simon and Schuster, 1982).
PG *The Power and the Glory* (New York: Viking, 1946).
TA *Travels with My Aunt* (New York: Viking, 1969).
WE *Ways of Escape* (New York: Simon and Schuster, 1980).

10. In response to a question about what God is like, Greene calls God "A mystery, an inexplicable force" (Cassis, *Graham Greene: Man of Paradox*, 334). Another interviewer asked him about God's intervention into human life. Greene replies (the ellipses are his): "Well . . . I don't know. I feel it's a mystery. There is a mystery. There is something inexplicable in human life. And it's important because people are not going to believe in all the explanations given by the Church" (ibid., 463). At another point, an interviewer asks Greene what religion means to him, and Greene replies (the ellipses and emphases are his): "'I think . . . it's a *mystery*,' he said slowly and with some feeling. It's a mystery which can't be destroyed . . . even by the *Church* . . . A certain *mystery*'" (ibid., 474).

11. Auberon Waugh, Evelyn Waugh's son, comments on Greene, "Smugness and certainty are the greatest enemies of religion, he believes." And in an interview, Greene says, "I think that the mere fact that you are doubtful about your attitude is

a very healthy one, because I think that doubt is the best quality in human beings" (Cassis, *Graham Greene: Man of Paradox,* 359, 369).

12. It is consistent with the orientation of his fiction to comprehensive space that Greene does not associate himself with a particular social or intimate place. Malcolm Muggeridge says of him: "Whatever his circumstances, he has this faculty for seeming always to be in lodgings, and living from hand to mouth. Spiritually, even physically, he is one of nature's displaced persons" (Muggeridge, "Nature's Displaced Person," 63). And in an interview, Greene says: "My roots are in rootlessness. Living out of a suitcase has never bothered me. In a way, my suitcases are my flat here and my place in Antibes. When I get on the move I can write in hotel rooms and feel quite at home with it" (Cassis, *Graham Greene: Man of Paradox,* 63, 196).

13. Conrad is often cited as an influence on Greene. Greene, however, stopped reading Conrad because he took him as a bad influence. James seems to have exerted a greater influence. As I have tried to point out, Hardy is, in my estimation, more important for understanding Greene than is either Conrad or James. And T. S. Eliot, as I have tried to point out, also has a specific relevance to Greene's work. However, Conrad's *The Heart of Darkness* retained a high position in Greene's estimation, and he took a copy of it along with him on his trip to the Congo.

14. Querry receives a letter from a former mistress, and Parkinson is able to unearth from his journalistic "morgue" information on two others.

15. There are many similarities between Querry and Greene. Greene was also estranged from his wife and distant from his children. He was quite candid about his many mistresses. In an interview, for example, he says: "'I have had close relationships with women for quite long periods: 12 years, 11 years, 3 years . . . 30 years!' A short laugh. 'They were not one-night stands, as it were. I've *had* one-night stands of course'" (Cassis, *Graham Greene: Man Of Paradox,* 472). Greene's picture, as did Querry's, appeared on the cover of *Time* in 1951. Querry and Greene are roughly the same age. In addition, when Rycker asks Querry if he prays, Querry tells him that he does in moments of danger and then "for a brown teddy bear" (ibid., 45). Greene was known for his adult attachment to a teddy bear. In addition, Greene admitted that he had grown tired of being hounded by Catholics who, discontent with the church, sought him out as a resource (see *WE,* 261). Finally, Greene thought that this novel would be his last. As he says, "I had finished *A Burnt-Out Case* with the depressing certitude that this would be my last novel" (*WE,* 296).

16. I tend to agree with this assessment of Greene's attitudes toward Western imperialism: "It would be difficult to think of any author who has written more often and more effectively about the bankruptcy of colonial and post-colonial regimes, the abuses of political power, the threat of unrestrained intelligence agencies, and the repression of personal and religious beliefs" (Mewshaw, "Graham Greene in Antibes," 257).

17. I think that it is characteristic of Greene's work that he does not present his characters, which are often aspects of himself or of his own experience, as providing

the principal sites of suffering caused by modern Western culture. While his characters register the negative effects of that culture, Greene is careful, I believe, to make clear that they, and he himself, have not suffered from those effects as much as have people who have been the unsuspecting and undeserving victims of modern violence and the habits of the culture's representatives.

18. Greene is careful to maintain a respectful distance between his European characters and the natives. For example, at one point Querry is surprised that one of the natives knows that a certain staff belongs to Deo Gratias even though there seem to be no outward signs of that identification. Querry recognizes that this is "just one more of the things they knew that he knew nothing about" (BOC, 62).

19. "'I was born in Monaco,' I said. 'That is almost the same as being a citizen of nowhere'" (C, 251).

20. "[T]he desire to talk openly, without reserve, after seven years of silence grew in him" (HF, 240).

21. "I was discovered to be—detestable term!—a Catholic writer." "Many times since Brighton Rock I have been forced to declare myself not a Catholic writer but a writer who happens to be a Catholic" (WE, 77).

22. "The only character in Journey Without Maps who comes close to resembling Kurtz is the Englishman [that is, Greene] who seems to think he is Marlow" (Shelden, Graham Greene: The Enemy Within, 165).

23. An adequately complex reading of Greene's elusive and ambiguous life, a reading that is also at several important points a refutation of Shelden's attack, is provided by West, The Quest for Graham Greene.

24. Greene's negative attitudes were not only a part of his personality. They were also a deliberate style or strategy that arose from his cultural assessments. He saw violence not only as a symptom or expression of modern culture but also as a productive means by which truth could be exposed. He seemed, for example, to welcome and to feel somewhat at home not only in places of real or potential violence but during and after bombing. He writes, for example, "The curious waste lands one sometimes saw from trains . . . they all demanded violence" (LC, 189). He is attracted by violence and destruction. For example, he felt, he says, "at home" in bombed cities "because life there is what it ought to be." Due to the war, "Life has become just and poetic, and if we believe this is the right end to the muddled thought, the sentimentality and selfishness of generations, we can also believe that justice doesn't end there" (LC, 191). Massive violence seems to be, for him, the only way by which the deceptions, hypocrisy, and comforts built up and secured by previous generations could be torn down and reality and truth once again restored.

Chapter 5. William Golding: Vision and the Spirit of Social Space

1. Baker, "An Interview with William Golding," 130.

2. Quotations from William Golding's works are cited in the text with the abbreviations listed below.

CQ   *Close Quarters* (London: Faber and Faber, 1987).

FDB *Fire Down Below* (New York: Farrar, Straus, Giroux, 1989).

FF   *Free Fall* (New York: Harcourt, Brace, and World, 1959).

HG *The Hot Gates* (New York: Harcourt, Brace, and World, 1966).

LF   *Lord of the Flies* (New York: G. P. Putnam's Sons, 1959).

MT *A Moving Target* (New York: Farrar, Straus, Giroux, 1982).

P   *Pincher Martin* (New York: Harcourt, Brace, and World, 1956).

S   *The Spire* (New York: Harcourt, Brace, and World, 1964).

3. On several occasions, for example, Golding speaks of his decision to write what became *Lord of the Flies* as an attempt to describe what boys are *really* like (see Golding, *MT,* 163; and *HG,* 88).

4. Although Golding tired of people comparing his work with Conrad's, those comparisons are often too narrowly gauged. When I compare his work with Conrad's, I am not stressing an emphasis on "darkness" or the concealed in human life or even the orientation to the sea. I mean primarily that the spatiality in his fiction has either obviously or by implication a social character.

5. Golding's admiration for Holland, for example, can be seen in his description of the way in which the Dutch built a society in defiance of the sea (see his "Through the Dutch Waterways," in *MT,* 20–35). In order to leave no doubt about his attitude toward the sea, let us keep in mind the following comment made by Golding to John Carey: "Anybody who knows the sea enough hates it. It's really incredibly hateful and loathsome; beautiful, grand, tremendous—god, it's hateful. You see it's really the cruelest bit of nature" (Carey, ed., *William Golding: The Man and His Books,* 181).

6. "Golding's novels admit no intimacy between himself and his reader. And this is a singular circumstance, for the opposite situation occurs so easily and naturally that novelist and reader are, as it were, accustomed to accept it without question" (Bayley, "The Impersonality of William Golding," 126).

7. The conjectures, associations, and conclusions that crowd the mind of Jocelyn throughout the novel and particularly at the end are the most difficult to judge in regard to Pangall and the mistletoe. Pangall is a major part of the cost of the spire not only because of his dignity but also because of his family's long association with the cathedral. In addition, the suggestive and ironic plays on the mistletoe are part of the novel's rich pattern of imagery, especially in relation to guilt and restoration or death and rebirth. But one should not, I think, elevate any one character, relationship, or image to primacy. This, I think, is what happens in Don Crompton's otherwise excellent essay on *The Spire* (see his *A View from the Spire: William Golding's Later Works,* esp. 47).

8. Golding: "I think of the shape of a novel, when I do think of a novel as having a shape, as having a shape precisely like Greek drama" (Baker, "An Interview with William Golding," 165).

9. Ibid., 150. Golding goes on, apparently, to approve of Frank Kermode's comment that the novel is really about writing a novel. Indeed, the stages of the construction of the tower and spire are aligned with the temporal pattern of the novel.

10. Berman, *All That Is Solid Melts into Air,* 64. Berman says of Goethe's Faust:

"the key to his achievement is a visionary, intensive and systematic organization of labor. . . . The crucial point is to spare nothing and no one, to overlap all boundaries" (64).

11. A more authentic visionary is Simon, "solitary, stammering, a lover of mankind, a visionary" who turns "part of the jungle into a church, not a physical one, perhaps, but a spiritual one" (Golding, *HG*, 98). But Simon is not an effective part of the social structure. Golding seems to indicate with Simon and this comment on him that in our society what visionaries and intuitive people we have, whether religious or artistic in their interests, tend largely to be removed from and ineffective relative to the social whole.

12. When considering the often-cited belief of Golding in original sin, it is helpful, I think, to keep in mind the understanding of original sin he is willing to accept from Julian Huxley, namely, "that man is a creature who suffers from an innate inability to live a proper and satisfactory life in a social circumstance" (Baker, "An Interview with William Golding," 134).

13. Carey, *William Golding: The Man and His Books*, 171, 174.

14. Boyd, *The Novels of William Golding*, 31–33.

15. Kinkead-Weekes and Gregor, *William Golding: A Critical Study*, 159.

16. Golding had complicated associations with Egyptian culture that arise from his youth and were fleshed out in his extended visit there. He writes, "I am, in fact, an ancient Egyptian, with all their unreason, spiritual pragmatism and capacity for ambiguous and even contradictory belief" (*MT*, 55).

17. Biggs, "*The Paper Man*," 160. Ms. Biggs's comment on balloons alludes to Golding's essay "Belief and Creativity" in which he compares the role of Marx, Darwin, and Freud in contemporary society to the balloons that dwarf the people that hold them during the Macy's Thanksgiving Day parade (see Golding, *MT*, 187).

18. Baker, "An Interview with William Golding," 160.

19. Golding says: "I think he's a silly ass, Colley. I think he is naïve rather than innocent" (ibid., 164).

20. Boyd, *The Novels of William Golding*, 190.

21. "I think an Englishman who is not aware of the classic disease of society in this country, that is to say, the rigidity of its class structure—he's not really aware of anything, not in social terms" (Baker, "An Interview with William Golding," 136).

22. John Fowles says, in reference to Golding, "Being possessed of one's own imagination, having the courage to let it dictate to technique, rather than the reverse, is to my mind one of the most enviable gifts or states a novelist can have or be in, for all its obvious dangers and penalties" (Fowles, "Golding and 'Golding,'" 152).

23. Kinkead-Weekes, "The Visual and the Visionary in Golding," 81.

Chapter 6. Taking Exception: Muriel Spark and the Spiritual Disciplines of Personal Space

1. Spark, "Edinburgh-born," 22.

2. Ibid., 22.

3. Quotations from Muriel Spark's works are cited in the text with the abbreviations listed below.

B   *The Bachelors* (Philadelphia and New York: Lippincott, 1960).
C   *The Comforters* (Philadelphia and New York: Lippincott, 1957).
CV   *Curriculum Vitae: Autobiography* (Boston: Houghton Mifflin, 1992).
H   *The Hothouse by the East River* (New York: Viking, 1973).
MM   *Memento Mori* (Philadelphia and New York: Lippincott, 1959).
OP   *The Only Problem* (New York: G. P. Putnam's Sons, 1984).
T   *The Takeover* (London: Macmillan, 1976).

4. See Walker, *Muriel Spark,* 3.
5. Spark, "My Conversion," 28.
6. Ibid., 26.
7. See Francis Russell Hart, "Ridiculous Demons," 29.
8. Page, *Muriel Spark,* 122.
9. Sproxton, *The Women of Muriel Spark,* 147.
10. Several critics notice the gradual decrease, especially after *The Mandelbaum Gate,* of the specifically Catholic language in her fiction (see, for example, Edgecombe, *Vocation and Identity in the Fiction of Muriel Spark,* 145).

Chapter 7. The Three Kinds of Place-Relations

1. Relph, *Place and Placelessness,* 8–28. Relph appears to privilege what I call personal space. He says, for example: "There is for virtually everyone a deep association with and consciousness of the places where we were born and grew up, where we live now, or where we had particularly moving experiences. This association seems to constitute a vital sense of both individual and cultural identity and security, a point of departure from which we orient ourselves in the world" (43).
2. Entrikin, *The Betweenness of Place,* 55. I recognize some overlap between Entrikin's three kinds and the three that I shall be elaborating in this chapter, but I also think that the difference between his kinds and those I shall develop is great.
3. Sack, *Homo Geographicus,* 84; see also 129. It seems that these characteristics of places and place-relations in Sack find their principal location in his philosophical anthropology, his tripartite analysis of human beings and experiences.
4. Raberg, *The Space of Man,* 34. Again, there are similarities between these kinds and the three that I shall propose, although I shall not be placing the kinds in some kind of hierarchical order.
5. Tuan, *Cosmos and Hearth.*
6. Tuan, *Space and Place,* 149.
7. Soja, *Thirdspace.* Soja takes "thirdspace" to be a recombination or extension of perceived and conceived space, to be, in other words, based on them. See, for example, page 6. However, it strikes me that spatial percepts and concepts are derived from lived (or what he calls "third") space.
8. Casey, "How to Get from Space to Place in a Fairly Short Stretch of Time," 44.

9. Henrietta L. Moore, *Space, Text, and Gender,* 85.

10. See Relph, *Place and Placelessness,* 23.

11. Lefebvre, *The Production of Space,* 70.

12. Ibid., 30–31.

13. See Coates, *Nature,* 3–4.

14. Meinig, ed., *The Interpretation of Ordinary Landscapes,* 37.

15. Sack, *Homo Geographicus,* 202–3.

16. Meinig, ed., *The Interpretation of Ordinary Landscapes,* 2.

17. Ibid., 34.

18. Ibid., 47.

19. Raberg, *The Space of Man,* 139.

20. Tuan, *Cosmos and Hearth,* 2.

21. W.J.T. Mitchell, "Holy Landscape," 219.

22. Buttimer, *Geography and the Human Spirit.*

23. Lefebvre, *The Production of Space,* 173.

24. Ibid., 201.

25. Ibid., 71.

26. See Turner, "Liminality and Communitas," in his *The Ritual Process,* 94–130.

27. Jameson, *Postmodernism, or, the Cultural Logic of Late Capitalism,* 49.

28. Weber, *Economy and Society,* 3:956–1136.

29. Timothy Mitchell, *Colonising Egypt.*

30. Pietz, "The Problem of the Fetish."

31. Timothy Mitchell, *Colonising Egypt,* 121–27.

32. Lefebvre, *The Production of Space,* 52.

33. Bourdieu, *Distinction.*

34. de Certeau, *The Practice of Everyday Life.*

35. Ibid., 225.

36. Giddens, *The Constitution of Society,* 1–40.

37. Baudrillard, *America.*

38. See, among other things, Harvey's many references to this sense of inevitability as a self-warranting ideology in the rhetoric of Margaret Thatcher (Harvey, *Spaces of Hope*).

39. Lefebvre, *The Production of Space,* 87.

40. Ibid., 142.

41. Rose, *Feminism and Geography,* 118.

42. Ibid., 133.

43. Thomas, *Spirit of Place,* 36.

44. Rose, *Feminism and Geography,* 40, 56.

45. Bachelard, *The Poetics of Space,* 8.

46. Ibid., 17–18.

47. Ibid., 61–63.

48. Ibid., 84.

49. Ibid., 7.

50. Woolf, *A Room of One's Own,* esp. 108.

51. Ibid., 35.
52. hooks, *Yearning: race, gender, and cultural politics,* 41–49.
53. Ibid., 42.
54. Ibid., 45.
55. Ibid., 45–47.
56. Blanchot, *The Infinite Conversation,* 13.
57. Blanchot, *The Writing of Disaster,* 107.
58. Blanchot, *The Infinite Conversation,* 207.
59. Blanchot, *The Step Not Beyond,* 38.
60. Sibley, *Geographies of Exclusion,* 94.

Chapter 8. The Two Sides of Place-Relations

1. Keith and Pile, eds., *Place and the Politics of Identity,* 4, 9, 23.
2. Soja and Hooper, "The Spaces That Difference Makes," 198.
3. Kant, "On the First Ground of the Distinction of Regions in Space."
4. Kant, "Dissertation on the Form and Principles of the Sensible and Intelligible World," 59.
5. Nethersole, "Writing Space," 128.
6. Kant, "Dissertation on the Form and Principles of the Sensible and Intelligible World," 65.
7. Casey, *The Fate of Place,* 332. I should add that this book is an invaluable survey of the roles in the history of Western philosophy of the categories of place and space. Casey, in this survey, laments the declining importance during the course of history of "place" and the increasing emphasis on "space." While I am sympathetic toward his point, I have not tried to deploy my theory with consistent loyalty to it. While I distinguish the two categories similarly, I have settled for a play between them that, while impure, seems to conform to most contemporary practice.
8. Casey, "How to Get from Space to Place in a Fairly Short Stretch of Time," 25.
9. Rose, *Feminism and Geography,* 33.
10. Quotations from Henri Lefebvre's *The Production of Space* will be cited in the text with the abbreviation *PS.*
11. de Certeau, *The Practice of Everyday Life,* 100.
12. Relph, *Place and Placelessness,* 47.
13. Thomas, *Spirit of Place,* 32.
14. Quotations from Joseph Frank's "Spatial Form in Modern Literature," in his *The Widening Gyre: Crisis and Mastery in Modern Literature,* will be cited in the text with the abbreviation *SF.*
15. Luke, "Simulated Sovereignty, Telematic Territoriality," 37.
16. Kong, "Religion and Technology."
17. Again, I am indebted to Paul Ricoeur for this sense of the two directions of language, a polarity that is basic to his hermeneutics.
18. See Raymond Williams, *The Long Revolution,* xiii. Quotations from Raymond Williams's works will be cited in the text with the abbreviations listed below.

CS   *Culture and Society: 1780–1950* (New York: Columbia University Press, 1983).

LR   *The Long Revolution* (London: Chatto and Windus, 1961).

ML   *Marxism and Literature* (Oxford: Oxford University Press, 1977).

PM   *The Politics of Modernism: Against the New Conformists,* ed. Tony Pinkney (London: Verso, 1989).

RH   *Resources of Hope: Culture, Democracy, Socialism,* ed. Robin Gable (London: Verso, 1989).

19. See Raymond Williams, *RH*, 33–36.
20. Soja, *Thirdspace*, 36.
21. van Baak, *The Place of Space in Narration,* 125.
22. See Raymond Williams, *ML*, 37–38.
23. One can see this shift in Eagleton, *The Idea of Culture* and, even more clearly, in several of the essays in Featherstone and Lash, *Spaces of Culture.*
24. Casey, "How to Get from Space to Place in a Fairly Short Stretch of Time," 19.
25. Ibid., 25.
26. Ibid., 34.
27. Ibid., 35.
28. Ibid., 27.

Chapter 9. The Single Norm of Place-Relations

1. Sack, "Place, Power, and the Good," 238.
2. Ian Baucom, in his book *Out of Place: Englishness, Empire, and the Locations of Identity,* discusses a rhetorical move that John Ruskin makes and that Baucom rightly sees as unwarranted. What Ruskin does, when he compares the guarding of one's home to the certification of the economic and political lines that relegate people to social spaces, is to confuse categories. The positive relation that a person has to intimate space cannot be taken as normative for the relations of groups in social space. In other words, a single norm for place-relations cannot cancel the differences that we already have established between kinds (see Baucom, *Out of Place,* 48–49).
3. See Relph, *Place and Placelessness,* esp. 79–114.
4. Entrikin, *The Betweenness of Place,* 57.
5. Kohak, "Of Dwelling and Wayfaring," 36.
6. Baudrillard, *The Ecstasy of Communication,* 131. While I take many of Baudrillard's points about human spatiality in a culture dominated, even determined, by modes of communication and transportation, I disagree with him on two points. First, he collapses all of human spatiality into social space. Second, he does not posit attachment to places in juxtaposition with mobility and rootlessness. I also am uneasy with his use of synecdoche in argument, that is, his use of particular items of the social scene as suggestive of the whole. In all of these ways, his work resembles that of Fredric Jameson.

7. Weil, *The Need for Roots,* 44, 99.

8. Ibid., 45.

9. Ibid., 12, 14.

10. Deleuze and Guattari, *A Thousand Plateaus,* 15.

11. Ibid., 76.

12. Entrikin, *The Betweenness of Place,* 57, 64.

13. Sopher, "The Landscape of Home," 146.

14. E. Relph, *Place and Placelessness,* 38.

15. Sarup, "Home and Identity," 96.

16. Ibid., 98.

17. Tuan, *Space and Place,* 182.

18. Casey, "Body, Self, and Landscape," 412.

19. Weil, *The Need for Roots,* 34.

20. Porteous, *Landscapes of the Mind,* 107.

21. See, for example, Altman and Low, eds., *Place Attachment.*

22. Ibid., 5.

23. Gold and Burgess, eds., *Valued Environments,* 5.

24. Meinig, ed., *The Interpretation of Ordinary Landscapes,* 34, 37, 47.

25. Porteous, *Landscapes of the Mind,* 202.

26. See Altman and Low, *Place Attachment.*

27. Leroy S. Rouner, ed., *The Longing for Home.*

28. Tuan, *Cosmos and Hearth.*

29. Tuan, "Cosmos versus Hearth," 322.

30. Entrikin, *The Betweenness of Place,*

31. J. E. Malpas, *Place and Experience,* 34. Malpas also implies distinctions between kinds of human places. On personal or subjective space, see 35; on social space, see 36; and on comprehensive space, see 62.

32. Raberg, *The Space of Man,* 34.

33. Porteous, *Landscapes of the Mind,* 107.

34. Sopher, "The Landscape of Home," 130.

35. Malpas, *Place and Experience,* 35.

36. Ibid., 36.

37. Ibid., 62.

38. See Smith, *To Take Place,* 105. I should add that Smith's study is excellent in many respects, not the least of which is the attention it gives to Kant and the bodily orientations that, for him, place and space allow.

39. See, for example, Hogan, *Dwellings: A Spiritual History of the Living World;* Hamma, *Landscapes of the Soul: A Spirituality of Place;* and Lane, *Landscapes of the Sacred: Geography and Narrative in American Spirituality.*

40. Tuan, *Cosmos and Hearth,* 6.

41. Lane, *Landscapes of the Sacred,* 20.

42. Sack, *Homo Geographicus,* 34.

43. Edward S. Casey, "How to Get from Space to Place in a Fairly Short Stretch of Time," 22.

44. Tuan, *Space and Time*, 141. It should be noted that Tuan in this passage is referring to what I call intimate or personal place-relations. I would apply this characteristic to place-relations of all three kinds.

45. Relph, *Place and Placelessness*, 41–42.

46. Rose, *Feminism and Geography*, 5.

47. Sack, "Place, Power, and the Good," 233.

48. Curry, "'Hereness' and the Normativity of Place," 99–100.

Conclusion: Freeing the City from the Factual Profane

1. James, *The Varieties of Religious Experience*, 396.

2. Ibid., 199.

3. See Owen, "Occultism and the 'Modern' Self in *Fin-de-Siecle* Britain"; and Thomson, "Psychology and the 'Consciousness of Modernity' in Early Twentieth-Century Britain."

4. Calthorpe, "The Pedestrian Pocket," 356.

5. Soja and Hooper, "The Spaces That Difference Makes," 216.

6. Linowitz, *This Troubled Urban World*, 3.

7. Ibid., 7.

8. Ley, "Co-operative Housing as a Moral Landscape," 132.

9. Harvey, *Spaces of Hope*.

10. Davis, "Fortress L.A.," 196.

11. Eyerman, "Moving Culture," 116.

12. Zukin, *The Cultures of Cities*, 1.

13. Rorty, *Philosophy and the Mirror of Nature*, 335.

14. Lewis, *Time and Western Man*, 428.

15. Berman, *All That Is Solid Melts into Air*, 89.

16. Marx, "Manifesto of the Communist Party," 207.

17. Engels, "The Great Town," 48.

18. See Eliade, *Cosmos and History*, esp. "The Terror of History," 141–75.

19. Eliade, *The Sacred and the Profane*, 10.

20. Ibid., 1.

21. Eade and Sallnow, eds., *Contesting the Sacred*, 5.

22. Ibid., 16.

23. Ward, *Cities of God*, 256. I am a bit uneasy about the level of agreement or similarity between these many theorists that listing them this way imputes. However, while the extent of agreement between them and between them and Ward may be a point of contention, there is no reason to suspect that if they, and a good number of others that Ward treats in the book and that he does not, were brought together into a single room there would be agreement among them that the city epitomizes what is wrong with modernity.

24. Ibid., 118–22.

25. John Agnew and James Duncan point out the dissociation that has occurred between "community" and social/urban space, one that, especially for social scien-

tists, relegates "community" to the private rather than the public sphere (Agnew and Duncan, *The Power of Place,* 16).

26. Ibid., 258.

27. Kitto, "The Polis," 36.

28. See, for example, Mumford, "What Is a City?" 92–96. We should keep in mind that Mumford's positive attitudes toward the potentials of cities were limited by his restrictions on the size of viable cities.

29. Byrne, *Understanding the Urban,* 36.

30. Wilson, *The Sphinx in the City,* 7.

31. Ibid., 11.

32. Ibid., 120.

33. Massey, "Politics and Space/Time," 150.

34. It was in the spirit of this newly developing positive attitude toward the city that Harvey Cox published his important book *The Secular City: Secularization and Urbanization in Theological Perspective.* In it, he celebrated the new freedom and challenges posed by urban space and the social changes that it produces. While overly optimistic in its assessments of the liberation offered people by the city and too willing to allow Christianity to conform to social changes wrought in and by the city, Cox's book, however dated, is an unusual, sustained orientation of Christian theology to and by urban space rather than by the allurements of its contrary, namely, the personal or subjective either individualized or projected as virtual church.

35. See Eagleton, *The Idea of Culture.*

36. Zukin, *The Culture of Cities,* 188, 254.

37. Rose, *Feminism and Geography.*

38. Fincher and Jacobs, eds., *Cities of Difference.*

39. Rogers, *Cities for a Small Planet,* 153.

40. Vattimo, *The Transparent Society,* 40.

41. Carrette, ed., *Religion and Culture,* 33.

42. Byrne, *Understanding the Urban,* 36.

43. Ley, "Modernism, Post-modernism, and the Struggle for Place," 52–53.

44. Sennett, "Growth and Failure," 23.

45. Hall, "The City of Theory," 370.

46. Davidoff, "Advocacy and Pluralism in Planning," 433.

47. Wheeler, "Planning Sustainable and Livable Cities," 438–39.

48. Bhabha, *The Location of Culture,* 170.

49. Ibid., 151.

50. Wilson, *The Sphinx in the City,* 158.

51. "In 1950 29 per cent of the world's population was urban. In 1965 it was 36 percent, in 1991 50 percent, and by 2025 it could be at least 60 per cent" (Rogers, *Cities for a Small Planet,* vii).

52. Talmy, *How Language Structures Space,* 6.

53. See my treatment of Ricoeur's use of these coordinates in *Story, Text and Scripture: Literary Interests in Biblical Narrative,* esp. 72–73 and 76–84).

54. Sheldrake, *Spaces for the Sacred,* 65.

55. Sedgwick, "Mapping an Urban Theology," introduction to *God in the City,* ed. Peter Sedgwick, xvi.

56. Harvey, "The Insurgent Architect at Work," in his *Spaces of Hope,* 233–56.

57. Orsi, ed., *Gods of the City,* 62.

58. Dougherty, "Exiles in the Earthly City," 111.

59. Cosgrove and Domosh, "Author and Authority," 37–38.

60. Adams, Hoelscher, and Till, eds., *Textures of Place,* xviii.

Bibliography

Adam, George. "A Pantheon of Contemporary Writers." In *Graham Greene: Man of Paradox,* edited by A. F. Cassis. Chicago: Loyola University Press, 1994.

Adams, Paul C., Steven Hoelscher, and Karen E. Till, eds. *Textures of Place: Exploring Humanist Geographies.* Minneapolis: University of Minnesota Press, 2001.

Advani, Rukun. *E. M. Forster As Critic.* London: Croom Helm, 1984.

Agnew, John A., and James S. Duncan, eds. *The Power of Place: Bringing Together Geographical and Sociological Imaginations.* Boston: Unwin Hyman, 1989.

Alcorn, John. *The Nature Novel from Hardy to Lawrence.* London: Macmillan, 1977.

Altman, Irwin, and Setha M. Low, eds. *Place Attachment.* New York and London: Plenum, 1992.

Bachelard, Gaston. *The Poetics of Space.* Translated by Maria Jolas. New York: Orion, 1964.

Baker, James R. "An Interview with William Golding." *Twentieth-Century Literature: A Scholarly and Critical Journal* 28, no. 2 (summer 1982): 130–69.

———, ed. *Critical Essays on William Golding.* Boston: G. K. Hall, 1988.

Baucom, Ian. *Out of Place: Englishness, Empire, and the Locations of Identity.* Princeton: Princeton University Press, 1999.

Baudrillard, Jean. *America.* Translated by Chris Turner. London: Verso, 1988.

———. *The Ecstasy of Communication.* Translated by Bernard and Caroline Schutze. Brooklyn, N.Y.: Autonomedia, 1988.

Bayley, John. "The Impersonality of William Golding." In *William Golding: The Man and His Books,* edited by John Carey. New York: Farrar, Straus, Giroux, 1986.

Beer, Gillian. "Finding a Scale for the Human: Plot and Writing in Hardy's Novels." In *Critical Essays on Thomas Hardy: The Novels,* edited by Dale Kramer, 54–73. Boston: G. K. Hall, 1990.

Benson, Donald R. "*Heart of Darkness:* The Grounds of Civilization in an Alien Universe." In *Joseph Conrad: Heart of Darkness,* edited by Robert Kimbrough. New York: Norton, 1971.

Berger, Sheila. *Thomas Hardy and Visual Structures: Framing, Disruption, Process.* New York: New York University Press, 1990.

Berman, Marshall. *All That Is Solid Melts into Air: The Experience of Modernity.* New York: Simon and Schuster, 1982.

Berthoud, Jacques. *Joseph Conrad: The Major Phase.* Cambridge: Cambridge University Press, 1978.

Bhabha, Homi K. *The Location of Culture.* London and New York: Routledge, 1994.

Biggs, Julia. "*The Paper Man.*" In *Critical Essays on William Golding,* edited by James R. Baker. Boston: G. K. Hall, 1988.

Blanchot, Maurice. *The Infinite Conversation.* Translated by Susan Hanson. Minneapolis: University of Minnesota Press, 1993.

———. *The Step Not Beyond.* Translated by Lycette Nelson. Albany: State University of New York Press, 1992.

———. *The Writing of Disaster.* Translated by Ann Smock. Lincoln: University of Nebraska Press, 1986.

Bold, Alan, ed. *Muriel Spark: An Odd Capacity for Vision.* London: Vision Press, 1984.

Bourdieu, Pierre. *Distinction: A Social Critique of the Judgement of Taste.* Translated by Richard Nice. Cambridge: Harvard University Press, 1984.

Boyd, S. J. *The Novels of William Golding.* New York: Harvester Wheatsheaf, 1988.

Bradbury, Malcolm, and James McFarlane, eds. *Modernism: 1890–1930.* Atlantic Highlands, N.J.: Humanities Press, 1978.

Brantlinger, Patrick. *Rule of Darkness: British Literature and Imperialism, 1830–1914.* Ithaca: Cornell University Press, 1988.

Bullen, J. B. *The Expressive Eye: Fiction and Perception in the Work of Thomas Hardy.* Oxford: Clarendon Press, 1986.

Buttimer, Anne. *Geography and the Human Spirit.* Baltimore and London: Johns Hopkins University Press, 1993.

Byrne, David. *Understanding the Urban.* Basingstoke and New York: Palgrave, 2001.

Calthorpe, Peter. "The Pedestrian Pocket" In *The City Reader,* 2d ed., edited by Richard T. LeGates and Frederic Stout. London and New York: Routledge, 1996.

Carey, John, ed. *William Golding: The Man and His Books.* New York: Farrar, Straus, Giroux, 1986.

Carrette, Jeremy R., ed. *Religion and Culture: Michel Foucault.* New York: Routledge, 1999.

Casey, Edward S. "Body, Self, and Landscape: A Geophilosophical Inquiry into the Place-World." In *Textures of Place: Exploring Humanist Geographies,* edited by Paul C. Adams, Steven Hoelscher, and Karen E. Till. Minneapolis: University of Minnesota Press, 2001.

———. *The Fate of Place: A Philosophical History.* Berkeley: University of California Press, 1997.

———. "How to Get from Space to Place in a Fairly Short Stretch of Time: Phenomenological Prolegomena." In *Senses of Place,* edited by Steven Feld and Keith H. Basso. Santa Fe, N.M.: School of American Research Press, 1996.

Cassis, A. F., ed. *Graham Greene: Man of Paradox.* Chicago: Loyola University Press, 1994.

Chatman, Seymour. *Story and Discourse: Narrative Structure in Fiction and Film.* Ithaca: Cornell University Press, 1978.

Coates, Peter. *Nature: Western Attitudes since Ancient Times.* Berkeley: University of California Press, 1998.

Collins, Deborah L. *Thomas Hardy and His God: A Liturgy of Unbelief.* New York: St. Martin's, 1990.

Colmer, John. *E. M. Forster: The Personal Voice.* London: Routledge and Kegan Paul, 1975.

Conrad, Joseph. *Chance.* New York: Norton, 1968.

———. *Heart of Darkness.* Edited by Robert Kimbrough. New York: Norton, 1963.

———. *Lord Jim: A Romance.* Harmondsworth, England: Penguin, 1949.

———. *Nostromo: A Tale of the Seaboard.* London: J. M. Dent and Sons, 1947.

———. *A Personal Record* and *The Mirror of the Sea.* London and New York: Penguin, 1998.

———. *The Secret Agent: A Simple Tale.* New York: Penguin, 1983.

———. *The Shadow-Line: A Confession.* London: John Grant, 1925.

———. *Typhoon and Other Stories.* New York: Knopf, 1991.

———. *Under Western Eyes.* New York: Penguin, 1985.

———. *Victory.* Garden City, N.Y.: Doubleday Anchor, 1957.

Cosgrove, Denis, and Mona Domosh. "Author and Authority: Writing the New Cultural Geography." In *Place/Culture/Representation,* edited by James Duncan and David Ley. London and New York: Routledge, 1993.

Cox, Harvey. *The Secular City: Secularization and Urbanization in Theological Perspective.* New York: Macmillan, 1965.

Crang, Mike, and Nigel Thrift, eds. *Thinking Space.* London and New York: Routledge, 2000.

Crompton, Don. *A View from the Spire: William Golding's Later Works.* Oxford: Blackwell, 1985.

Culler, Jonathan. "*Fabula* and *Sjuzhet* in the Analysis of Narrative." *Poetics Today* (spring 1980): 27–37.

Curle, Richard. *Joseph Conrad: A Study.* New York: Russell and Russell, 1968.

Curry, Michael R. "'Hereness' and the Normativity of Place." In *Geography and Ethics: Journeys in a Moral Terrain,* edited by James D. Proctor and David M. Smith. London: Routledge, 1999.

Daunton, Martin, and Bernhard Rieger, eds. *Meanings of Modernity: Britain from the Late-Victorian Era to World War II.* Oxford: Berg, 2001.

Davidoff, Paul. "Advocacy and Pluralism in Planning." In *The City Reader,* 2d ed., edited by Richard T. LeGates and Frederic Stout. London and New York: Routledge, 1996.

Davis, Mike. "Fortress L.A." In *The City Reader,* 2d ed., edited by Richard T. LeGates and Frederic Stout. London and New York: Routledge, 1996.

de Certeau, Michel. *The Practice of Everyday Life.* Translated by Steven Rendall. Berkeley and Los Angeles: University of California Press, 1984.

Deleuze, Gilles, and Felix Guattari. *A Thousand Plateaus: Capitalism and Schizophrenia.* Translated by Brian Massumi. Minneapolis: University of Minnesota Press, 1987.

Derrida, Jacques. "Architecture oue il desiderio puo abitare." *Domus* 671 (1986): 17–24.

Dougherty, James. "Exiles in the Earthly City: The Heritage of Saint Augustine." In *Civitas: Religious Interpretations of the City,* edited by Peter S. Hawkins. Atlanta: Scholars Press, 1986.

Duncan, James, and David Ley, eds. *Place/Culture/Representation.* London and New York: Routledge, 1993.

Eade, John, and Michael J. Sallnow, eds. *Contesting the Sacred: The Anthropology of Christian Pilgrimage.* London and New York: Routledge, 1991.

Eagleton, Terry. *The Idea of Culture.* Oxford: Blackwell, 2000.

Edgecombe, Rodney Stenning. *Vocation and Identity in the Fiction of Muriel Spark.* Columbia: University of Missouri Press, 1990.

Eliade, Mircea. *Cosmos and History: The Myth of the Eternal Return.* Translated by Willard R. Trask. New York: Harper and Row, 1959.

———. *The Sacred and the Profane.* Translated by Willard R. Trask. San Diego, New York, London: Harcourt, Brace, and World, 1959.

Engels, Friedrich. "The Great Town." In *The City Reader,* 2d ed., edited by Richard T. LeGates and Frederic Stout. London and New York: Routledge, 1996.

Entrikin, J. Nicolas. *The Betweenness of Place: Towards a Geography of Modernity.* Baltimore: Johns Hopkins University Press, 1991.

Erdinast-Vulcan, Daphna. "'Sudden Holes in Space and Time': Conrad's Anarchist Aesthetics in *The Secret Agent.*" In *Conrad's Cities: Essays for Hans van Marle,* edited by Gene M. Moore. Amsterdam and Atlanta: Rodopi, 1992.

Eyerman, Ron. "Moving Culture." In *Spaces of Culture: City, Nation, World,* edited by Mike Featherstone and Scott Lash. London: Sage, 1999.

Featherstone, Mike, and Scott Lash, eds. *Spaces of Culture: City, Nation, World.* London: Sage, 1999.

Feld, Steven, and Keith H. Basso, eds. *Sense of Place.* Santa Fe, N.M.: School of American Research Press, 1996.

Fincher, Ruth, and Jane M. Jacobs, eds. *Cities of Difference.* New York and London: Guilford, 1998.

Fogel, Aaron. "The Fragmentation of Sympathy in *The Secret Agent.*" In *Joseph Conrad,* edited by Elaine Jordan. New York: St. Martin's, 1996.

Forster, E. M. *Howards End.* New York and London: G. P. Putnam's Sons, 1911.

———. *The Longest Journey.* Norfolk, Conn.: New Directions, 1922.

———. *Marianne Thornton: A Domestic Biography.* New York: Harcourt, Brace, 1956.

———. *Maurice.* New York: Norton, 1971.

———. *A Passage to India.* New York: Harcourt, Brace, 1924.

———. *A Room with a View.* Norfolk, Conn.: New Directions, 1922.

———. *Two Cheers for Democracy.* Harcourt, Brace, 1951.

———. *Where Angels Fear to Tread.* London: Edward Arnold, 1924.

Foster, Hal, ed. *The Anti-Aesthetic: Essays on Postmodernist Culture.* Port Townsend, Wash.: Bay Press, 1983.

Foucault, Michel. *Discipline and Punish: The Birth of the Prison.* Translated by Alan Sheridan. 1977. Reprint, New York: Vintage Books, 1995.

———. "Of Other Spaces." Translated by Jay Miskowiec. *Diacritics* 16, no. 1 (spring 1986): 22–27.

———. *The Order of Things: An Archaeology of the Human Sciences.* New York: Random House, 1970.

———. *Power/Knowledge: Selected Interviews and Other Writings, 1972–1977.* Translated by Colin Gordon et al. New York: Pantheon, 1980.

Fowles, John. "Golding and 'Golding.'" In *William Golding: The Man and His Books,* edited by John Carey. New York: Farrar, Straus, Giroux, 1986.

Frank, Joseph. *The Widening Gyre: Crisis and Mastery in Modern Literature.* New Brunswick, N.J.: Rutgers University Press, 1963.

Fraser, J. T., ed. *The Voices of Time: A Cooperative Survey of Man's Views of Time As Expressed by the Sciences and by the Humanities.* New York: George Braziller, 1966.

Gadamer, Hans-Georg. *Truth and Method.* Translated by Garrett Barden and John Cumming. New York: Seabury, 1975.

Gates, Henry Louis Jr., ed. *"Race," Writing, and Difference.* Chicago: University of Chicago Press, 1986.

Genette, Gérard. *Figures of Literary Discourse.* Translated by Alan Sheridan. New York: Columbia University Press, 1982.

Giddens, Anthony. *The Constitution of Society: Outline of the Theory of Structuration.* Berkeley and Los Angeles: University of California Press, 1984.

Gold, John R., and Jacquelin Burgess, eds. *Valued Environments.* London: Allen and Unwin, 1982.

Golding, William. *Close Quarters.* London: Faber and Faber, 1987.

———. *Darkness Visible.* New York: Farrar, Straus, Giroux, 1979.

———. *Fire Down Below.* New York: Farrar, Straus, Giroux, 1989.

———. *Free Fall.* New York: Harcourt, Brace, and World, 1959.

———. *The Hot Gates.* New York: Harcourt, Brace, and World, 1966.

———. *The Inheritors.* New York: Harcourt, Brace, and World, 1955.

———. *Lord of the Flies.* New York: G. P. Putnam's Sons, 1959.

———. *A Moving Target.* New York: Farrar, Straus, Giroux, 1982.

———. *The Paper Man.* New York: Farrar, Straus, Giroux, 1984.

———. *Pincher Martin.* New York: Harcourt, Brace, 1956.

———. *The Pyramid.* New York: Harcourt, Brace, and World, 1967.

———. *Rites of Passage.* Farrar, Straus, Giroux, 1980.

———. *The Spire.* New York: Harcourt, Brace, and World, 1964.

Goode, John. "Hardy and Marxism." In *Critical Essays on Thomas Hardy: The Novels,* edited by Dale Kramer. Boston: G. K. Hall, 1990.

Goodin, George, ed. *The English Novel in the Nineteenth Century: Essays on the Literary Mediation of Human Values.* Chicago: University of Illinois Press, 1972.

Greene, Graham. *Brighton Rock.* New York: Viking, 1948.

———. *A Burnt-Out Case.* London: Heinemann, 1961.

———. *The Comedians.* New York: Viking, 1966.

———. *Doctor Fischer of Geneva or the Bomb Party.* New York: Simon and Schuster, 1980.

———. *The End of the Affair.* New York: Viking, 1951.

———. *The Heart of the Matter.* New York: Viking, 1948.

———. *The Honorary Consul.* New York: Simon and Schuster, 1973.

———. *The Human Factor.* New York: Simon and Schuster, 1978.

———. *Lost Childhood and Other Essays.* New York: Viking Press, 1951.

———. *Monsignor Quixote.* New York: Simon and Schuster, 1982.

———. *The Potting Shed.* New York: Viking, 1957.

———. *The Power and the Glory.* New York: Viking, 1946.

———. *Travels with My Aunt.* New York: Viking, 1969.

———. *Ways of Escape.* New York: Simon and Schuster, 1980.

Gregor, Ian. *The Great Web: The Form of Hardy's Major Fiction.* London: Faber and Faber, 1974.

Hall, Peter. "The City of Theory." In *The City Reader,* edited by Richard T. LeGates and Frederic Stout. London and New York: Routledge, 1996.

Hamma, Robert M. *Landscapes of the Soul: A Spirituality of Place.* Notre Dame, Ind.: Ave Maria, 1999.

Handyside, John, ed. *Kant's Inaugural Dissertation and Early Writings on Space.* Chicago: Open Court, 1929.

Hardy, Florence Emily. *The Early Life of Thomas Hardy: 1840–1891.* London: Macmillan, 1928.

Hardy, Thomas. *Desperate Remedies.* New York and London: Harper and Brothers, 1905.

———. *Far from the Madding Crowd.* New York and London: Harper and Brothers, 1905.

———. *Jude the Obscure.* New York: Harper and Brothers, 1896.

———. *The Mayor of Casterbridge: A Story of a Man of Character.* New York: Rinehart, 1948.

———. *The Return of the Native.* 2 vols. New York and London: Harper and Brothers, 1905.

———. *Tess of the D'Urbervilles: A Pure Woman.* New York and London: Harper and Brothers, 1920.

———. *Under the Greenwood Tree.* New York: Oxford University Press, 1985.

Hart, Francis Russell. "Ridiculous Demons." In *Muriel Spark: An Odd Capacity for Vision,* edited by Alan Bold. London: Vision Press Ltd., 1984.

Hart, William D. *Edward Said and the Religious Effects of Culture.* Cambridge: Cambridge University Press, 2000.

Harvey, David. *The Condition of Postmodernity: An Inquiry into the Origins of Cultural Change.* Oxford: Blackwell, 1989.

———. *Spaces of Hope.* Berkeley and Los Angeles: University of California Press, 2000.

Hawkins, Peter S., ed. *Civitas: Religious Interpretations of the City.* Atlanta: Scholars Press, 1986.

Hawthorn, Jeremy. *Joseph Conrad's Language and Fictional Self-Consciousness.* London: Edward Conrad, 1979.

Hay, Eloise Knapp. "*Nostromo.*" In *The Cambridge Companion to Joseph Conrad,* edited by J. H. Stape. Cambridge University Press, 1996.

———. *The Political Novels of Joseph Conrad.* Chicago: University of Chicago Press, 1963.

Herz, Judith Scherer, and Robert K. Martin, eds. *E. M. Forster: Centenary Revaluations.* Toronto and Buffalo: University of Toronto Press, 1982.

Hewitt, Douglas. *Conrad: A Reassessment.* London: Bowen and Bowen, 1975.

———. *English Fiction of the Early Modern Period: 1890–1940.* London: Longman, 1988.

Hogan, Linda. *Dwellings: A Spiritual History of the Living World.* New York: Norton, 1995.

hooks, bell. *Yearning: race, gender, and cultural politics.* Boston: South End Press, 1990.

Hutcheon, Linda. *A Poetics of Postmodernism: History, Theory, Fiction.* New York and London: Routledge, 1988.

Hynes, Joseph, ed. *Critical Essays on Muriel Spark.* New York: G. K. Hall, 1992.

Isenberg, Noah. *Between Redemption and Doom: The Strains of German-Jewish Modernism.* Lincoln and London: University of Nebraska Press, 1999.

James, William. *The Varieties of Religious Experience.* New York: Collier Macmillan, 1961.

Jameson, Fredric. *The Geopolitical Aesthetic: Cinema and Space in the World System.* Bloomington: Indiana University Press, 1992.

———. "Postmodernism and the Cultural Logic of Late Capitalism." *New Left Review,* no. 146 (1984): 53–92.

———. *Postmodernism, or, the Cultural Logic of Late Capitalism.* Durham: Duke University Press, 1991.

Jedrzekewski, Jan. *Thomas Hardy and the Church.* London: Macmillan, 1996.

Kamenka, Eugene, ed. and trans. *The Portable Karl Marx.* New York: Penguin, 1983.

Kant, Immanuel. "Dissertation on the Form and Principles of the Sensible and Intelligible World." In *Kant's Inaugural Dissertation and Early Writings on Space,* edited and translated by John Handyside. Chicago: Open Court, 1929.

———. "On the First Ground of the Distinction of Regions in Space." In *Kant's Inaugural Dissertation and Early Writings on Space,* edited and translated by John Handyside. Chicago: Open Court, 1929.

Keith, Michael, and Steve Pile, eds. *Place and the Politics of Identity.* London and New York: Routledge, 1993.

Kermode, Frank. "A Reply to Joseph Frank." *Critical Inquiry* 4, no. 3 (spring 1978): 579–89.

———. *The Sense of an Ending: Studies in the Theory of Fiction.* New York: Oxford University Press, 1967.

Kestner, Joseph A. *The Spatiality of the Novel.* Detroit: Wayne State University Press, 1978.

Kimbrough, Robert, ed. *Joseph Conrad: Heart of Darkness.* New York: Norton, 1971.

King, Francis. *E. M. Forster and His World.* London: Thomas and Hudson, 1978.

Kinkead-Weekes, Mark. "The Visual and the Visionary in Golding." In *William Golding: The Man and His Books,* edited by John Carey. New York: Farrar, Straus, Giroux, 1986.

Kinkead-Weekes, Mark, and Ian Gregor. *William Golding: A Critical Study.* London: Faber and Faber, 1967.

Kitto, H.D.F. "The Polis." In *The City Reader,* 2d ed., edited by Richard T. LeGates and Frederic Stout. London and New York: Routledge, 1996.

Knowles, Owen. "Conrad's Life." In *The Cambridge Companion to Joseph Conrad,* edited by J. H. Stape. Cambridge: Cambridge University Press, 1996.

Kohak, Erazim. *The Embers and the Stars: A Philosophical Inquiry into the Moral Sense of Nature.* Chicago: University of Chicago Press, 1984.

———. "Of Dwelling and Wayfaring: A Quest for Metaphors." In *The Longing for Home,* edited by Leroy S. Rouner. Notre Dame: University of Notre Dame Press, 1996.

Kong, Lily. "Religion and Technology: Refiguring Place, Space, Identity and Community." *Area* 33, no. 4 (December 2001): 404–13.

Kort, Wesley A. *Modern Fiction and Human Time: An Essay in Narrative and Belief.* Tampa: University of South Florida Press, 1986.

———. *Story, Text, and Scripture: Literary Interests in Biblical Narrative.* University Park: Pennsylvania State University Press, 1988.

———. *"Take, Read": Scripture, Textuality, and Cultural Practice.* University Park: Pennsylvania State University Press, 1996.

Krajka, Wieslaw. *Isolation and Ethos: A Study of Joseph Conrad.* New York: Columbia University Press, 1992.

Kramer, Dale, ed. *Critical Approaches to the Fiction of Thomas Hardy.* London: Macmillan, 1979.

———. *Critical Essays on Thomas Hardy: The Novels.* Boston: G. K. Hall, 1990.

Laclau, Ernesto, and Chantal Mouffe. *Hegemony and Socialist Strategy: Towards a*

Radical Democratic Politics. Translated by Winston Moore and Paul Cammack. London and New York: Verso, 1985.

Lane, Belden C. *Landscapes of the Sacred: Geography and Narrative in American Spirituality.* Mahwah, N.J.: Paulist Press, 1988.

Lefebvre, Henri. *The Production of Space.* Translated by Donald Nicholson-Smith. Oxford: Blackwell, 1991.

LeGates, Richard T., and Frederic Stout, eds. *The City Reader.* 2d ed. London and New York: Routledge, 1996.

Lemon, Lee T. "The Hostile Universe: A Developing Pattern in Nineteenth-Century Fiction." In *The English Novel in the Nineteenth Century: Essays on the Literary Mediation of Human Values,* edited by George Goodin, 1–13. Chicago: University of Illinois Press, 1972.

Lester, John. *Conrad and Religion.* New York: St. Martin's, 1988.

Lewis, Wyndham. *Time and Western Man.* Boston: Beacon, 1957.

Ley, David. "Co-operative Housing as a Moral Landscape: Re-examining the Postmodern City." In *Place/Culture/Representation,* edited by James Duncan and David Ley. London and New York: Routledge, 1993.

————. "Modernism, Post-modernism, and the Struggle for Place." In *The Power of Place: Bringing Together Geographical and Sociological Imaginations,* edited by John A. Agnew and James S. Duncan. Boston: Unwin Hyman, 1989.

Linowitz, Sol M. *This Troubled Urban World.* Claremont: Claremont Colleges, 1974.

Lodge, David. "Thomas Hardy as a Cinematic Novelist." In *Thomas Hardy after Fifty Years,* edited by Lance St. John Butler. London: Macmillan, 1977.

Lothe, Jakob. "Conradian Narrative." In *The Cambridge Companion to Joseph Conrad,* edited by J. H. Stape. Cambridge: Cambridge University Press, 1996.

Luke, Timothy W. "Simulated Sovereignty, Telematic Territoriality: The Political Economy of Cyberspace." In *Spaces of Culture: City, Nation, World,* edited by Mike Featherstone and Scott Lash. London: Sage, 1999.

Lutwack, Leonard. *The Role of Place in Literature.* Syracuse: Syracuse University Press, 1984.

Lyotard, Jean-François. *The Postmodern Condition: A Report on Knowledge.* Translated by Geoff Bennington and Brian Massumi. Minneapolis: University of Minnesota Press, 1979.

Macdonell, Diane. *Theories of Discourse: An Introduction.* Oxford: Blackwell, 1986.

Malmgren, Carl Darryl. *Fictional Space in the Modernist and Postmodernist American Novel.* Lewisburg, Pennsylvania: Bucknell University Press, 1985.

Malpas, J. E. *Place and Experience: A Philosophical Topography.* Cambridge: Cambridge University Press, 1999.

Martin, Robert K., and George Piggford, eds. *Queer Forster.* Chicago: University of Chicago Press, 1997.

Martin, Wallace. *Recent Theories of Narrative.* Ithaca: Cornell University Press, 1986.

Marx, Karl. "Manifesto of the Communist Party." In *The Portable Karl Marx,* edited and translated by Eugene Kamenka. New York: Penquin, 1983.

Massey, Doreen. "Politics and Space/Time." In *Place and the Politics of Identity,* edited by Michael Keith and Steve Pile. London and New York: Routledge, 1993.

McDowell, Frederick P. *W. E. M. Forster.* Boston: Twayne, 1982.

Meinig, D. W., ed. *The Interpretation of Ordinary Landscapes.* New York: Oxford University Press, 1979.

Mewshaw, Michael. "Graham Greene in Antibes." In *Graham Greene: Man of Paradox,* edited by A. F. Cassis. Chicago: Loyola University Press, 1994.

Meyers, Jeffrey. *Joseph Conrad: A Biography.* New York: Charles Scribner's Sons, 1991.

Miller, J. Hillis. *Thomas Hardy: Distance and Desire.* Cambridge: Harvard University Press, 1978.

Mitchell, Timothy. *Colonising Egypt.* Berkeley and Los Angeles: University of California Press, 1991.

Mitchell, W.J.T. "Holy Landscape: Israel, Palestine, and the American Wilderness." *Critical Inquiry* (winter 2000): 219.

Moore, Gene M., ed. *Conrad's Cities: Essays for Hans van Marle.* Amsterdam and Atlanta: Rodopi, 1992.

Moore, Henrietta L. *Space, Text, and Gender: An Anthropological Study of the Marakwet of Kenya.* Cambridge: Cambridge University Press, 1986.

Morton, Peter. *The Vital Science: Biology and the Literary Imagination, 1860–1900.* London: Allen and Unwin, 1984.

Muggeridge, Malcolm. "Nature's Displaced Person." In *Graham Greene: Man of Paradox,* edited by A. F. Cassis. Chicago: Loyala University Press, 1994.

Mumford, Lewis. "What Is a City?" In *The City Reader,* 2d ed., edited by Richard T. LeGates and Frederic Stout. London and New York: Routledge, 1996.

Najder, Zdzislaw. *Joseph Conrad: A Chronicle.* Cambridge: Cambridge University Press, 1983.

Nethersole, Reingard. "Writing Space." *JLS/TLW* 10 (March 1994): 128.

Orsi, Robert A. "Introduction: Crossing the City Line." In *Gods of the City: Religion and the American Urban Landscape,* edited by Robert A. Orsi. Bloomington: Indiana University Press, 1999.

Owen, Alex. "Occultism and the 'Modern' Self in *Fin-de-Siecle* Britain." In *Meanings of Modernity: Britain from the Late-Victorian Era to World War II,* edited by Martin Daunton and Bernhard Rieger. Oxford: Berg, 2000.

Page, Norman. *Muriel Spark.* New York: St. Martin's, 1990.

Parini, Jay. "Getting to Know Graham Greene." In *Graham Greene: Man of Paradox,* edited by A. F. Cassis. Chicago: Loyola University Press, 1994.

Parry, Benita. *Conrad and Imperialism: Ideological Boundaries and Visionary Frontiers.* London: Macmillan, 1983.

Pietz, William. "The Problem of the Fetish." *Res* 9 (spring 1985): 5–17; 13 (spring 1987): 23–45; and 16 (autumn 1988): 105–23.

Pinian, F. B. "The Ranging Vision." In *Thomas Hardy after Fifty Years,* edited by Lance St. John Butler. London: Macmillan, 1977.

Piper, Karen. *Cartographic Fictions: Maps, Race, and Identity.* New Brunswick, N.J., and London: Rutgers University Press, 2002.

Porteous, J. Douglas. *Landscapes of the Mind: Worlds of Sense and Metaphor.* Toronto: University of Toronto Press, 1990.

Pratt, Mary Louise. "Scratches on the Face of the Country; or, What Mr. Barrow Saw in the Land of the Bushmen." In *"Race," Writing, and Difference,* edited by Henry Louis Gates Jr. Chicago: University of Chicago Press, 1986.

Proctor, James D., and David M. Smith, eds. *Geography and Ethics: Journeys in a Moral Terrain.* London: Routledge, 1999.

Purdy, Dwight H. *Joseph Conrad's Bible.* Norman: University of Oklahoma Press, 1984.

Rajberg, Per. *The Space of Man: New Concepts for Social and Humanistic Planning.* Stockholm: Almquist and Wiksell International, 1987.

Relph, E. *Place and Placelessness.* London: Pion, 1976.

Ricardo, David. *The Principles of Political Economy and Taxation.* London: J. M. Dent and Sons, 1973.

Ricoeur, Paul. *The Conflict of Interpretations.* Edited by Don Ihde. Translated by Kathleen McLaughlin, et al. Evanston: Northwestern University Press, 1974.

———. *Time and Narrative.* Vol. 2. Translated by Kathleen McLaughlin and David Pellauer. Chicago: University of Chicago Press, 1985.

Robertson, George, et al., eds. *Travellers' Tales: Narratives of Home and Displacement.* London: Routledge, 1994.

Rogers, Richard. *Cities for a Small Planet.* Boulder, Colo.: Westview, 1998.

Rorty, Richard. *Philosophy and the Mirror of Nature.* Princeton: Princeton University Press, 1979.

Rose, Gillian. *Feminism and Geography: The Limits of Geographical Knowledge.* Minneapolis: University of Minnesota Press, 1993.

Rosecrance, Barbara. *Forster's Narrative Vision.* Ithaca: Cornell University Press, 1982.

Rosenfield, Claire. *Paradise of Snakes: An Archetypal Analysis of Conrad's Political Novels.* Chicago: University of Chicago Press, 1967.

Rouner, Leroy S., ed. *The Longing for Home.* Notre Dame: University of Notre Dame Press, 1996.

Sack, Robert David. *Homo Geographicus: A Framework for Action, Awareness, and Moral Concern.* Baltimore and London: Johns Hopkins University Press, 1997.

———. "Place, Power, and the Good." In *Textures of Place: Exploring Humanist Geographies,* edited by Paul C. Adams, Steven Hoelscher, and Karen E. Till. Minneapolis: University of Minnesota Press, 2001.

Said, Edward W. *Culture and Imperialism.* New York: Knopf, 1994.

———. *The World, the Text, and the Critic.* Cambridge: Harvard University Press, 1983.

Sarup, Madan. "Home and Identity." In *Travellers' Tales: Narratives of Home and Displacement,* edited by George Robertson et al. London: Routledge, 1994.

Schwartz, Daniel R. "Beginnings and Endings in Hardy's Major Fiction." In *Critical Approaches to the Fiction of Thomas Hardy,* edited by Dale Kramer. London: Macmillan, 1979.

Scott, Nathan A. *Craters of the Spirit: Studies in the Modern Novel.* Washington, D.C.: Corpus, 1988.

Sedgwick, Peter, ed. *God in the City: Essays and Reflections from the Archbishop's Urban Theology Group.* London: Mowbray, 1995.

Sennett, Richard. "Growth and Failure: The New Political Economy and its Culture." In *Spaces of Culture: City, Nation, World,* edited by Mike Featherstone and Scott Lash. London: Sage, 1999.

Shelden, Michael. *Graham Greene: The Enemy Within.* New York: Random House, 1994.

Sheldrake, Philip. *Spaces for the Sacred: Place, Memory, and Identity.* London: SCM Press, 2001.

Sibley, David. *Geographies of Exclusion: Society and Difference in the West.* London and New York: Routledge, 1995.

Smith, Jonathan Z. *To Take Place: Toward Theory in Ritual.* Chicago: University of Chicago Press, 1987.

Smith, Neil, and Cindi Katz. "Grounding Metaphor: Towards a Spatialized Politics." In *Place and the Politics of Identity,* edited by Michael Keith and Steve Pile. London and New York: Routledge, 1993.

Smitten, Jeffrey R., and Ann Daghistany, eds. *Spatial Form in Narrative.* Ithaca: Cornell University Press, 1981.

Soja, Edward W. *Postmodern Geographies: The Reassertion of Space in Critical Social Theory.* London and New York: Verso, 1989.

———. *Thirdspace: Journeys to Los Angeles and Other Real-and-Imagined Places.* London: Blackwell, 1996.

Soja, Edward, and Barbara Hooper. "The Spaces That Difference Makes." In *Place and the Politics of Identity,* edited by Michael Keith and Steve Pile. London and New York: Routledge, 1993.

Sopher, David E. "The Landscape of Home." In *The Interpretation of Ordinary Landscapes: Geographical Essays,* edited by D. W. Meinig. New York: Oxford University Press, 1979.

Spark, Muriel. *The Bachelors.* Philadelphia and New York: Lippincott, 1960.

———. *The Comforters.* Philadelphia and New York: Lippincott, 1957.

———. *Curriculum Vitae: Autobiography.* Boston: Houghton Mifflin, 1992.

———. *The Driver's Seat.* New York: Knopf, 1970.

———. "Edinburgh-born." In *Critical Essays on Muriel Spark,* edited by Joseph Hynes. New York: G. K. Hall, 1992.

———. *A Far Cry from Kensington.* Boston: Houghton Mifflin, 1988.

———. *The Girls of Slender Means.* New York: Knopf, 1963.

———. *The Hothouse by the East River.* New York: Viking Press, 1973.

———. *Loitering with Intent*. New York: Coward, McCann, and Geoghegan, 1981.

———. *The Mandelbaum Gate*. New York: Knopf, 1965.

———. *Memento Mori*. Philadelphia and New York: Lippincott, 1959.

———. "My Conversion." In *Critical Essays on Muriel Spark*, edited by Joseph Hynes. New York: G. K. Hall, 1992.

———. *Not to Disturb*. New York: Viking, 1971.

———. *The Only Problem*. New York: G. P. Putnam's Sons, 1984.

———. *The Prime of Miss Jean Brodie*. Philadelphia: Lippincott, 1962.

———. *The Public Image*. London: Macmillan, 1968.

———. *Robinson: A Novel*. London: Macmillan, 1958.

———. *Symposium*. Boston: Houghton Mifflin, 1990.

———. *The Takeover*. London: Macmillan.

———. *Territorial Rights*. New York: Coward, McCann, and Geoghegan, 1979.

Spencer, Sharon. *Space, Time, and Structure in the Modern Novel*. New York: New York University Press, 1971.

Springer, Marlene. *Hardy's Use of Allusion*. Lawrence: University of Kansas Press, 1983.

Sproxton, Judy. *The Women of Muriel Spark*. New York: St. Martin's, 1992.

Stape, J. H., ed. *The Cambridge Companion to Joseph Conrad*. Cambridge: Cambridge University Press, 1996.

St. John Butler, Lance, ed. *Thomas Hardy after Fifty Years*. London: Macmillan, 1977.

Stock, Brian. "Reading, Community and a Sense of Place." In *Place/Culture/Representation*, edited by James Duncan and David Ley. London and New York: Routledge, 1993.

Stone, Wilfred. *The Cave and the Mountain: A Study of E. M. Forster*. Stanford: Stanford University Press, 1966.

———. "E. M. Forster's Subversive Individualism." In *E. M. Forster: Centenary Revaluations*, edited by Judith Scherer Herz and Robert K. Martin. Toronto and Buffalo: University of Toronto Press, 1982.

Talmy, Leonard. *How Language Structures Space*. Berkeley: University of California Cognitive Science Program, 1983.

Taussig, Michael. "The Beach (A Fantasy)." *Critical Inquiry* 26, no. 2 (winter 2000): 248–78.

Thomas, Alan G., ed. *Spirit of Place: Letters and Essays on Travel*. New York: Dutton, 1969.

Thomson, Mathew. "Psychology and the 'Consciousness of Modernity' in Early Twentieth-Century Britain." In *Meanings of Modernity: Britain from the Late-Victorian Era to World War II*, edited by Martin Daunton and Bernhard Rieger. Oxford: Berg, 2000.

Tindall, Gillian. *Countries of the Mind: The Meaning of Place to Writers*. Boston: Northeastern University Press, 1991.

Tolley, Christopher. *Domestic Biography: The Legacy of Evangelicalism in Four Nineteenth-Century Families*. Oxford: Clarendon Press, 1997.

Tristram, Philippa. *Living Space in Fact and Fiction.* London: Routledge, 1989.

Tuan, Yi-Fu. *Cosmos and Hearth: A Cosmopolite's Viewpoint.* Minneapolis: University of Minnesota Press, 1996.

———. "Cosmos versus Hearth." In *Textures of Place: Exploring Humanist Geographies,* edited by Paul C. Adams, Steven Hoelscher, and Karen E. Till. Minneapolis: University of Minnesota Press, 2001.

———. *Space and Place: The Perspective of Experience.* Minneapolis and London: University of Minnesota Press, 1977.

Turner, Victor W. *The Ritual Process: Structure and Anti-Structure.* Chicago: Aldine, 1966.

van Baak, J. J. *The Place of Space in Narration: A Semiotic Approach to the Problem of Literary Space.* Amsterdam: Editions Rodopi B. V., 1983.

Vattimo, Gianni. *The Transparent Society.* Baltimore: Johns Hopkins University Press, 1992.

Venturi, Robert, et al. *Learning from Las Vegas: The Forgotten Symbolism of Architectural Form.* Cambridge: MIT Press, 1977.

Walker, Dorothea. *Muriel Spark.* Boston: Twayne, 1988.

Ward, Graham. *Cities of God.* London and New York: Routledge, 2000.

Weber, Max. *Economy and Society: An Outline of Interpretative Sociology.* Translated by Ephraim Fischoff et al. New York: Bedminster, 1968.

Webster, Harvey Curtis. *On a Darkling Plain: The Art and Thought of Thomas Hardy.* Chicago: University of Chicago Press, 1947.

Weedon, Chris. *Feminist Practice and Poststructuralist Theory.* Oxford: Blackwell, 1987.

Weil, Simone. *The Need for Roots: Prelude to a Declaration of Duties toward Mankind.* Translated by Arthur Wills. New York: G. P. Putman's Sons, 1952.

West, W. J. *The Quest for Graham Greene.* London: Weidenfeld and Nicolson, 1997.

Wheeler, Stephen. "Planning Sustainable and Livable Cities." In *The City Reader,* 2d ed., edited by Richard T. LeGates and Frederic Stout. London and New York: Routledge, 1996.

Williams, Merryn. *Thomas Hardy and Rural England.* London: Macmillan, 1972.

Williams, Raymond. *Country and City in the Modern Novel.* Swansea: University College of Swansea, 1987.

———. *Culture and Society: 1780–1950.* New York: Columbia University Press, 1983.

———. *The English Novel from Dickens to Lawrence.* London: Chatto and Windus, 1971.

———. *The Long Revolution.* London: Chatto and Windus, 1961.

———. *Marxism and Literature.* Oxford: Oxford University Press, 1977.

———. *The Politics of Modernism: Against the New Conformists.* London: Verso, 1989.

———. *Resources of Hope: Culture, Democracy, Socialism.* London: Verso, 1989.

Wilson, Elizabeth. *The Sphinx in the City: Urban Life, the Control of Disorder, and Women.* Berkeley and Los Angeles: University of California Press, 1991.

Winter, Jay. *Sites of Memory, Sites of Mourning: The Great War in European Cultural History.* Cambridge and New York: Cambridge University Press, 1995.

Woolf, Virginia. *A Room of One's Own.* San Diego, New York, London: Harcourt Brace, 1981.

Wright, T. R. *Hardy and the Erotic.* New York: St. Martin's, 1989.

Wright, Walter F. *Romance and Tragedy in Joseph Conrad.* Lincoln: University of Nebraska Press, 1949.

Zukin, Sharon. *The Cultures of Cities.* Oxford and Cambridge, Mass.: Blackwell, 1995.

Index

Wesley A. Kort is professor of religion, chair of the Department of Religion, and convener of the religion and modernity field in the graduate program in religion at Duke University. He is the author of many articles and nine books that relate the study of religion to literary and cultural studies. He is presently working on a study of autobiography and religious identity in contemporary America.